MORE PRAISE FO

"More than one hundred years after Thoreau lived and wrote on Walden Pond, Thomas Rain Crowe went deep into the woods in western North Carolina, along the Green River, where he lived and wrote. No electricity, no calendars and clock, no modern conveniences, and totally alone. *Zoro's Field* is Crowe's telling of what he learned, how he managed his daily life, and his observations on nature and the human's place in it. For my money, this book is sacred writ." —*Knoxville News-Sentinel*

"I have known Thomas Crowe for thirty years or so, as poet, writer, editor, and community activist. Before he returned to North Carolina he was a neighbor in my part of California. I have always respected his work and dedication as someone who has truly found both his place and his work, and recommend him highly. His writing speaks from a fluency with landscape and an ease with language like water. At home in both." —GARY SNYDER, author of *The Practice of the Wild*

"*Zoro's Field* evokes a longing for escape from the rat-race cycle of earn and spend. Crowe's rich narrative of his homesteading experiment is engaging, informative and humorous. Reading this memoir will make you think about how you live your life, whether it's the life of quiet desperation Thoreau admonished or one of true freedom and self-sufficiency." —BOBBI BUCHANAN, Editor, *New Southerner*

"Having taught Thoreau for many years, what I liked about *Zoro's Field* was the terrific honesty. This books moves in this tradition with a very durable and authentic spirit and genius. Annie Dillard's *Tinker Creek* was my favorite book in the tradition of Thoreau until I read this book." —JAMES W. CLARK, North Carolina State University

"One of the best books I've seen in the tradition of Thoreau's *Walden*. So good, in fact, that I've read the book twice, and find myself gushing about it to friends and people coming through the store here at Walden Pond, where it is a featured, staff-recommended book."
—JIM HAYDEN, Thoreau Society Shop at Walden Pond

"I found *Zoro's Field* a total joy to read. I'm not sure which impressed me most, Crowe's ability to live by himself and off the land for four years, or his ability to tell about it. His account of these four years is counterbalanced by his own steadfast grasp of the Zen of the moment. Quite an achievement." —BILL BELLEVILLE, author of *River of Lakes*

"Being seventy-seven and having grown up in the North Carolina woods, I relate to every inch of *Zoro's Field*. It's a grand slam."
—WILFORD CORBIN, author of *A World Apart: My Life among the Eskimos of Alaska*

"*Zoro's Field* is a beautiful book—like a draught of good home brew from Crowe's root cellar. It is as sturdy and sure as an oak, and as light and flexible as a reed. Now that's alchemy!" —RICHARD CAMBRIDGE, author of *Pulsa: A Book of Books*

"*Zoro's Field* will appeal to anyone (and we are many) who has imagined unhinging from the cumbersome structures of 'progress' and consumerism in order to know the rhythms of quiet work and nature." —ALISON HAWTHORNE DEMING, author of *The Edges of the Civilized World: A Journey in Nature and Culture*

Zoro's Field

Thomas Rain Crowe

Zoro's Field

MY LIFE
IN THE
APPALACHIAN
WOODS

Foreword by Christopher Camuto

The University of Georgia Press   Athens and London

Paperback edition, 2006
Published by the University of Georgia Press
Athens, Georgia 30602
© 2005 by Thomas Rain Crowe
All rights reserved
Designed by Sandra Strother Hudson
Set in 10.8/14 Dante
Printed and bound by Maple-Vail
The paper in this book meets the guidelines for permanence
and durability of the Committee on Production Guidelines for
Book Longevity of the Council on Library Resources.

Printed in the United States of America
06 07 08 09 10 P 5 4 3 2 1

The Library of Congress has cataloged the hardcover edition
of this book as follows:

Library of Congress Cataloging-in-Publication Data
Crowe, Thomas Rain.
Zoro's field : my life in the Appalachian Woods / by Thomas Rain
Crowe ; foreword by Christopher Camuto.
p.   cm.
ISBN 0-8203-2734-4 (alk. paper)
1. Crowe, Thomas Rain—Homes and haunts—Appalachian Region,
Southern. 2. Crowe, Thomas Rain—Homes and haunts—North
Carolina—Polk County. 3. Poets, American—Homes and
haunts—North Carolina—Polk County. 4. Poets, American—
Homes and haunts—Appalachian Region, Southern. 5. Wilderness
areas—North Carolina—Polk County. 6. Wilderness areas—
Appalachian Region, Southern. 7. Poets, American—20th century—
Biography. 8. Appalachian Region, Southern—Biography. 9. Polk
County (N.C.)—Biography. 10. Solitude. I. Title.
PS3553.R5924Z478 2005
811'.54—dc22   2005000964

Paperback ISBN-13: 978-0-8203-2862-1 / ISBN-10: 0-8203-2862-6

British Library Cataloging-in-Publication Data available

Do not go where the path may lead, go instead
where there is no path and leave a trail.

RALPH WALDO EMERSON

Two roads diverged in a wood, and I—
I took the one less traveled by,
And that has made all the difference.

ROBERT FROST, "The Road Not Taken"

For Zoro Guice and Gelolo McHugh

CONTENTS

ACKNOWLEDGMENTS

I wish to thank: Gary Snyder for putting me on the path of the real work. Thomas Berry for the great work. The McHugh family for their generosity and hospitableness and for the opportunity to live simply and well for four years on their land. The Guice family for accepting me and for sharing with me their lives and wisdom. The Saluda, North Carolina, community for tolerating the eccentricities of my ways and my desire to live a different kind of life. The Dave and Debbie Thomas family for their friendship and unconditional help during tough times. Paul Rhodes for his inspiration and his wild wit. Gary Pace for the stove. Horace Pace for his invaluable lessons on the river. Muff Dickson for the homemade biscuits and for saying no. Blake Dickson for his always present smile and love of bees. John Lane for kicking me in the seat of the pants and for blazing the trail. Jim Kilgo, Janisse Ray, Franklin Burroughs, Chris Camuto, Susan Cerulean, Jan DeBlieu, Dorinda Dallmeyer, Bill Belleville, Ann Fisher-Wirth, and the whole Southern Nature Writers gang for putting up with my lethargy and having to listen to me whine. Christa Frangiamore: the messenger, who believed. Will Harlan for his marathon-sized support. Nan Watkins, my soup chef during the long days and nights at the end. Scott McLeod for his belief in the validity of this work and for keeping his promise each month for the past two years. John Meyers for the fan mail when I needed it most. Michael Wren Steele for his alter-egolessness and as someone who has been there too. Sam Gray for the shots of single malt and reminding me that poets can take poetic license even when writing prose. Joe Napora, straight shooter and sidekick from the start. And Bob Jones, copyeditor from on high and providence's gift to this book.

FOREWORD

From One End of the Road to Another

Christopher Camuto

It happens that the last literary thing I'm going to do before moving from Highland Farm, my own rustic home of fourteen years, is to write a few porch words on behalf of Thomas Rain Crowe's *Zoro's Field: My Life in the Appalachian Woods*, a thoughtful, well-wrought volume which celebrates Thomas's rustic life in western North Carolina. Thomas knows my country here in Virginia's Blue Ridge and I know his; our kinship runs deep through the rivers and bedrock of the southern Appalachians, a country unto itself for those who know it and one that continues to inspire lives and literature in equal measure. I could hunt grouse south and Thomas could chase his bees north, and we'd bump into each other somewhere in the New River Valley and have plenty to talk about, mostly how the land we both love guides living and schools writing—step by step, word by word.

Zoro's Field bears—and repays—careful reading because this country of ours, the southern Appalachians, bears and repays living in. And with rural America—true rural America—in danger everywhere of disappearing into the maw of development or the travesty of gentrification, it is important that some literal, as well as literary, ground is still held by people like Thomas who keep bees, split wood, hoe beans, and follow the flight of birds familiar and strange through woods they know by heart.

"In the woods," Emerson writes, "we return to reason and faith." Thomas lives and writes in that tradition, and the account of his life—a life of practical action and patient thought—that you will find in the leaves of this book will entertain (quietly), instruct, and suggest in myriad ways how the nature of an ordinary (extraordinary) countryside remains the surest guide we have to the beauty and truth in things and in ourselves. References to Thoreau are almost always trite, but Henry would dig this humble, honest book, which takes up the business of life and death with gentle, well-earned wisdom.

Thomas, who is a genuine literary pastoralist (not some hit-and-run city slicker or media celeb slumming in the country), has paid his dues to the solitude and rigors of country life. Each year he lives up to its demands and puts up its rewards. He knows the cost of living and bears the expense with grace and wit. A classicist in many respects, his occupations and preoccupations are as noble as Hesiod's in *The Works and Days*. His voice is original and clear—strong as a Carolina wren's.

Thomas's prose shows the calluses and sinewy strength of days lived plainly and well doing the wild work of a new native guided by many mentors living and dead. Thoreau writes somewhere in *A Week on the Concord and Merrimack Rivers* that a writer's sentences should somehow convince the reader that their author could plow a deep, straight row. Thomas writes like that. His account of the practical and intellectual side of his honorable and radical pastoralism will appeal—I think, I hope—to many readers who would love to get themselves to the end of the road where, given half a chance, life and lives grow well.

Thomas Rain Crowe—a mossy-looking poet of a man—is a true son of the wild rural South. The wonderful book that follows is now a valuable part of our beleaguered landscape.

Highland Farm
Rockbridge County, Virginia
June 2004

Zoro's Field

RETURNING

I will arise and go now, and go to Innisfree,
And a small cabin build there, of clay and wattles made;
Nine bean rows will I have there, a hive for the honey bee,
And live alone in the bee-loud glade.

WILLIAM BUTLER YEATS
"The Lake Isle of Innisfree"

*W*hile sitting on his front porch looking out over the hills surrounding the Green River Gorge where his kin had farmed and fought the landscape and the elements for generations, local legend and mountain sage Zoro Guice turned to me and said, "The best way to learn about life, nature, and these mountains is to just go out into the woods and set down in one spot and let the nature and the teachings come to you. A man don't need to go searching for God or answers. Why go searching for something you can't find? All you need is a little patience. If a man goes out in the woods and just sets down in one place for long enough, all of nature and everything he needs to know will eventually pass before him like a parade."

Just as Zoro suggested, I have planted myself in this little cabin beside his old family homestead garden field and watched as the world of Nature and its parade of weather and wildlife have passed by like chapters in the book of these years spent in a writer's solitude on the extreme outer edge of the civilized world. And here I remain.

This place in the woods where I am living is part of what was once a mountain farm. Near the town of Saluda in Polk County, it was settled, owned, and worked for several generations by the Guice family, who migrated to America from Germany and then made their way from New York, down the Appalachians, into this region by foot and ox-drawn wagon to settle within a loose community of Scots-Irish immigrants along the ridgetops above the Green River just off the historic Drover's Road that went from Tennessee all the way to the Atlantic coast, crossing the Green River at a shallow ford just north of here where Zoro's grandfather, Peter Guice, would build the first bridge, and for whom the giant Green River Bridge is now named.

I never meant to come here. It all happened rather serendipitously — a lark that led to something stronger, more compelling, profound. I did what Joseph Campbell has called following your bliss — which led me here to the outskirts of a mountaintop farm and a small clearing surrounded by poplars and pines. I have been here, now, for a little over three years, scratching out an existence from the field that once fed the Zoro Guice family with rhubarb, mustard greens, Irish potatoes, and pole beans, and that now feeds me.

During these years of hibernating from humanity, I have come to believe that we must go home again. Whether home is literally where we are native or where our place-based imagination resides. To re-turn as "new natives" to do the work. "The real work," as my California friend and mentor Gary Snyder says. The work that puts blisters and then smooth calluses on the hands and mind as we strive to work reciprocally and in balance and harmony with the native people and the land. The kind of work that is collected and referenced in the libraries of the lives of elder men and women who have spent long lifetimes in one place learning and applying that knowledge to an agrarian and nature-based style of life. Knowledge taught and learned, protected and passed down from generation to generation as part of a culture soon to disappear — bits of which are now being passed down to me, as I struggle willingly and with wonder at self-sufficiency, becoming a "future-primitive" — someone who has gone back from the techno-cultural mainstream to the land.

I have come home again. Come back to the rural essences of my boyhood — where my early friends had been sons of farmers, or mill hands who grew large gardens, and where I had grown up in tobacco fields and potato patches, picking beans, shucking corn, and carrying water from a well. Back to the rural mountain highlands of western North Carolina where things are familiar and from where I now write.

I had been living in northern California working on a mountain farm in the Sierra foothills when I made the decision to come back east to the mountains of my boyhood and where I had spent much time during my college years. At some point while in college I had made my way up into Polk County looking for a mythic bridge that had been built across the Green River between two mountains. I ended up getting lost and landed in the front yard of an old mountain homestead where an elder mountain man named Walt Johnson was living with his dog Mac. I became friendly with Walt, and he later introduced me to Dr. Gelolo McHugh, who had bought the original Guice family farm and for twenty years or more had been prepping it for his impending retirement during long summer stays with his family. Dr. McHugh, who was, and is, a psychologist of some renown, took a liking to me, and so I began spending time with him during my truant visits to Saluda and the Green River watershed.

After I had finished school and spent a year in France working as a convent gardener and another working as a hired hand on a large family farm in Indiana, and after Walt had died, Dr. McHugh wrote to me saying that I could come and live in Walt's little cabin next to "the garden field." At the time, I was not ready to make this kind of move from the West Coast, where I was completely ensconced in movements both literary and bioregional. When the day did come that I found myself ready to make the leap, the cabin and the field were there for me. "Mac," as he is called by all his close friends (and after whom Walt's loping bloodhound was fondly named), had become, during those earlier years when I was still in school, like a father as well as a teacher and friend, creating the foundation for the relationship we share today—one that approximates that of Emerson and Thoreau, since Mac owns the land on which my little cabin stands, and since he is the wise, older mentor and patron. In a word, Mac is my Emerson. Without his generosity, patience, and insightful understanding, I wouldn't be here. Because I have a place to live where I don't pay rent and a garden where I can grow my food, I have been able to eke out a marginal living, to learn and live from the fruits of my labor and my natural surroundings, and to write—much as Thoreau did at Walden Pond.

Thinking of Emerson reminds me of when I was not much more than a boy reading a passage from one of his essays, in which he says, "You shall not tell me by languages and titles a catalogue of the volumes you have read. You shall make me feel what periods you have lived." These words have stayed with me over the years, and I have taken them to heart when I put pen and pencil to paper in an effort to scribe the nature of my thoughts and experiences as I have lived them here in the woods.

Emerson's ideas come back to haunt me pleasantly these days, as I stand at rest in my garden field leaning on my hoe or I prepare the fire to cook my evening meal, and I wonder if it wasn't these same lines that drove Thoreau also into the woods. In this sense Emerson has been an inspiration and catalyst to us both — a torchlight and helping hand to Thoreau's two years spent on Walden Pond and a guide and muse to these years I have labored and slept in my mountain cabin by Zoro's field. Trying to complete what Thoreau started one hundred fifty years ago, I want to take his experience of the body and its toil of work and reflections deeper into the heart and soul of the woods . . . in amongst the big trees and dark hollers of the natural world and the world of the human spirit. It is my goal to live at least twice the time he did at the edge of Walden Pond and to give myself a realistic opportunity to take the *Walden* experience and a life of relative seclusion a step further — two full seasonal cycles deeper into the heart and spirit of self-sufficiency and simple living to discover the soul of the wild. To find firsthand the path to a greater sense of self-confidence, with hopes of replacing an unnatural urban psychological fear with familiarity and serenity based on common sense. By "familiar" I mean recognizing and knowing myself and excelling in a natural environment in which I am truly and profoundly aware of my surroundings. This ideology is based on the premise of living in one place for a long time and knowing that place well.

So, after years of wandering North America and Europe, I have returned to the woods, where I live along the Green River near the great granite geologic confluence known as "the Blue Wall" and the North Carolina–South Carolina border. For almost four years, with the gift of a roof over my head, a small woodstove, and enough cleared land to garden, this has been my home.

My physical year has consisted of, firstly, nine months of laboring with and in the earth. Sowing seeds. Stewarding a wild / domestic life in a small ecosystem that is my sustenance, my habitat. Harvesting and laying by food and firewood for the winter. This is the work of living in the wild from March through November.

With the onset of cold weather late in the fall I am more than ready for the three months of hard labor within the confines of the cabin and the walls of the mind — months that nurture reading, writing, pondering (what the mountain people call "studying"), and walking the woods to let ideas settle like the rich lees in an old mountain jug of scuppernong wine. To allow mental gravity to bring me to rest in a place of calm understanding. The winter months are a time of exploring the wild world of image, symbol, and metaphor as well as the genesis of imagined speech, and of inquiring into what my Cherokee friends call the Great Mystery.

Then, with the first signs of green and red buds on the trees and vines in late March — and exhausted from mind work, with my body calling out for exercise and attention — I have, year after year, emerged from the cabin with hoe in hand. Drawn again to the dirt. "Poems on the back of a hoe . . ." my friend Jack Hirschman wrote to me recently from San Francisco referring to new poems I had sent him from the woods, poems mirroring a voice that has found its wisdom in the nine-and-three-month annual calendrical cycle of letting the body and the mind live freely and simply at nature's pace. A memory dance that my body and my mind play here in the wild Polk County woods and its subterranean world of silence that is not only familiar but genetic; is lyrical, is song.

As I sit here writing these words, it seems to me as if I've been here my whole life — such is the way time has stood still for me these past three years, stretching out to meet the seasons one at a time until life has become almost timeless and everything seems to merge into a larger, seamless kind of clock. A clock that never ticks yet whose hands keep on turning. Now the years seem to me more like days were when living in the world of machines and commerce, and days expand quietly and slowly into gentle years. Here in these woods the pace of nature has slowed life down from a car race to a stroll. From a rush to a ripple on the wind. What a difference this is! What a change it has made in my overall perspective on things and in my state of mind!

Here the deer and the dove go about their business at the same speed. Neither wearying of the other's proximity, they seem content to share the same space — neither possessive nor greedy for the right to food or a quiet place to graze and sleep. Watching them I have tried to learn the hospitality of their ways, their acceptance of one another, their willingness to share. How much we humans can learn from our wilder neighbors! There are lessons for us in everything they do. In this we would often do better to use a little less of the rational side of our enlarged brain and act according to the dictates of our cellular memory. Let the wildness of our distant beginnings guide us as we make our way through life and the world around us. At least, these are my thoughts as I live through the days that make up the seasons of each year and the necessary, yet gratifying, work that fills these days in this small green universe of plants and animals next to Zoro's field.

RETURNING HOME

Coming home is
where winter
is the eyes of an old man
near death.
Freedom
only a flame
in the heart of these hills.

Where I saw a falcon fly
down low near a school of fish.
Saw wind
color all the maples, red.

Here, the earth is as black
as the sky is blue.
As white as
my love for love
in an inch of snow.

Sun,
moon,
a shower of rain.

These three and the wind.
Corners of a square
in a circle's bane.
As I return.
Up over the rock ledges.
Home.

SOLITUDE

To go into solitude, a man needs to retire as much from his
chamber as from society. I am not solitary whilst I read and write,
though nobody is with me. But if a man would be alone, let him
look at the stars. . . . In the woods too, a man casts off his years,
as the snake his slough, and at what period soever of life,
is always a child. In the woods, is perpetual youth.

RALPH WALDO EMERSON
"Nature"

*I*t all began with this quote from Emerson's essay "Nature," which
is echoed by Thoreau in *Walden* where he writes: "I love to be alone. I
never found the companion that was so companionable as solitude."

From an early age these words of Emerson and Thoreau were for
me as much a mantra as a dare. A challenge to take my self-motivat-
ing sense of self-confidence and self-sufficiency and put it to the test.
Now, almost twenty years later, I am calling their bluff, living alone
here in the woods, retired from chamber as well as society, from time
and technology, staring at the stars.

How have I done it, and what have I done? Let me begin by saying that to live in solitude and to do what I am doing/have done, a
person must, first of all, be at peace with himself. He must enjoy his
own company. He must be comfortable with the lack of clatter of so-
called civilization or the chatter of the human voice. He must be able
to live with himself as a solitary, embracing silence and defying bore-
dom, restlessness, and constant stimulation coming from anywhere
but from within himself. Therefore solitude is not for everyone. I have
met very few who I expect could (or would) live as I do with silence
as my counterpart and counterpoint to conversation that only sometimes reaches the lips in a singular and solitary debate with the self.

Among the hurdles for those who would wish themselves into the
wild for a self-sufficient sojourn such as mine, is, foremost, overcoming one's fear of darkness. During the day, when we can see our potential adversaries and, in seeing, minimize the unknown, we are fairly
confident of our competence and ability, if nothing else, to retreat.

But at night in the country, when a black veil is lowered over sight and world, confidence falls away and even the smallest sounds seem expanded, are exaggerated to our ears, causing mind and imagination to run wild with hallucinations of conspiracy and ill will. Small rodents suddenly become flesh-hungry bears, moths become rabid bats, and foraging skunks become predatory wolves. To live alone in the wild, one must come to grips with darkness and, in fact, must learn to see at night. In order to adjust the eyes, one must begin by getting out and walking at night—first with full-moon light and then gradually making forays by the dark of the moon into the woods, as do my neighbors on a nightly basis: the screech owl, opossum, skunk, and raccoon. With time and practice eyes will adapt, retinal patterns change, fears subside, and one is well on his way to overcoming the insecurities about the world of shade and shadow comprising that half of our life that is naturally without light.

Perhaps even more important than being inwardly strong and independent, to live the solitary life one must be a good listener. Must be curious, have insatiable hunger for knowledge, be inherently unenamored of the sound of one's own voice.

"To be a good writer, you have to be a good reader," Mac once said to me, years ago, rightly perceiving my lack of discipline and my short attention span. In a parallel sense, if a person aspires to solitude, self-sufficiency, or to be someone who may have something one day to say, he must first be a good listener. This axiom is never truer than when one is living self-sufficiently, alone in the woods. Every synapse, nerve-ending, and sense mechanism in one's body must be in a constant state of alert, as much for self-preservation as for clarity of awareness, in order that the daily lessons offered by the natural world not be missed because one was not cognizant enough to recognize and receive them.

These days, when the economic lure of urban society is taking almost everyone to the cities and few are living simply or in the wild, there has become an exaggerated and romanticized idea of going back to the land. For the wrong person, an attempt to live remotely and away from one's peers and family may prove to be an exercise in futility at best and a waking nightmare at worst. This loner's life I have embraced, while being a vehicle for the most grand education one could ever hope to receive, comes at great price, even to those who are both at home with themselves and the silence and also agile at building a life in the wild. The wilderness is no place for the starry-eyed, the uncoordinated or uninitiated, as potential peril lurks over every hillock and around every river's bend. Let this warning be a strong one, and let me also testify that while turkey and fox on some days seem competent and even complete company, there are other days, even for the strong-hearted and the hardheaded, when the desire for human conversation or a lover's arms is palpable.

As I write these words I am smiling with the memory of having been here for only a short time and walking up a thin path in the woods at night to the little mountain home of an old bachelor who lived alone and whom I had lately befriended. As I approached, I heard a voice coming from inside the shack. Thinking that the old man must have visitors, and because I was coming uninvited and unannounced, I almost turned back. But since I had walked a long way to see my aging friend and since I harbored a healthy dose of curiosity, I walked ahead until I reached the near corner of the house. The voice inside grew louder as, like the Peeping Tom I was undoubtedly named for, I peered into the window. There, in the bright light of a single hundred-watt bulb that hung from the ceiling by a thin wire, was the old fellow holding forth and in fine voice. While I listened to what was more the measure of a sermon than simple social banter, I raised up, peering through the window to get a better look at whom he was preaching to. It didn't take long to realize that there was no one else in the small, lighted room other than his aging hound. After eavesdropping on one of the most entertaining, if not most bizarre, Southern Baptist–style sermons ever delivered to a canine audience of one, and not wanting to interrupt his diatribe or to embarrass him in any way, I turned around in the moonlit night and headed back out the same little bootworn path in the direction I had come.

While I was at first a little taken aback, even shocked, at having encountered my old friend talking to himself there alone in the deep woods, I had learned a valuable lesson: that even those who live alone and self-sufficiently for a lifetime can eventually fall victim to the siren's song of their own soliloquy as an occasional respite from the ineffable silence of a life lived at more than arm's length from their own kind.

In truth, one of the things that I cherish most about this life I lead in solitude, and despite my earlier and more monkish and naive aspirations regarding silence, is the unself-conscious freedom to talk to myself. In cities amongst throngs of people and their oversocialized notions and patterns of accepted behavior, people are made to feel more than guilty should they be caught talking to themselves. The looks on the faces of those nearby question the very sanity of anyone who is caught talking to less an audience than another soul. But in the country or in the wild, one constantly talks to himself! Talks to the trees, to the birds, to the wind and sky, to the earth and dirt that he digs to plant seeds or uncover fruit. And he talks in many languages—soliloquy, conversation, and song—as he walks along the water's edge, singing in trills and hums as he mimics the tunes of birds, the cry of fox and mating skunk. In all manner of ways does the human voice get a workout and opportunity to express itself. And all done without so much as a thought of self-consciousness or being ill at ease with what might be thought of in other circumstances as aberrant behavior. In fact he feels invigorated, satisfied with having done so.

My major source of conversation, however, during these past years, has come by way of an almost obsessive correspondence. The rural route mailman is for me a mythic Messenger as well as simply the bringer of mail. In that sense he is a silence-breaker, a link to the outside world, a revered and trusted friend. It would not be an overstatement to say that all the time I have been holed up here in my mountain shack I have been living on mail. And it has become a necessary nourishment and tonic in much the same way my evening meal has allowed me to get through the night in preparation for work the next day. My correspondence, this act of writing, is nothing less than sustenance for body and soul.

No matter what one's resolve, the human heart (and body) yearns for human companionship, and mine is no different from that of anyone else, no matter how much I may romanticize my own self-sufficiency. Behind all my posturing machismo and bravura, there are a million years of DNA coding that has, in our species, necessitated human touch. And even if, during long periods of drought, I am being touched only with the long, thin fingers of typewriter keys or smudged from the lipstick residue of ribbon ink from an old Smith Corona, the caress of my faraway friends is, on those days when I am gifted with mail, like a passionate embrace, a balm for untouched skin.

Again today there has been no mail. All this is but a reminder of the fact that in the end we are truly alone. Even amongst our families, friends, and crowded cities, we essentially wander the inner and outer worlds of this existence as solitaries. Our progression and progress through life is done on a thinly worn path through the woods of our experience (our karma and dharma) alone, where no one else has trod, from birth till death. And no illusion of romantic or unconditional love nor all the familial affection on Earth can alter the fact of our aloneness. Yet, paradoxically, it seems that as a result of our social instincts we are able to traverse, albeit roughly, this solitary and continuing initiation that is our life. On this thin path of paradox we are sometimes able to make physical and mental ends meet as we work to grow consciously or merely to survive, even though this relative solitude may not be of the quiet kind.

Yet, with all the inherent aloneness of a life lived in solitude, we are not quite literally alone, as I have a great deal of company—in both house and field. In winter I have the mythic and generational battle between old blacksnake and young squirrel going on in the ceiling above my bed. The rolling around of walnuts and acorns at night, to the accompanying patter of racing, chasing feet. And then the slither and slide of the old snake as it moves into position to tangle with the young and unsuspecting squirrel—until the battle is on and there is, for the rest of the winter, a squirrelly silence of nut-noise or the sleep-stopping patter of little feet.

The mice, too, have, as they do each year, come inside to weather the winter. And an occasional mole will show up following the avenues of entrance from the outside created by the mice. The house spiders take over in winter and put up their hard-to-see hammocks in every corner and cranny of the cabin, as if these right-angle paradigms of geometric perfection were designed with the Araneae species in mind. Even the space between rocker leg and the nearest wall is not safe from their loomlike instincts, as in a night's work they re-weave their webs that I destroyed in my rocking the previous evening while reading myself into the mood for sleep.

In the mornings I am wakened not only by the light of the sun but by the songbirds and the crows who perch themselves in limbs overhanging the roof of my cabin and make fun of my lethargy and my slow ascent into another day. Another reminder of how, in my aloneness, I am never by myself yet, at the same time, am in soli-tude. When the birds are singing and the turkeys cackling, I am in solitude. When the snake slithers and the squirrel scurries, I am in solitude. When the fox yelps and the skunk whines, I am in soli-tude. When the raccoon crashes and the opossum clumps, I am in solitude. When the rain beats down on the tin roof sounding like a million tiny drums and the north wind blows through the rainspout like a flute, I am in solitude. When the river roars over rocks and the spring branch trickles through twigs and leaves, I am in solitude. When the engine of the mailman's small blue car struggles unseen up the hill, with the sound of balding tires etching out new ruts in the slick dirt road and the clack of the door to my mailbox banging shut echoes through the woods, I am in solitude.

Alone, yet, like Thoreau, no more lonely than a dandelion in the pasture or a bean leaf in the garden row, the snowflake in a snowdrift or the honeybee in the hive, I have been here in this little house now for three years, and not one day have I felt sorry for myself or even en-tertained the idea of wandering away from here and back to the world of machines and men. Here in this solitude I am granted indulgences that are rarely, if ever, offered those in the outside world: lying in the grass on the south side of the garden field like a sleepy old dog, soak-ing up the afternoon rays of the sun, daydreaming; dashing clothes-less through the woods to the outhouse in the morning—soles flying over the frost to keep feet from freezing; sitting for long periods of time (maybe even hours) in the middle of a workday watching an ant-hill or a hive of wild bees; and, of course, talking to oneself. Distanced from time and human social strictures, one feels truly free and experi-ences a kind of pure anarchy. A return to childhood. Yet, consciously, becoming one with the wild.

Day by day I am increasingly aware of the gift that I have been given: to live in this way. Even with all the invitations and the possibilities for travel and a life in other places—which I must say are, on some days, pleasant sources for daydream—there could be no better life for me now than the life I have carved out for myself here in these woods. Here, with the seasons and the solitude, I have the best of this world. I relish this, knowing that this may be my only chance to live in this way. I've always said and believed, timing is everything. During these years of relative youth, I have chosen to be here as much as this place seems to have chosen me. In many ways, now, I have two of the things that I have wanted all my life: a place (without the psychic and fiscal encumbrances of ownership) and meaningful work. The third and more elusive variable in my ideal equation, a companion, is not an option now, for I still have much to learn from living here as an apprentice to the natural world. Another body in this small cabin would not only tip the scales of carrying capacity but would be a grave distraction from the kind of focus I have achieved the past few years, thanks to the utter simplicity of my daily pace and the freedom I have gleaned from being in one place for all this time.

As the sun each day rises and sets, Zoro's wise words keep coming back to me, echoing Emerson's—that everything a person needs and would want to know is right here and available to him in the world of nature. Every association and skill can be learned from watching and taking part in the dance of diversity and in the natural cycles of the wild world. Subsequently I have come to realize that there is no need for formal schooling other than to learn, maybe, a little practical math and to read and write. (And there are even times when I question the ultimate wisdom of these so-called civilized skills and the path they have mapped out for humankind since their inception.) For the most part, I value the perception I share with the rural mountain people that everything we need to know is right here in this natural classroom, if we are curious enough and patient enough to wait, watch, and listen in order to take it all in. There is no need to walk, like the seventh-century Chinese monk Hsüan-tsang did, across Asia searching for Truth. Truth can easily be found right where we are. If one stays in one place, quietly, for long enough, what one doesn't know will appear when one is ready. I believe this and have experienced this dynamic many times in the past few years here in these woods. Zoro's platitudes of common sense remind me of the lines of the ghazal (poem/song) of the fourteenth-century Persian poet Hafiz of Shiraz, who writes:

Now that I have raised the glass of pure wine to my lips,
The nightingale starts to sing!

Go to the librarian and ask for the book of this bird's songs,
And then go out into the desert. Do you really need college to read this book?

Break all your ties with people who profess to teach, and learn from the Pure Bird.
From pole to pole the news of those sitting in quiet solitude is spreading.

The great poets and contemplative minds have been thinking about the practice of solitude for a long time. Monks and yogis, solitaries and sages have gone out into various wildernesses of the world to seek out the needed and necessary quiet in order to let their minds and bodies focus on the natural rhythms, the universal harmonies that set everything silently swinging in this great life of ours. Having experienced a healthy dose of this kind of living and its indigenous knowledge, dreaming of being anywhere else than where I am right now serves no constructive purpose. And frankly I don't long to be elsewhere, or with others, as I am quite happy being here, in just one — this one — place, at the edge of Zoro's field.

LIVING ON MAIL

It's not only hope,
it's the letters have kept me alive
all these years.
My mailbox
like a big black belly,
always hungry,
always dying of thirst.

Rumbling and grumbling for
only the best of food.

Sometimes, during periods of draught,
there is not enough ink in the world
to go around.
My mailbox shrinks.
My body weakens.
And a time of darkness comes.

But bad times,
like my old friend says,
are the same as good times.
Neither lasts.

So I pick up thick books.
Take long walks.
And swim all day in the river nearby —
Until the groans from my middle
and my mailbox cease.
And there is mail.
And a flicker's unchained laugh
echoing wildly through the woods!

SUN TIME

Time is but the stream I go a-fishing in.

HENRY DAVID THOREAU
Walden

For him the sun was a sign, a symbol.
He bowed in prayer to what was behind the sun.
He made songs and dances to the makers and movers of the sun.

CARL SANDBURG
"Cahokia," *Honey and Salt*

*H*ere, at the end of what was once an old drovers' road—a foot-path for the Catawba, Creek, and Cherokee turned into a wagon-wheel concourse stretching from Knoxville, Tennessee, to Charleston, South Carolina, now known as Old Howard Gap Road—time stands almost still. Stands still in the sense that I am not living according to man-made time. Rather, I am living by the signs and the seasons. By the light- and heat-providing presence of the sun. By the phases of the moon. Zoro calls it "sun time." When he uses this phrase he means living a life that is off the clock. A reality guided by nature, alone. A calendar determined and dictated by daily and seasonal cycles that become ingrained, encoded, and therefore instinctual with each passing year of experience in the wild.

Not only am I off the clock, but I am also off the grid. No electric power, no phone line, no piped-in water or gas—nothing from the outside to which I am attached or obligated in terms of dependency or financial debt. As in Amish country, there are no power lines coming from the road and attaching to my house. There are no radio or TV antennas disrupting the natural line of this landscape. There are no bills hiding among the letters in my mailbox. This disconnected life at times feels like what it must feel like to free-fall through the air after jumping from a plane. What it must feel like to float weightless in space. It's a kind of physical and mental freedom that can't accurately be described with words. One has to have lived this anti-umbilical experience, I think, to know the feeling of essentially being unplugged and culturally adrift.

In *Walden*, Thoreau talks eloquently, even matter-of-factly (even sarcastically), about the need for a greater awareness and appreciation of the chapters of the day. "Morning air!" he exclaims. "If man will not drink of this at the fountain-head of the day, why, then, we must even bottle up some and sell it in the shops for the benefit of those who have lost their subscription ticket to morning time in this world." Echoing Thoreau's words, Whitman too celebrates the morning sun with words found in *Leaves of Grass* in the narrative and autobiographical poem "Song of Myself":

> along the fields and
> hill-sides,
> The feeling of health, the full-noon trill, the song of me rising from bed
> and meeting the sun.

With no clock or calendar in my cabin, I get up and go to bed with the sun. My body has become attuned to this pattern—so when the sun goes down every night, my body reacts, weariness sets in, and I am ready to sleep. And in the morning, when night's dark shroud is broken by the first rays of the sun, I'm wide awake—as if the sun were some kind of solar alarm clock. The pages in the chapters of a season's book turn as do the colors of the leaves in fall, as the solar cycle goes on day after day, night after night, thank goodness, without change or failure.

It is similar with the seasons. I don't need to turn the pages of any calendar to know when it is spring. The birds, the butterflies, the blossoms on the trees and flowers, the greening of the grasses, the warming of the wind . . . all these things and more tell me of the arrival of the new season. The same is true in summer, fall, and winter. The signs make themselves evident, and the mind and body take note and make the necessary adjustments. The body feels the shift and the mind begins thinking of corresponding seasonal things—like the exact day to go out under the apple trees to look for morels. While it doesn't hurt to know, from years of observation, that the return of the hummingbirds generally coincides with the appearance of this prince of the fungal world, the idea pops into the mind on the precise day that morel mushrooms will appear over in the orchard. As uncanny as it may sound to the uninitiated, this is how it works. I'll walk across

Zoro's field to the pine trees and through the pines to the logging trail that goes up into the woods and, beyond, to the orchards, and beneath the limbertwigs there they'll be! The whole process is autonomic. Signals are triggered, neurological connections are made, and programmed thought patterns appear on the screen of the mind, getting me ready for the wild work ahead for that season, until the signs and the signals shift again in about three full moons.

I much prefer nature's clock to the other methods and devices of keeping time. I've owned and worn a watch only once in my life, and that was for a few days as a teenager, having received a cheap wristwatch for a birthday present when I was thirteen. No sooner had I put it on than I began checking the time almost incessantly, neurotically. Every few minutes, it seemed, I would twist my wrist or push up my sleeve and look at my watch. I remember always being aware of the time, to the point that it was an ever-present and ominous specter that hung over me everywhere I went and with everything I did. I remember feeling imprisoned by this device on my wrist and what it represented. It quickly became so pervasive and preoccupying (even keeping me from sleep) that I took off the watch and threw it away (much to the dissatisfaction of its donor). I've never worn or owned another watch since. Being a prisoner to time for those few days during my youth parallels my experiences in subsequent years when I've worked in factories or at other jobs that necessitated punching a time clock at the beginning and end of the workday. This sort of relationship with time made me feel like little more than a number, albeit a body, chained to a huge and ominous System to which I had become enslaved.

Here in the woods along the Green River, with no watches, clocks, or calendars, there is none of that feeling of enslavement. Rather, and in direct opposition to that, there is a feeling of freedom, even flight. I am master of my time and my movements. I live entirely in the moment rather than by the clock. The past, the present, and the future seem somehow part of the same time-space continuum. The present seems never-ending and includes the past, taking it along for the ride like a companion or lifelong friend.

When I watch the wild turkeys that often wander into the garden field, they go about their business of searching for grain, foraging through the compost pile, pecking at the fall grapes low to the ground in the arbor, and just searching in general in a timeless fashion. They are not scurrying about as if at any moment a whistle will blow or a bell will ring to remind them of another deed that needs doing. Going about their business, they just ARE there in the field and, in that sense, at one with the field, their work, and the day. I can't help but laugh at the thought of my wild friends strutting around my garden field adorned with wristwatches, as if they were shopping at the supermarket before having to hurry off to pick up the kids at school. Fact is, I find that I've become more like these turkeys than I am like the folks I run into in town, who are always rushing about as if a pack of wolves were at their heels. Never graceful, never comfortable where they are and doing what they are doing, they seem to be always on edge and a little off balance, as everywhere, all around them and attached to their bodies, they are reminded of their obligations to the Great God of Time.

Here in Zoro's field I think back to ancient civilizations — the animistic and pagan cultures — which almost universally worshipped the sun as a primary deity. Having lived on sun time now for over three years, it's easy for me to understand the ancients' fascination with and devotion to that round, warm orb that comes up in the east and sets in the west each day. It provides light and heat — the true essentials for all life on earth. What could be more natural than to pray to and pay tribute to that which provides us with life? The great Egyptian sun god Ra lords over that culture like a true luminary, putting the illusive hominoid Christian God of time, guilt, and treachery to shame by comparison. Temples, pyramids, and massive statues were built, and elaborate ceremonies were choreographed throughout pre-Christian history in honor of various sun gods — all as, really, nothing more than a reminder that the natural world, and especially the sun, is worthy of man's worship and praise.

The way I see it, this business of sun worship is also part of my work here in Zoro's field. My prayers and my planting cycles are all dictated by the sun, with the moon as a monitor and a night-light for my sleep. I keep track of months by keeping watch on the waxing and waning of the moon. I keep track of the seasons by taking notice of the amount of heat that is generated during the earth's orbit around the sun. The respect and reverence we pay to both moon and sun is, or should be, equal to the time we spend in the field or in the woods and streams doing what we do to survive. The more pagan I have become (from *paganus* and the Latin root meaning "country dweller"—later modified into the French *pays* meaning "land" or "country"), the more the work of celebration and ritual goes hand in hand with the work I do with hoe, axe, or spade. Nothing that is done is taken for granted, and I am always finding myself in meditation and prayer—giving thanks to the sun, to the moon, for their roles in this wild life I live.

In his gnomic, gnostic, and slightly pantheistic poem "Waving Adieu, Adieu, Adieu," Wallace Stevens writes:

What is there here but weather, what spirit
Have I except it comes from the sun?

Sun time. Time for the sun. Time of the sun. Time with the sun. Keeping time to the sun. Time spent in the sun. Time orbiting the sun. Everything I do revolves around the sun. It is at the center of my life.

Here in this world away from blowing whistles, ringing bells, and ticking timepieces I am, ironically, more aware of time than those who live and are enslaved by it. In fact, I've found that when pressed by my infrequent and time-conscious visitors from the outside world as to what time it is, I can usually come within one or two minutes of the actual time—just from noticing the position of the sun in the sky, the amount of shadow cast by trees or buildings on the ground, or the temperature and the barometric pressure. My visitors think this to be some sort of magic when performed, but assuredly it is not sleight of hand. Rather it's that my sensory system (my body) has become so finely and intuitively tuned that my response to time is automatic, autochthonous—much the same as a few remarkable musicians I've known who are sensitive to pitch and can call out keys from hearing a single note.

Being in place (in with place) means being in the moment, of the moment. Living in the wild, in nature, I am truly in place. In this place there is ONLY the moment. It is a long, slow moment, to be certain. But it's always there and I am always a part of it. And in this sense, I know where and who and WHEN I am. There is no confusion. There is no uncertainty. There is no hesitation. There is no rush. There just IS. And that is IT. I am HERE. And the time is NOW. What else can there be?

TIME

Slow down!
Where are you going in such a rush?
To the supermarket of your last dime?
Is the sound of pencil-lead on paper
too much for your ears?

At fifty miles per hour
the butterfly on the rose by the side of the road
is as invisible
as a wish for the answer to prayers.
As you run through your best years
watching the road.

Faster than the speed of life.

THE WILD WORK

It's good to work—I love work, work and play are one. All of us
will come back again to hoe in the ground, or gather wild potato
bulbs, or hand-adze a beam, or skin a pole, or scrape a hive—
we're never going to get away from that. We'll always do
that work. That work is always going to be there.

GARY SNYDER
The Real Work

When Gary Snyder signs his letters to me, "yours in the wild
work," I know what he means. He's talking about organizing a local
watershed institute, preparing presentations for the board of county
commissioners, participating in forest-fire training sessions with the
volunteer fire department, writing another poem for his *Mountains
and Rivers without End* cycle . . . planting a garden, making a firebreak,
splitting firewood, sewing beads onto a peyote-meeting fan, putting a
water pump on his old flatbed truck. The highbrow and the lowbrow
of the work of self-sufficiency. The intellect intensely engaged alongside the forearm.

I watched him and his neighbors attentively during my years living
up on the San Juan Ridge—the way they worked as solitaries and the
way they worked as a community. It was no easy thing scratching a life
out of the rough climate and terrain of the Sierra foothills along the
Yuba River. And the word "work" took on a new meaning for me as I
wiped the sweat from my brow working and playing alongside Gary's
friends and my new neighbors.

But there's work and then there's "the wild work." While it's a fine
line that separates the two (if, indeed, they should be separated at all),
the wild work, for me, is more about time spent in thought and deed
in the wild world. In the world of nature. In the wilderness. This emphasis on wildness and wilderness comes from my own upbringing
and my memories of those years.

Those memories are juxtaposed with days like today, when the
wind is blowing from the west and I can hear the incessant roar of
the trucks on I-26 all day long—which, even though a long way from

the cabin, with the windows open sounds like it's right outside my door. This particular unpleasant disruption puts me on the defensive, and I yearn for an even simpler, quieter life—even farther from the fray and noise of the world and even deeper into the undeveloped and uninhabited woods that, ironically, are owned by Duke Power Company and border the Green River.

My initiation into the world of wildness came during my childhood years growing up on Snowbird Creek in Graham County, North Carolina. Snowbird Creek, the woods, the abundant wildlife, and the free-form, free-ranging relationship the young Cherokee boys and I had with this natural world were all there in my backyard—just outside the door of the little house where I was reared, irrespective of my parents' livelihood and values, as a child of nature.

My own essential and permanent social and environmental values were formed during those years, as were friendships, some of which have also lasted a lifetime. And it was there, I believe, that wildness became a part of my own personal bloodline—part of my genetic coding. Those were the barefoot years, running unimpeded and uninhibited through a seemingly boundless, wooded, watery, loamy, mossy, fern-resplendent, and blooming photosynthetic Eden. Surrounded in every direction by clean air, drinkable water, and the green silence and great solitude of the woods, my friends and I used the creeks and forests as a playground, where we were as free and at ease as were the animals.

While a good many families in our little mountain community eked out their livings working in the lumber industry—the main employer in the county—I was living a charmed life, oblivious to the unpleasant issues associated with the logging business and such specters as clear-cutting, which is on the tip of every tongue here in western North Carolina these days. The wilderness that surrounded my home across the road from Snowbird Creek was the source of my sense of freedom. In the shadows of the deciduous rain forest, I became conscious for the first time of the paradox of being anonymous there amongst the trees and, at the same time, of being so very visible, vulnerable, and known as a part of the community of wild animals and species that lived there so freely. At that point I began living, consciously, a dual life: the life I lived when I was with my family, when I was in school, when I was at church—in short, the life I lived in and around the human community—and the life I lived on my own when I was alone in the woods.

When I think back on those years, I think it has to be that pristine boyhood experience that has led me to these woods and this experience along the Green River here in Polk County. Why else would I be here? Why else would I have left northern California and the camaraderie of kindred kind? The answer to these questions could be nothing other than an arcane yet symbiotic calling that has come psychogenetically from my memories of wild youth spent not all that far from here. What other explanation could there be for my bizarre behavior? For leaving behind a congenial nature-based community for this hermit's life in the woods of conservative Southern Baptist North Carolina?

When Gary Snyder told me to "go home," at first I felt insulted, spurned. I took it to mean that he thought I was out of place there in the San Juan community. That I wasn't welcome. Didn't fit in. An outsider—something I had felt most of my life after being uprooted from my Graham County home as a boy. So, I rebelled by burying his remark in my subconscious and ignoring it, or at least trying my best to, which was no easy thing, as it had come from someone I looked up to as a mentor and teacher. Yet here I am, back in the North Carolina mountains. Home. Where now I am sitting, thinking back in the other direction, over a time-bridge that has lengthened from months to years, to when I lived on the site of an old Maidu ceremonial village, rich with old oaks (from which the natives had gathered acorns to make *ooti*—a kind of porridge that was their main dish), artifacts, and spirits-of-place who, more often than not, made themselves known in all manner of unpredictable if not unsettling ways. Back then I lived alongside a very different community of wildlife from what is familiar to me here—coyote, cougar, condor, eagle, weasel, and what seemed an overabundance of rattlesnake and deer.

I lived in that place in a Plains Indian tipi under a five-hundred-year-old cedar tree amidst a community of humans that included farmers, home builders, moccasin makers, musicians, river rafters, magazine editors, and Zen meditators. In that community I was allowed to live a kind of Anglo-Indian fantasy, where I rode a wild stallion bareback over and through the northern California hill country, coming home from those riding excursions to tend fields of comfrey, popcorn, and garlic and to make cheese and yogurt from the milk of goats.

As I sit here looking back on it, I can see that not only was that period something of a return to my past and the pristine connections I had made with the natural world here in western North Carolina as a boy, but it served as a means of making even deeper impressions on my inner psychic and psychological wildernesses. Having developed a more mature and objective eye by the time I arrived in the Sierra foothills, I was able, in that wild yet nurturing environment wedding human with nature, more clearly to search for and see the Big Picture where the Natural Universe was concerned, and how it played off the microcosmic world with relative ease and balance.

I sit here in my rocker, with the woodstove lit and the front door of the cabin wide open, in a warm womb, and think fondly of those Maidu village days and of the re-inhabitory community into which I was accepted. And out of which I was thrown, gently and lovingly, in order that I might find my way back to my true home here in the Green River woods.

The years of experience and awareness garnered in the back country of the Sierras and earlier during my Graham County boyhood, I have brought back with me into this one-room cabin that Walt Johnson and I built many years ago while I was still in college down in Greenville, South Carolina, at the foot of the Greenville watershed, which has its headwaters just south and east of Saluda. For almost four years this has been my home, where I am again amongst the familiar faunal faces of my youth: black bear, wild turkey, hedgehog, peregrine falcon, gray fox, ruffed grouse, blacksnake, copperhead, and the ever-present crows. With the gift of a roof over my head, enough cleared land to garden, and few interruptions or temptations from the outside world, I have set up house and garden to take Thoreau's *Walden* experience even more self-sufficiently into the deep woods. To try to discover firsthand the organic and natural rhythms of the God-given world, as well as the ritual essences of self-sufficiency, self-confidence, and the purging of psychological fear. Where on full-moon nights I sit by the fire in deep thought, contemplating a physics of wildness based on commonsense familiarity and observation borne of a life lived at the (true) speed of life. A speed borne of wilderness. A life lived doing the wild work.

The wild work, like "the real work" Snyder talks about, is borne of necessity and caring. Caring for what lives around us and what sustains us. Caring implies protecting. For if we should not protect that which sustains us, then what are we left with but our own wits and clumsy devices that feign to approximate what the natural world does as a matter of course? The real and wild work is what we humans do with our intellect and efforts to organize and improvise ways of maintaining some modicum of balance with the natural world, allowing us a life of relative peace and possibility and, in good times, even a sense of security. Without this inner peace that comes with a deep inner knowing that we are at one with the wild world around us, there can really be no sense of security, and therefore we are not at rest but rather are rest-less, fearful, tired. And we know from history what havoc is wreaked from fear and fatigue. So, while fear and fatigue are inherently present in those few of us who attempt to live self-sufficiently on the land, we do try to minimize those weakened and deluded states of body and mind by giving ourselves a fair chance at a noble life of living at peace amidst the ordered anarchy of the wild.

Snyder himself defines the real work as being:

What we really do. And what our lives are. And if we can live the work we have to do, knowing that we are real, and that the world is real, then it becomes right. And that's the "real" work: to make the world as real as it is, and to find ourselves as real as we are within it. It is what is to be done. To take the struggle on without the least hope of doing any good. To check the destruction of the interesting and necessary diversity of life on the planet so that the dance can go on a little better for a little longer.

Taking life one day at a time is what I think he's getting at here. For my part, I have taken and given, on this day, all that I have. I've fed the wild birds, created a five-day stew that I have simmering on the woodstove, chopped up a week's worth of kindling and night wood, sewed buttons back on my winter vest, walked to the top of the orchard hill and back after checking the spring, and written it all down in the detailed journal I am keeping of the seasonal transition from winter to spring. It has all been done wildly, yet with love.

It's past dark and time for bed. I stick one last round of ironwood into the small box woodstove, shut down the air vent and the damper for the night. My last act of wild work for the day.

OCCAM'S RAZOR

for Wendell Berry

"Work is the health of love."
The best path.
Something as simple as wood.
As wild
as a tree. Or
the perfect essence of space —
These ways.
Like the magic of hands:
    gone, without trace . . .

In a small world,
I live with the things I grow.
Careful of what comes.
Letting nothing go.

JOHNSON'S POND

A lake is the landscape's most beautiful and expressive feature.
It is earth's eye; looking into which the beholder
measures the depth of his own nature.

HENRY DAVID THOREAU
"The Ponds," *Walden*

I met Walt Johnson many years before I moved into the cabin he had once inhabited next to Zoro's field. I was going to school in Greenville, South Carolina, and had borrowed a friend's car and driven up into the Greenville watershed to try to locate an enormous bridge I had been told had been built over the Green River, sans road, somewhere in the vicinity of the town of Saluda. I had taken Old Macedonia Road, missed the bridge, lost my way, and found myself in the dirt yard of an old mountain house that sat on the edge of a small, jade-colored lake. No sooner had I driven up into the yard than an old man emerged from the quaint board-and-batten house. This was Walt Johnson, who, in his late sixties, was living alone in his family home-place. After asking directions to the "big bridge between two mountains in the middle of nowhere" (the Peter Guice Memorial Bridge on I-26 between Saluda and Flat Rock), I was invited into the house and introduced to his bloodhound, who answered to the name of Mac. After I had drunk a glass of springwater and answered a lot of questions as to who I was, where I was from, and what my intentions were, Walt took me back outside, where we began to walk around the eastern perimeter of the lake.

Immediately I was struck by the quiet calm and serene beauty of the place. At the time, I had not, as yet, been to Thoreau's Walden Pond in Concord, Massachusetts. But as I walked around the perimeter of this pristine green body of water reflecting the color of the pines, with Walt chattering and giggling at his own jokes, I thought to myself: "Walden Pond! A cabin sitting on the edge of a perfect pond surrounded by nothing but nature—this is what Thoreau's haven away from the world must look like." And it was at that moment

29

that the old Johnson home-place and its body of quiet water became my Walden Pond.

During the three years I remained in Greenville following that serendipitous day, I guess I spent more time with Walt and Mac on Johnson's Pond than I did at school. My studies seemed almost insignificant in comparison with what I was learning in the woods and on the pond not far from the Green River. It turned out that Walt was an unlikely mentor, but despite his puckish nature, he was a teacher nonetheless. I learned about pond life and small watershed ecosystems in ways that I could never have learned in introductory biology courses at school, as Walt, Mac, and I searched the underbrush and the grass around the pond for duck eggs, which would, with grits, make up our morning meals. For dinner we often had catfish I'd caught on a long bamboo pole baited with worms. Walt would laugh as I cut my fingers on the fins while trying to skin the catfish with a pair of pliers. In this and other work around the place, I became something of a willing servant to Walt's whims. I think he enjoyed watching my awkward attempts to master basic life skills long held by the mountain people of this region, and he would often tease me mercilessly when I made a fool of myself, time and time again, trying to do the simplest of chores. But it wasn't long before I could catch and fry up a large catfish that was at least edible and seemed good enough to satiate our appetites, excluding Mac, of course, who had no taste for fish.

Looking back on these first days at Johnson's Pond, I can appreciate Walt for the character he was. I remember that at some point early on, I brought a lovely blond girl, whom I was dating at the time, with me on one of my quick getaways to Saluda. No sooner had we driven into the yard than Walt had us inside the house, offering us a meal of corn bread, boiled potatoes, and black-eyed peas. As he dished up the plates for our late-afternoon supper, he turned to me with a twinkle in his eye and asked me whether I'd ever eaten "red okra." I hadn't and told him so, which sent him into the bedroom in the back of the house. He emerged holding what looked like dried red okra in his left hand. "Here," he proclaimed, playing to his captive audience, holding the pods of okra up in the air for my young guest to see, "is some of the best red okra you'll ever eat." I should have contemplated the slight smile peeking out from under his lips as he made his pronouncement, but I didn't, being more concerned with making a good impression on my friend. As he placed our plates of mountain gruel in front of us on the small, rough-hewn oak-top table in the room that tripled as dining room, kitchen, and parlor, he handed me one of the long, thin red pods, inviting me to "take a big bite." Taking delight in my inexperience and lack of knowledge of southern Appalachian cuisine, he smiled as I took the red pod from his extended hand and bit about three inches off the tip. Three seconds later I was on my feet and headed out the door toward the springhouse. As I hit the yard I could hear Walt laughing inside, my mouth ablaze from the heat of the hot pepper. In the springhouse, my whole head went under water as I struggled to extinguish the fire in my gullet.

Feeling like the fool I was for having been suckered by such a prank, I went back to the house, where Walt was parading around the room and looking very proud of himself while making a mockery of me to my friend: "What do you think of a man who would eat a hot pepper thinkin' it was okra?" Embarrassed, I picked at my meal, wondering what else he had slipped into the supper while I wasn't looking. My girlfriend seemed to enjoy Walt's little joke, which made the whole episode all the more demeaning. Even the dog seemed to have a wry grin on his baggy snout.

Such were the early years and the adventures with Walt during my days of internship and idyll at Johnson's Pond—a saga that ended one weekend when I arrived at the Johnson farm to find the old home-place reduced to ashes. It was still smoldering, with only the large stone chimney standing like a lone fireman poking at embers in hopes of discovering some relic or memento of the past.

As I got out of my borrowed car, Walt and Mac emerged from the woodshed, where they had been sleeping the past two nights since the house had burned. "Electric fire," was all Walt said when I asked him what had happened. "Them old wires in the kitchen. Never was put in right. I knew they was bad, but I never had anyone come in and rewire the place. Never had the money." I still remember the sight of the standing chimney and the smoldering ashes as one of the saddest I've ever seen. Paradise lost. Burned, at least. Even today I can't go down the road to the old Johnson place and stand by the edge of the pond without experiencing a rush of memory of all-night conversations between Walt and me on evenings when it was too cold to go to bed or the *likker* was too good, or without feeling a sting of sadness for the loss of the classic sawmill shack that once looked out over the lake like a proud fisherman contemplating his catch.

It wasn't long before Walt and I were at work building the cabin beside Zoro's field where Walt would spend the next ten years while I was off living in France and then on the West Coast as one of the Baby Beats. Only after I'd returned, and after Walt had died, did I learn the truth about the fire: Walt had burned down his own house. He had apparently gotten into some kind of disagreement with the folks from Florida to whom he had sold the old family farm, a land deal that left him as the caretaker of the place for as long as he lived. It had something to do with money that he felt was owed him by the new owners and that they were apparently unwilling to pay. So, in stereotypical mountain style, he retaliated by burning down the house, thinking it would deprive the Florida family of its value while allowing him an out from under the contract/deed he had signed. Homeless, he lived for a time in the woodshed, until Mr. McHugh offered to put up the money for materials so that Walt could build a little bungalow in exchange for help with the upkeep of the orchard and property, which had belonged to the Guice family during an earlier era when generations of Guices and Johnsons had lived in proximity as neighbors.

These days, with little traffic or use from the owners in Florida, the pond is pretty much as it was in the days of my first visits as a college student up into the North Carolina hills. A sanctuary for wild birds, forest animals of all kinds, and a diverse population of fish. I go down to the pond by way of a trail that follows a spring branch through a wee glen of trillium, wild sarsaparilla, and Solomon's seal and ends at the water on a west bank, where, in the shallows, bream make their beds and breed in the muddy bottom. Where trout and bass jump, biting at insects invisible to the eye. Where mallards and wild geese lay their eggs under the boxwoods and in the high grass, and turtles wander around almost aimlessly as if drunk on their own muse. So quiet, so serene, so filled with a sense of the bucolic is the energy (what Buddhists call "chi" and what geomancers call "ley") of this place. I come here, as I did as a student, to witness the windfall of nature's wealth in beauty. I love this place and its ongoing continuity of self-sufficiency and subsistence—all carried on without the assistance of human hands. The balance it has achieved is a kind of perfection that inspires me in my daily tasks of trying to scrape together a crude life for myself up the road amidst much rougher terrain.

It is spring and I have come down the hill from the cabin to be beside the pond. I park myself on a south-facing bank in a soft bed of crowfoots and moss and just lie, for the sake of lying, in the noonday sun. I spend an afternoon watching the Rorschach of clouds, the migration of birds, the way the wind choreographs the dance of the upper limbs of white pine, tulip poplar, and silver maple on the ridgetops that surround. Propped up on an elbow, chewing on a blade of long, green grass, I can see the large snappers coming up from the bottom of the pond for air. Their long necks and small heads poking out of the water like apostrophes renegade from words. A water snake swims leisurely, undulating, creating ripples, as it makes its way into reeds on the opposite side of the pond. A ruffed grouse drums somewhere off in the woods to the north. A pond frog tries, like an aging rock star, to sing . . .

When Thoreau wrote about Walden Pond, it was often from the perspective of his boat. A small canoe. Sitting in the still water, looking down, watching the perch play on the ribbed bottom, while playing the flute. Charmed by the fish and his own music. Lying beside my pool of water, my Walden Pond, I feel as Thoreau must have felt, agreeing that my pond, like his, is "a perfect forest mirror." Would that I could write like Thoreau—could write down the things I think and feel in my idyll by my Green River pond with such resplendent passion. I wonder if, maybe, feeling is enough. But I know it's not—for someone like me whose blood boils over, gushing with words.

What I know is that each time I come into this watery clearing in the woods, whether I enter by dusty roadway or by way of the spring-branch path, I feel the same expansive opening and sense of well-being. It feels a lot like what I felt at Walden Pond during a single day there a few years ago, swimming, hiking, and sitting amongst beech trees in a grove. I could almost hear, that day, Thoreau's words, just the way I remembered them today as I came up to Johnson's Pond—his voice loud and clear, echoing my own thoughts: "Why, here is Walden, the same woodland lake that I discovered so many years ago. The same thought is welling up to its surface that was then; it is the same liquid joy and happiness to itself and its Maker, ay, and it may be to me." Each time I return to Johnson's Pond, it is like the first time I laid eyes on it. Fresh, new, timeless.

I took a smooth white rock from the bottom of Walden Pond the day I swam there. That stone now sits on my writing desk in the cabin. It is a tangible link between Walden Pond and Johnson's Pond. Between north and south. Between past and present. Between Thoreau and Crowe.

As I think these thoughts I am pulled from my reverie by the sight of a large water snake at the center of the pond. It is moving fast. In a straight line. As it gets closer I can see that its eyes are fixed on me. It is coming at me! Closer still, I begin to sense it is not happy with my being sprawled out in this particular place. Am I near its nest of young? It swims faster, closer. Right at me. The snake is now no more than twenty yards out in the water from where I sit. From this distance I can see the dark brown blotches in alternating bands on the back of the snake. I've seen this kind of snake before, and Walt called it a moccasin. Is this indeed a cottonmouth water moccasin? Or just a northern watersnake (*Nerodia sipedon sipedon*), what is more commonly called the banded watersnake? In a place where everything green is referred to as either laurel or ivy, the name moccasin is also applied to almost every kind of large brown water snake. Knowing that the likelihood of a cottonmouth water moccasin appearing in a small lake in western North Carolina at an elevation of almost 2200 feet is slim, if not impossible, and that banded watersnakes are often mistaken for cottonmouths, makes little difference, as the aggressive-ness of this particular snake coming at me from across the lake has pressed my fright-and-flight button. A sense of wild instinct and pres-ervation sets in. Taking no chances on the true identity of the snake, I jump to my feet and flee . . . the snake having by now reached land and started through the grass. I hit the path on the south side of the pond, running. Looking back as I run, I see it pursuing me. I run faster and don't stop until I've reached the old homesite that looks down on where I had spent the afternoon reclining in the sun. There is no sign of the moccasin, only a patch of Devil's Bit, its white catlike tails sticking above the ground cover of crowfoots and fiddlehead ferns. The snake must have found its den—which for most banded watersnakes is usually in a burrow of some sort in the overhanging embankment, in shoreline vegetation, or in an old log. Glad, in any case, to be out of range of the snake—no matter what its phylum, genus, species, or common name—I blow a sigh of relief. Winded and breathing hard there in the yard where the old mountain house once stood and where all my subsequent Green River adventures began, I perceive the incident with the snake as a kind of sign, a message for me to end my idyll and go home. Not wanting to retrace my steps and venture too close to the snake's lair, I decide to go back the long way and take the path around the east edge of the pond past black pools of frog eggs that ring the shoreline like a living necklace, then walk over the rustic bridge that crosses a feeder-branch, go up a thin path made by wild turkeys who come down to the water to drink, and scale the ridge to an old logging road that cuts through a large stand of poplars at the edge of Zoro's field.

A POND IN THE WOODS

There are answers in the ponds at night.
Like the silence of fish.
How many wheels are turning in these woods?
Little lives
unseen in the dark
as I walk alone by the lantern-light presence of moon.

For those who don't die,
their lives are like the time that is locked up in rocks.
Stones thrown sleeping into
the bottom of the pond
where bream bed and are born
to the water in flight.
This night
like remembered moonlight
reflected in the eyes of owls.

TOOLS

We had our hands full the first ten years just getting up walls and
roofs, bathhouse, small barn, woodshed. A lot of it was done the
old way: we dropped all the trees to be used in the frame of the
house with a two-man saw, and peeled them with drawknives.

GARY SNYDER
"Kitkitdizze," *A Place in Space*

By cutting wood with an axe,
the model is indeed near at hand.

LU JI
"Essay on Literature," fourth century AD

*T*he very best friends to anyone who would attempt to live the
self-sufficient life are his tools. Without the proper tools, a man
is as useless to this life as any member of the natural order would be
in trying to reinvent itself as a human and take on the manners and
customs of the upright race.

I am remembering an experience I had with Zoro, not long after
beginning my life here in the woods, and the important lesson learned
on that day. As on many previous occasions, I had traveled by foot up
Old Macedonia Road to Guice Road and Zoro's farm to lend him and
Bessie a helping hand with chores. Helping them with various labor-
intensive tasks was a way of showing my thanks for all the hospitality
they had shown me and for the practical education and advice they
had given me on woodslore and the business of simply getting by. On
this particular day, after sweeping a winter's worth of pine needles
from the tin roof and gutters of the house, hoeing out new rows for a
second planting in the garden, and cultivating the early potatoes, I was
set to the task of splitting kindling for Bessie's wood-fired cookstove.
Bent over the woodblock, a small axe in one hand and a thin poplar
limb in the other, hacking off twelve-inch lengths that would be used
as tinder for starting fires or for adding heat to an already ignited firebox (which she used in all seasons despite the heat or the fact that she

had a brand new electric range there in her kitchen, donated by her children, that she had never used), I had already accumulated a generous pile of kindling from a huge pile of limbs Bessie had dragged up on one of her scavenging forays into the woods, when I was startled by the sudden presence of Zoro. He had walked up behind me and was standing over my right shoulder, watching as I hacked away at the branches with a novitiate, zealous, one-handed awkwardness. No sooner had I noticed him than he reached over my shoulder and grabbed the small kindling axe out of my hand, as if taking a dangerous object away from a curious toddler. Taking a quick glance at the business end of the axe, and with an expression that was at once disgusted and fraught with pain, he peered down on me kneeling there amidst the woodchips and sawdust and said: "I can't bear to watch for nary another minute a man make so much work of such a simple job! How do you expect to cut anything with a dull axe? As tired as I am from just watchin' you, I may as well be out here doin' this for myself!"

Embarrassed by Zoro's scolding and by the fact that I hadn't thought to check the blade of the axe for sharpness, I remained silent, having nothing to say in my own defense. As I knelt there in myopic mute self-examination, Zoro pulled a long thin filing blade from his overalls, laid the head of the axe on the chopping block in front of me and began to file smooth, steady strokes over the edges of the axe. As the axe blade started to take on a bright silver sheen, and after he had lifted it up from the woodblock and tested its sharpness with his thumb, drawing a thin line of dark red blood, and then running the filed edge against the contour of the backside of his forearm — cutting the hair on his arm as he went, like a scythe mowing wheat — Zoro looked down at me with something of a twinkle in his eye, handed me the axe, and said: "A man's no better than his tools. If'n he don't take care of his tools, keep 'em looked after and sharp, he'll end up workin' himself to death before his time. A sharp tool saves a man time, strain, and adds years to his life." With that proclamation he turned and walked in the direction of the barn and returned within a few minutes with an armload of old tools that looked to have been used for generations — so worn and filed down as to be barely recognizable as anything that might have originally been store-bought or new.

"Since you're settin' there filing that axe, I've got these here other tools that need a few licks from that file of yours. It'll get you in the practice," Zoro concluded. He laid down the load of tools that included a shovel, mattock, sling-blade, hoe, hatchet, and threshing scythe and turned and headed back for the house with a knowing grin on his face.

I remember sitting there on that chopping block for the rest of the afternoon filing Zoro's tools. I had watched Zoro file the axe and so made quick work of finishing his job, as well as sharpening the hatchet. But with the other tools I had to discover on my own the proper stroking angles and technique by trial and error. After a couple hours of filing, with forearms aching and fingers bleeding from missed strokes, I was whipped. As I got up from my knees and reached for the brush pile to test the newly sharpened axe on a limb, there was Zoro standing beside me like an apparition, with a huge hunk of corn bread and a glass of sweet tea in his outstretched hands. "I don't never ask a man to do anything without pay," he said, standing there smiling with that all-knowing look on his face. A little less embarrassed than at our previous encounter, I smiled back. As he sauntered away to the house, I made quick work of both the corn bread and the tea.

Walking home down Macedonia Road at dusk, I noticed that I was feeling satisfied with myself. Not only from having done a day's work to help the Guices, but from something much less immediately tangible than a day's wages paid in corn bread and tea. I wasn't going home that evening empty-handed. I had been paid with knowledge and given a lesson that I knew would accrue interest over the course of a lifetime. In that sense it would prove priceless.

It's spring again and two years since that day I spent in front of Bessie's branch pile filing tools. This time of year, when the weather begins to stay warm from day to day in longer stretches, the morels and hummingbirds appear, the spring rains come to soften up the garden soil that has been freezing and thawing all winter, and there are fewer and fewer fires to be built in the woodstove for the purpose of providing heat, I get out my tools and begin the ritual of filing them down to that Zoro-sharp edge. Zoro's lesson of a couple of springs ago has become a seasonal ritual as well as part of my kinesthetic memory. A reflex action that comes on the heels of the blooming of the ornamental pear trees in the Revis family yard down the road, of the first sight of bluebirds and the return of chipmunks and woodchucks from their underworld winter dens. The longing for the sound and feel of metal on metal hits me like a hunger, and I know from this impulse, this yearning that comes from arm muscle and ear, that it is time to take care of the tools.

For the small mountain farmer such as myself, there are a few essential tools that are as important as good health and the food we eat to keep ourselves alive. Tools that, in all honesty, spend most of the year in the slab-sided toolshed I've built on the far side of the garden field. A few of these tools I have inherited as gifts from Zoro. I don't embrace them as keepsakes but rather have, in some cases, re-handled them from grip-sized sourwood saplings and made them a part of my arsenal of friendly weapons with which I fight the good fight of self-sufficiency. I carry on the hand-tool tradition that has been passed down through at least two generations with Zoro's hoe, its blade barely half the original size, so much of it having been filed off by either rasp or loamy red-clay mountain soil.

The list of tools that stand at attention in neat, orderly rows in my toolshed reads like a who's who in the history of agrarian domesticated life on the planet Earth: hoe, axe, mattock, maul, wedge, scythe, shovel, sledge, handsaw, crosscut saw, pitchfork, rake, hammer, hand drill, and level. Like businessmen sitting in raised chairs on the corner of a city street on a summer morning waiting for their shoes to be shined, my tools wait for their spring makeover and a call to arms from the raspy blade of my silver file.

This spring, like those that have come before, with the honeybees out of their hives and working the golden surfaces of the dandelions for pollen, each tool will take its turn out on the chopping block and will be sharpened carefully and properly until it has received a razor-sharp edge — allowing it to penetrate either earth or wood easily, as if it were a foot sliding into a pair of familiar shoes. The *hoe* will emerge from its session with file, its multigenerational blade yet another eighth of an inch shorter, and make its way to the north end of the garden to furrow shallow rows for early spinach, leeks, spring onions, cabbage, parsnips, rutabagas, and Jerusalem artichokes. The *axe*, with a fresh edge and maybe a new hickory handle after a rough winter's workout, will find its way into the nearby woods to cut dead branches a manageable length from fallen or standing-dead trees, branches that will become kindling for fires for cooking corn bread or simmering a cast-iron pot of stew. The *mattock* will leave the sharpening block to find its way to the south end of the garden, where it will turn up mulched cabbage, carrots, beets, and other tubers and hearty vegetables that have wintered over and need to be harvested before the warm soil and rain cause them to rot. It will also be used to dig out around the spring, to rid the springbox of silt and to open up the spring so that it can freely flow. The *shovel* will begin the spring turning the compost one last time before going into the rows where seed potatoes will be dropped. It will dig deep holes where the germinated tomato seeds, as slips, will be heeled-in later in the spring. It will dig postholes for the locust poles that will carry the heavy weight of half-runner green beans as they mature and spread out on the trellises during the summer months before becoming ripe and being picked by the bushel. The long tines of the *garden rake* are filed in a circular motion to get their tips almost to the likeness of icepicks, so they will glide through the turned earth creating waves of soil covering the planted and sown seed and will clear the paths through the woods and around the cabin of a winter's worth of matted and rain-soaked leaves and twigs. The working edges of the *splitting maul* and *wedge* also will be sharpened to take that first bite into a round of wood still needing to be split for the last fires of the season or to create the poplar and pine kindling for woodstove firings for cooking during the spring and summer. A good edge to the *scythe* takes only a few minutes, with the thin metal being honed to a clean silver glaze and sharp sparkle in several long licks of the file, thus readying it for the clearing and maintenance work of keeping the briars and brambles at bay during the warmer months when untended grasses and weeds dominate the woods, orchard, arbors, and fields.

Last but not least are the garden, kitchen, and pocket knives, which demand oil and a sharp edge by way of my whetstone. The smaller pocketknife demands special attention, as it is a constant companion—like a lover carried all year long against my hip. It is not uncommon to meet an old-timer here in this community who has carried a single familiar penknife his whole life—one that was given to him by his father and that belonged to his father's father before that. These knives carry with them the weight and bearing of a rite of passage amongst the male members of the community and are carried and brought out for show, conversation, and trade with pride and bragging rights.

Added to those already mentioned, yet of a different family, is another tool that is part of one's essential cache: the *fishing rod*. With the annually stocked wild and scenic Green River nearby, mountain trout has, along with squash, apples, corn, tomatoes, and potatoes, become one of my dietary staples. It is just a fifteen-minute hike down to a section of river that is rarely visited or fished because of the steep and rocky terrain. There I can always catch my limit of trout—for smoking, for fish jerky, or for the instant gratification of an evening's meal. The short plastic pole I own is handy in getting around through the thickets and laurel hells down by the river and has allowed me to add a bit of soft meat and protein to my otherwise vegetarian diet.

Here in the woods of Polk County, I treat my tools as I would a family, an automobile, or a mule, if I had such things to be responsible for. I remember Zoro telling me a moving story about his mule, who had lived for over thirty years and had, in essence, fed and provided for his family during all that time. When the old mule finally drew its last breath, Zoro walked out of the barn and sat down by the side of his house and spent the rest of the day crying, unable to be comforted—so much a part of him and his family, so much a friend had that old mule been.

With this same kind of loyalty anyone who would live self-sufficiently must bond with his tools. Without them, without their being healthy, clean, and sharp, one is an all but helpless freak in these woods. My tools, like Zoro's mule, are my friends. I talk to them the same as I would talk to my neighbors, the rural-route mailman, or the animals that make their homes in these woods. I love to go into the shed in the winter and commune with my half-hibernating tools, the rakes and scythes hanging from their nails against a backdrop of veined and weathered balsam boards. Like old-timers sitting around a pot-bellied stove in the general store, we swap stories and lay plans for the coming spring. The tarrying tools in the shed are a portent of the warm weather to come, of movement and exercise, and the welcome work of getting one's hands, feet, and whole body back into the dirt.

By taking good care of the tools I have and learning how to use them efficiently, I have been able to be here, warmed and well fed, through three winters. (Admittedly I have been blessed with good physical health.) My tools are evidence of my wealth. Though I have no money, I can hold up my tools as currency. Currency I would not trade for the bank account or the life of any man who is not living in the wild.

I've always thought it interesting that in some tribal or more traditionally agrarian cultures, to steal tools is a crime punishable by death. To steal the tools of another is tantamount to murder, since the victim wouldn't be able to survive without them. Thusly are tools in these cultures valued. With this kind of care and with this sort of ethic in mind, I keep my tools in good condition. For the same reasons, I follow the ethic that is practiced here in these mountains: that it is impolite to ask to borrow someone's primary tools, as no one wants to risk having someone else damage something that is essential to his family's well-being. By the same token I don't want to be responsible for having broken or damaged anyone else's tools. We keep our tools to ourselves and close to home. While the members of my immediate neighborhood are only too happy to offer a hand to anyone in need, I don't think I have heard of a native in this community who has lent out either his chainsaw or his mule for someone else to use. The chainsaw especially is a sacred cow in the social ethic of tools and the lending of tools because of the delicate and variable nature of the tool itself and its potential for breakage, its costliness, and the impact it has as a laborsaving device. One might, coming from the urban, outside world, find such attitudes and behavior amongst the mountain farmers of this region strange. But those of us living in the mountains on little or no monetary income and dependent upon our tools to make it from one day to the next would only

laugh at outsiders who might make fun of such "selfish," "old-fash-
ioned" eccentricities. Eccentricities and epithets aside, I have made
a good life for myself here in these woods—a life that I wouldn't
trade for any other—all thanks to good health, good neighbors, and
my tools.

TOOLS

Silver and slick as velvet
the edge of the old hoe glistens,
    how I've filed away this day—

GATHERING WOOD

Every man looks at his wood-pile with a kind of affection.
I loved to have mine before my window, and the more chips
the better to remind me of my pleasing work.

HENRY DAVID THOREAU
"House-Warming," *Walden*

A man can't have too much wood laid up for winter," Zoro says as he watches me split a big round of white oak with a single blow. "I've usually got two or three winters' worth, just in case of bad times or a bad winter. One never knows when he might need the extra wood to help himself or his neighbor. And with Bessie using wood for her cookstove all year long, we're always piling in small stuff as well as anything else we can cull from the woods." Looking up from what I'm doing, I can see the huge, over-head-high pile of branches that Bessie has dragged out of the woods and stacked up against the garage-become-woodshed.

"Yep," I answer, knowing the wisdom in his words.

With winter coming on, I'm helping Zoro get a start on his wood supply. At his age it's too much for him to manage by himself, and this has been the nature of our relationship all along—I help, he teaches. The barter of survival. The currency of community.

"That maul sharp enough fer ye?" Zoro asks, seeing I could use a break.

"Yep," I answer with my usual restrained response. "You want all of this white oak split first, or do you want me to get into that locust today?" I ask.

"Best to stick with the oak for now," Zoro replies. "It's good an' dry. Been in the woodshed since last winter. That locust is still a little green, so we'll not mess with it until the cold sets in for good."

Zoro wanders over to the garage, which is full of stacked firewood, tools, and old furniture, looking over what he's got already split and stacked for the winter, and comes back to where I stand leaning on his maul and taking a drink of water from a plastic milk jug Bessie has brought me from the house. "Yep," is all he says and makes his way back toward the house. I look at the yard full of rounds, give one more tug on the water jug, and get back to work. A red-tailed hawk soars low overhead, searching the garden field for something that might move and provide a late lunch.

Ever since my first winter, when I came up short of firewood around the end of February and spent the rest of the winter in the woods around the cabin cutting deadwood and dragging in downed pines, I've stayed ahead with my woodlot. While I may not have the three-year reserve that Zoro has, I've learned my lesson the hard way and have been at least one year on the safe side of frostbite, which has given me dry, seasoned wood for the duration of each subsequent year.

Like Thoreau, I have come to love the work of gathering firewood for the winter. A kind of unlikely aerobics, it builds the body. A kind of active meditation, it clears the mind. And being in one place in the woods for the better part of a day, one is more likely than not to witness all kinds of events of nature that serve as schooling that one stores as knowledge and upon which one builds a life in the wild. And, at the end of the day, there is a reward in being able to see firsthand the result of one's labor.

In the woods alone with saw, axe, or maul in hand and wood chips flying, sweat saturating my shirt and running off my brow, I love the rhythm of this work. It somehow blends, in time with the wind, the trees, the birds. Becomes almost a silent song—the chorus of the cells in the body singing to the swinging arc of the wood and metal tool, the pitch and key of the blade as it strikes its target, and the refrain of the chips as they land nearby in the dry leaves. "You can't find this kind of work in the city," as Zoro would say, reciting one of his stock expressions, and I agree. There is no more satisfying or pleasing work than the splitting and stacking of wood. Assuming that one likes to work, of course. And I do. Using the body for what it does best: move. Muscle and bone, tendon and cartilage bending and stretching to the drumbeat of the will as it makes love to this wilderness the way lovers lock lips and embrace. "Work is the health of love," Wendell Berry has written in one of his poems from his farm in Kentucky. I love the work of splitting wood. I love the sound of the wood cracking as the axe passes through its sinewy inner grain. I love the ring of the wedge as it receives the blunt end of the maul. I love the smell of the opened round as it meets, for the first time, the cool air—the sweet smell of locust, the loamy aroma of oak, the fruity scent of apple, the musky odor of slightly rotted walnut and pine. And I love the colors of the newly exposed wood. The urine yellow of the locust. The deep red of cherry. The skinlike pink of poplar. The golden epidermis, the rich purple vein that surrounds the heartwood, and the dark brown inner core of walnut. A feast for the senses is this working with wood.

When I go into the forest in the autumn of the year just before the leaves begin to fall, I make a habit of looking up into the canopy of trees. Search the heights for holes, for shades of brown in the green ceiling of the woods—evidence of trees that have died. These will be marked in memory as future firewood. The closer they are to the cabin, the sooner I will return to them and the sooner they will come down. Cut with crosscut saw into manageable lengths to drag, under-arm, to the woodpile, they will be cut again into rounds and then split and stacked for next year's use. Since I have been here beside Zoro's field, I've never cut a living tree for firewood. There has been enough deadwood within close range that I've had more than enough wood for winter heat. Softwoods and hardwoods. Kindling and night logs. A "gracious plenty," as the mountain saying goes. My open-air wood-shed built of pine poles and tin has never been anything other than full since the first winter. The business of scouting, marking, felling, cutting, splitting, and storing firewood never ends, as this spontaneous cycle is renewed again each year by process of observation and per-ceived need. During the hot summer months, one generally refrains from this kind of strenuous work, leaving the business of gathering wood for early spring and late fall. A constant and continuous process worked in with other seasonal chores, with the wood making its way from woods to woodshed, and from woodshed to a substantial pile stacked up by the front door under the overhang of the roof, and from there into an apple crate in the cabin, and eventually into the belly of my stove.

It wasn't much more than a week after I had arrived here in the Green River woods when Gary Pace showed up with a little black stove in the bed of his big Ford truck. He'd traded up for a better stove for himself and thought maybe I could use his old Box woodstove, which was just the right size, he figured, for my little cabin. Gary, like his father Horace, is a jack-of-all-trades and a real woodsman. He is also generous and offered me the stove with no mention of payment or nonmonetary reimbursement. He obviously knew my situation, as well as my intentions of living as best I could here on this ridgetop farm without benefit or burden of modern currency. The stove was a welcoming gift from the Saluda community. And a welcome gift it was, since I had no stove for the winter and no capital in a nonexistent bank account or a buried mason jar to purchase one.

I helped Gary unload the comparatively lightweight black stove from the truck, and together we brought it across the field and up to the cabin, where we set it inside in the corner with its back to the cinder-block chimney. A little embarrassed, I thanked him and asked him what I owed him. "Nothin'," he replied. "I had this old 'un and had no use for it, and Horace told me that you were livin' out here with nothin' to heat with. With winter comin' on, I figured you might could use this while you got settled in and until you got something better. No need to worry about being beholden for it, as it's not worth much anyway. But it should warm up this little house of yours just fine. You're going to need some stovepipe, and you should get you one of those ovens that hook up with the pipe. I'll come by here next week, and we'll go over to Hendersonville. I know a place that used to sell those ovens over there. I'll call 'em up when I get home and see if they've got any left." He tipped his seed cap as he went out the door, and I watched him cross the field to his truck.

The next week, true to his word, Gary took me to town, and I spent the last of the money I had brought with me from California, returning to the cabin with a brand new cylindrical, double-walled cookstove oven and ten feet of stovepipe. About a foot across and two feet deep, the oven was the perfect size for my box stove, with two flanges on top and bottom, fitting snug into the sections of six-inch pipe. I positioned the oven on the stovepipe about three feet above the flat top of the stove. About a foot above the oven, the pipe took a right-angle turn and ran about three feet before disappearing into a hole in the face of one of the gray blocks of the chimney. With my woodstove and oven in place, I was ready for winter—prepared to cook corn bread, baked potatoes, roastin' ears, or anything else that suited my fancy. All I needed now was some wood.

Trees come in many shapes, sizes, and names in the mountains of western North Carolina. Oak, locust, walnut, ironwood, dogwood, poplar, beech, sycamore, mountain and sugar maples, hawthorn, alder, elm, blackhaw, chinkapin, sourwood, basswood, persimmon, buckeye, ash, hickory, box elder, pine, and hemlock . . . all grace the hills at the southern end of the Blue Ridge. Softwoods, hardwoods, and everything in between. A multiflorous, multifarious, multiform arbor with multifold potential for giving shade, rain-forest oxygen, home, and serenity to humans and animals alike. What a woodlot I've got!

While all are beautiful and useful in their own way, not all trees are fit for firewood. Conifers, for instance—all pine, spruce, fir, hemlock, cedar, and juniper—while burnable, are minimal and problematic fodder for a woodstove. All being softwoods, they ignite and burn quickly, and hot. Their resin generates an excess of creosote in both firebox and stovepipe, creating a cleaning nightmare, as well as the potential for disastrous flue fires. While pines tend to die on the stump or be blown over by wind on a regular basis—and so are always available for scavenging nearby—one burns pine and its kinfolk only in situations of emergency or as a last resort.

Slightly higher on the list of usable softwoods are poplar, beech, buckeye, basswood, and birch. These, I've found, are good as starter wood, kindling. Poplar rounds are split with hardly any effort, and one can split the smaller, quartered pieces into thin strips by using a smaller limbing axe or hatchet. So easily does the tender wood split with the grain, that it takes only the weight of the raised hatchet, and no real force, to do the job. A hefty pile of good poplar or buckeye splits is a necessary part of the wood larder, and a hefty pile under shelter will last all winter.

Between the hardwoods and softwoods is an intermediary group that includes walnut, maple, sweet gum, and elm. While these are good woods to burn for heat, they tend to be harder to find in this immediate ecosystem and are more difficult to split, and so one doesn't bring these trees to the woodpile in abundance. But when I can get them, I use them, as they burn plenty hot and a good deal slower than the poplars and other softer woods.

Hardwoods within easy dragging distance of my cabin include oak, locust, ironwood, sourwood, sycamore, hickory, and dogwood. These are the Cadillacs of the firewood larder. The night wood. Logs that can be laid into the stove in the evening before going to bed, that give essential heat during the night and leave a decent bed of coals in the morning to rekindle the fire. While these woods are the most sought-after, they are also the most rare and, with the exception of the white oak and locust, tend to split with difficulty. Here in this second-growth forest most slow-growing hardwoods are still fairly small in diameter. This being the case, the dead ones I bring into the yard to cut into smaller logs don't usually need splitting, which is fine with me. Also one must be sure when burning wood such as locust, ironwood, and hickory that the woodstove dampers are shut all the way. If given too much air, these woods can burn extremely hot. As a novice pioneer during my first winter here, more than once I was driven out of the cabin by the heat. On these occasions the stove had gotten so hot that I had to open the windows and doors to get relief from the saunalike heat. Thinking I had properly banked the fire for the night, I left the front damper open partway when I went to bed and woke up in the middle of the night in a sweat from the extreme temperature inside the cabin. The use and maintenance of a woodstove demands more than the usual amount of diligence, not to mention sensitivity and skill. It is a machine, as well as a tool, and in that sense it demands a certain amount of savvy and skill regarding its operation. Over time, however, one learns to run it almost on instinct—albeit with a healthy dose of respect.

During that first winter here in the woods, I liked to sit in my old cane-bottomed rocker in the dark and just watch the coals and hardwood logs slowly burning through the stove's open door. Sitting there, I was mesmerized by the sound of the popping wood and the way the light would flicker on the walls and ceiling creating designs and illusions—the woodstove acting as surrogate campfire within the haven of my cabin walls. To my eye, everything inside the cabin looked better in that light. The old chair, the rustic table I use as a desk, the rough-cut oak bookshelves, even the glass jars of canned beans and applesauce on the larder shelf looked elegant, rich, and refined in the firelight—reminding me of the wealth of my existence here. How a man who is poor in money can be rich in his surroundings.

As I sit here during my third winter next to Zoro's field, I remember the first fire I built in my little black stove. The trepidation I felt in striking the first match to ignite the tinder and twigs. How I worked the stove and its dampers like an old engine—full of gears and levers. How the flames and heat rose and subsided. Went out. My feeling of accomplishment when the fire finally took and I could damp it down and sit back in my rocker and enjoy the heat. I sat for a long time that day, waiting and watching to see what the fire would do. It felt a little like I had just discovered fire and now was learning how to keep the flame and the embers aglow, so as never to let them go out. After three years, two of which have produced long, cold winters, I know what Zoro means when he says, "Firewood is like havin' money in the bank." It's simply a comfort to know the wood is there.

Like the first skillet of corn bread that came out of my little oven three years ago, a pone is cooking as I write these words. When its crust has hardened to a golden brown and it's ready to eat, I'll put my pen down from this page and fix my supper—which, as usual, will be boiled potatoes and green beans, corn bread and applesauce, and some springwater to wash it down. While everything is constantly changing here by Zoro's field, some things stay pretty much the same. My diet is one of those things. But there is a comforting consistency in the mundaneness of my meals. Like old friends, the jars of string beans and applesauce come off the shelf, the potatoes from out of the wood and screen box in the root cellar, and the pone of corn bread from out of the woodstove oven door. Again and again. Like a Zen koan or a Hindu mantra. This food. This fire. This love-work that keeps me healthy, wealthy, and warm.

SEEING BY THE LIGHT OF THE STOVE

On a dark winter night
I sit staring into
my woodstove's open door.

As I look at the fire,
I see
translucent sparks turning to roses
and baby birds
shooting out from the flames . . .

Can this all be anything
other than what it is?
Or have wry woodspirits
cast a scampish spell?

Whether illusion or the real world,
it doesn't get any better than this.
Solitude
and steady heat.
If you don't believe what I say,
then try this trick:
Close your eyes quickly and keep them shut
after taking in everything you can see.
Now open them.
Would you rather be living in
the glow of this woodstove light
or
in that close-eyed netherworld of night?

DIGGING A ROOT CELLAR

Grandma had her a little cellar dug under the floor, right next to
the fireplace, where she kept her sweet 'taters. She had a trap door
to it. It held twenty five bushels and she'd fill it full and cover
them with leaves and they'd last all winter.

ALEX STEWART

Alex Stewart: Portrait of a Pioneer

The first two months of my first year in the woods were spent
down on my knees. Not in prayer, but under the floor joists of the
north side of the cabin with pick and mattock in hand, digging a root
cellar. Digging an underground room. A red-clay pantry in which to
store my food. The cabin, it turned out, was built on a shelf at the base
of a small hill that was composed almost entirely of sandy shale and
hard red clay. Since I had to start the root cellar on my knees—there
was barely four feet of clearance from the ground to the floor joists,
which rested on locust posts—the use of a shovel was not only im-
practical but impossible owing to the density of the soil. Day after
day for several weeks I chipped away at the shelf of shale, removing
the compacted sandy gray and red earth in smaller than hand-sized
chunks and then dumping the dug earth and rock (when there was
enough to fill a five-gallon bucket) out onto and over the small bank I
was consequently building up at the foot of the cabin.

Looking back, those two months may have been some of the most
grueling work I've ever done. Above- and below-ground mining is
what it was, in fact. Nothing less. While I wasn't getting black soot
on my face and inhaling coal dust into my lungs, I breathed enough
clay and shale dust to make a few bricks and, in the process, wore
out a couple pairs of jeans. I don't think that the work I did several
years ago swinging a fifteen-pound hammer and laying track for the
Philadelphia, Bethlehem & New England Railroad was as hard as the
pick and mattock work it took to create the root cellar. Neither was
the work I experienced in Indiana as a hired hand on a family farm.
Nor the heat-exhausted months I worked on slate roofs in the summer sun of Pennsylvania as a roofer, nor de-barking trees eight hours

a day at a Virginia veneer plant. Nor anything that I've done here since. But it had to be done. I needed a place to store food efficiently for the winter months, and unfortunately the cabin had been built first—the cart before the horse—and so my pick-and-mattock plight seemed destined.

As I picked and plucked at the hard earth there beneath the cabin floor, careful not to dig too close to the locust posts that served as the foundation for the small building, my knees ached, my arms were sore, my hands were bruised and blistered, and my mind was blank with the meditation of repetition and with no thought of anything having to do with the actual work at hand, especially any notions of the future or how much more digging there was to do. If ever I was in the moment, it was while I was there down on my knees praying to the god of all miners and the deity of all mattocks. No one who might have wandered by and seen what I was about during those weeks (and thank God no one did) would have believed what they were witnessing. Such rigorous and seemingly pointless labor—to dig an eight-by ten-foot hole that was eight feet deep to store a few bushels of potatoes, a couple bushels of onions, and several shelves of canned goods. Unthinkable! I'm sure even Zoro would have been amused at my almost adolescent ambition and the zeal with which I attacked the job. But once I had dug down to level and had actually begun to create a small chasm in the soil, there was no turning back. With every laminated layer of claylike fissile rock I encountered, there was an equal number of grunts to accompany choice declarative phrases—a muted mantra, a wild work song to keep mind and body moving in repetition, time and time again, until back and buttocks ached enough that I had to get out from under the house and stand up and move about, allowing the blood that had gotten blocked in bent limbs to flow again, to breathe.

Like slow-moving frames on a reel of 16mm film, the hours and days of digging on my knees continued. After a little more than three weeks, weeks that seemed like an eternity, having barely enough room to swing the pickaxe authoritatively enough to break the surface of the shale-gray soil, my arms and shoulders getting sorer but stronger, I finally got the hole about three feet deep and was able to take a full swing with the mattock from a standing position. While this was a welcome relief, as I was able to get much more force into every roundhouse swing of the pick, all it served to do really was to transfer the constant pain from my knees to my lower back, which was soon sore from the bending and the torque that went into every thrust. But despite the pain the work went more quickly, and soon I was truly standing in a hole, out of which I peered into Zoro's field. I could also now use a shovel to toss out the loose dirt from the hole, which saved me from having to go about the whole business of filling the bucket and carrying it out of the hole to dump over the ever-enlarging bank.

Soon the day came when I had dug the hole so deep that I could no longer turn and look out into the field. I could see only the lower limbs of the pine trees on the far side of the field and a couple very small patches of sky. At this point, instead of shoveling in sunlight, I was digging in the dark. Because of the east-west arc of the sun over the field, by the middle of the afternoon there was hardly enough light in the cellar hole for me to see. This was not only dangerous, but depressing. So work on the root cellar was done from 10:00 a.m. to about 3:00 p.m. each day (except for the occasional days when I would give my body and mind a rest by doing less formidable work) until, finally, the hole was roughed out and deep enough to begin with the finish work, as it were.

The finish work consisted of squaring and leveling the dirt walls and floor, first of all, and creating a temporary stairway out of some cinder blocks I'd borrowed from Mac that he'd had up in his barn as extras from a retaining wall job done some years previous. The primitive cinder-block stairs allowed me to get in and out of the hole, albeit cautiously. Once the room was square by eyesight, I worked on the mental design of a set of permanent wooden steps and took some measurements for future reference. With this much accomplished and the pick and shovel work essentially done, I began appraising the open areas around the top of the hole and began planning the carpentry phase of the project—the actual boxing-in of the hole from the outside world and weather.

After coming up with a crude carpentry design that I sketched on a sheet of lined notebook paper from a loose-leaf binder I used for writing and taking notes while reading, I began making a list of materials I would need to do the job. I would need rough-cut lumber (framing and siding), which I could get at a family sawmill at the end of Macedonia Road for the price of hauling it away. I would need nails—some ten-penny as well as some spikes—for the actual framing, a roll or two of six-inch insulation to put up under the cabin floor between the joists, and a roll of roofing felt to serve as a barrier to keep the weather from coming in between the cracks. For these items of hardware I would have to barter. Either that or I would have to run up a bill at Pace's General Store in Saluda, which I didn't want to do. In the end I was able to work out a deal with Mac, trading the hardware (which he had an excess supply of left from building an outdoor porch on his house) in exchange for some pruning and fertilizing that still needed to be done in his orchard. A good deal for me, as it would give me the materials I needed to enclose the root cellar and I would be getting all these materials in exchange for work that I actually enjoyed doing—the pruning and orchard work. This would allow me to do a good bit of tree climbing, something I still enjoyed as a carryover from my childhood.

With the building materials nearby, I was able to begin at once with framing and enclosing the cellar. After the weeks of agonizing manual labor, the framing job was like play in comparison. I was also able to put my mind to work in figuring out the details, angles, and problems presented by this particular room. It was pretty easy, since it was for a marginal space that wouldn't be part of the actual living space of the house. This being the case, I was able to cut corners and improvise in ways that a true finish-carpenter wouldn't have been able to. In a matter of a few days I had the framing studs in place and the three-quarter-inch by six-inch rough-cut pine boards nailed up, closing in everything but a four-and-a-half-foot opening for a doorway leading down into the cellar.

Before I built the door I tacked the roofing felt to the walls, which not only sealed the room from the outside but would also help maintain a constant fifty-five degrees throughout the year, and installed the fiberglass insulation between the floor joists on the underside of the cabin floor. Finally I had what I could call a room. Except for the door, which I built and hung in about an hour's time a day or so later, I had accomplished the job of creating a functional room underneath the house. Something that would act as both refrigerator and storage shed for my food. A naturally conceived and constructed stable-temperature environment that would allow me to preserve certain foods during the cold and warm months of the year.

With the door on and the root cellar built, I was ready for the job of furnishing it with shelves and containers for the various foods that would satisfy my hunger and culinary desires during the coming years. But the finishing touches would have to wait, as an ignominious and ironic event was about to occur . . . On the day that I was set to begin work on the shelving and storage bins, and the day after I'd built and hung the door, I walked out the door of the cabin with a tape measure in one hand, planning to measure the dimensions of the root cellar for space considerations. I opened the root cellar door with my free hand and took a first step into the dark room onto what I thought was the first block of my makeshift cinder-block stairway. My thoughts taking that first step were admittedly a little clouded by the extra mug of homebrew I'd had before going to bed—something I took some evenings to relax or at the very least to soothe the muscular aches and pains—and were focused on the potential location of the shelves and on the measuring process and not on where I was placing my foot. It was so dark in the closed-in hole that even with the door swung back a couple feet or so, I couldn't see down into the room at all. The adage "watch out for that first step, it's a killer" doesn't begin to describe what I was about to experience as I went airborne, that first step taking me to the bottom of the hole. I had forgotten that I'd built the temporary steps on the right side of the room, with the first block beneath only half the doorway, and I had stepped down into the room to the left and center of the door—missing entirely the first step. In my next conscious moment, I was lying on my back in the dirt, looking up at the sunlight coming through the open door above and feeling a terrible pain in my left ankle. Dazed and a bit in shock from the fall, I assessed my situation and my condition, coming to the conclusion that I was in trouble and that my ankle could very well be broken. Feeling around my ankle to make sure no bones had punctured the skin, I concluded that everything seemed intact. But the shooting pain told me I had sustained a serious injury.

As I came to my senses I realized that it was going to be no easy feat getting myself out of the root cellar. In my fall I had caught enough of the makeshift stairway to send it flying in the other direction. The cinder blocks were strewn and broken at my side. I was at the bottom of an eight-foot hole with a badly injured ankle and no immediate way out. I imagined myself being stuck until such a time as someone might wander by on an unannounced and unscheduled visit, which could be weeks. But rather than focusing on the negative, I set my mind to work on a way to get myself out. The only way to do that, I figured, would be somehow to restack the cinder blocks to make a crude stairway and then drag myself up the steps and out of the hole. Doing so took considerable time and endurance, as the pain in my ankle was throbbing and extreme, so that most of the lifting and placing had to be done on my knees or, more awkwardly, on one foot. But finally after an hour or so I was able to rebuild a rickety facsimile of the block stairway, which I crawled up like a wounded spider into what was, by then, the late-afternoon daylight.

The next three weeks were spent in a state of disagreeable yet self-imposed idyll, reading or lounging around the field in the afternoon sun — dreaming of the day when I could become active again and get back to work on the root cellar as well as other garden and life-sustaining chores. The ankle was not broken but had suffered a severe sprain, and so I hobbled around cabin and field, doing necessary chores and performing bodily functions with the help of a stout crook-handled walking cane I'd constructed from a small sourwood sapling growing near the cabin. During those weeks of convalescence, I saw no one and received no mail. So the period was a lonely one, giving me more than ample time to imagine what might have been if I'd injured myself so severely from the fall into the cellar that I could not have gotten myself out.

Having survived the fall and the convalescence, by the end of the month I was back in the root cellar building a safe and substantial set of steps from the remaining rough-cut wood I'd gleaned from the sawmill. After finishing the steps, I built a set of shelves, all the while imagining them stacked with canning jars full of applesauce, jellies, and beans. After the shelves were done, I engineered and built several large boxes for storage of potatoes and other root crops. These I constructed out of the scraps of lumber and some heavy-duty screening I'd gotten from Mac as part of our materials-for-labor trade. The screening was necessary to allow the tubers to breathe, helping to deter rot or putrefaction as well as to keep the critters out. With wood and screen in alternating layers making up the four sides of each box, I fashioned a top that would serve as a secure lid, further insuring my precious stash of food from any would-be pilfering invaders.

These days I look back on those weeks of building the root cellar in relief and almost in amazement, when I think of the amount of work and even peril I experienced in bringing it about. With my ankle as good as new and with a better pair of jeans, the story of building the root cellar makes for jovial conversation and an occasional good laugh for those who have since heard it and have made my foible the brunt of their jokes. But the joke is on them, as my root cellar is full of canned goods, and my boxes full of potatoes, Jerusalem artichokes, onions, apples, hearty cabbage, and beets. And I must say it has worked like a charm. Even on the coldest of winter days these past few years, the temperature in the cellar has stayed right at, or at least around, fifty-five degrees. Never has the temperature gotten to or below freezing. And I've never lost a single bite of food to either weather or varmint. In fact, the only critters I've seen in the root cellar all these years have been the small community of blue-tailed lizards that moved in right after I finished building it, the wolf spiders that seem to take to the dark and the constant cool, and a single old black-snake that found its way there trying to get out of the cold one night that first year in the early fall. These critters live here now too. In the basement, as it were. As tenants they pay no rent but are a comfort to me in the constancy of their being there. With their presence I am reminded that I am never alone, either in my cabin or outside in the wistful woods.

THE ROOT CELLAR

Where will this food go
that I have grown and gathered
all year long?
Will I eat it all

in a great meal that never ends?
Will I put it in cases
covered with glass in town
like trophies for all to see?
Or will I gather it in colorful mountains
and raffle it off to the animals
or the putrefaction of all my needs?

In the old days,
strangers or those who were on hard times
and were hungry and in great need,
would be fed.
Women went outside
to cellars dug in the dirt.
Where food was hidden.
Where wealth was stored in
bins of potatoes and urns of grain.
In glass jars that let sweet fruit sleep.

Having learned from those who have
gone before,
I gather the feast of what I have been given
into my own eyes:
beet-fire, beer-water, onion-earth, and corn-shucks of air.
Waiting among roots and red dirt
to fill my belly with food
and my mind with these withy words.

A MOUNTAIN GARDEN

I came to love my rows, my beans . . . They attached me
to the earth, and so I got strength like Antaeus.

HENRY DAVID THOREAU
"The Bean-Field," *Walden*

Breaking Ground

The first thing I planted in Zoro's field was several rhubarb roots
that Zoro had given me from his garden over at his home on the
Guice Road farm. He wanted me to have some of the plants from his
plentiful rhubarb bed because the field in which I would be gardening was once, he hinted, a plethora of rhubarb. "I want you to take
some of this rhubarb home with you and put it in that field of yours.
When I was growin' up, that field was almost plumb full of rhubarb.
That was our rhubarb patch. More rhubarb pies came out of that
patch than a man could count. This rhubarb in my garden is the same
stock that came out of that field next to where you're livin' now. I
guess some of these roots are older than you are." Hearing this, I
was only too happy to accept Zoro's gift and watched while he put
several beet-red stalks he had dug from the edge of the garden into a
brown burlap sack. Handing me the sack, he said, "That's some of the
best 'barb you'll ever eat. Take 'em home and put 'em in the ground
right away. And give 'em plenty of water. Water 'em every day until
they're rooted in." Knowing the history of the rhubarb connection
to my field, I practically ran all the way home to put Zoro's rhubarb
ceremoniously in the ground. With this auspicious beginning, and
with rhubarb returned to the old Guice rhubarb patch (to a special
area I cleared and double-dug that would be devoted only to the sour,
stalky plant, along with several volunteer asparagus plants that had
gone wild and, yet, after many years, were still growing in the far end
of the field), I began the work of putting in my first garden.

Since my garden was going to be my major source of sustenance,
there was much to do in those first days and weeks to get both garden

and gardener ready for planting in the spring. The field needed to be plowed and disked, seeds purchased, and a schema drawn up for efficient use of space. Luckily I had arrived in Polk County with a small stash of money in my pocket and so could buy a few of the necessities for getting my garden started. Some of this money would go to paying one of the Revis boys, who lived out the old dirt road and owned a small tractor and a set of plows, to plow and disk the field. The second major job in getting ready for the spring garden would be much more difficult and would demand much more time and effort on my part—the clearing of a small field down the hill (close to where an old drovers' inn and corral had been located almost a century before) in order to grow corn for the making of cornmeal. Because I had arrived in early winter and therefore still had time before warm weather when everything would burst into bloom, I hoped the remaining winter weeks would give me enough time to clear out the fenced-in field down by the old drovers' inn site and get it worked up in time for spring planting.

After Zoro's field had been plowed and disked, for the next two months when weather would allow I worked with bush axe, mattock, and crosscut saw down at the half-acre field at the drovers' inn, cutting trees, hacking down briars and vines, and digging out roots. After this backbreaking work had been done I dragged all the trunks, branches, and vines to large piles for burning. Then on a cold, wet winter day I dowsed the piles with kerosene, lit a torch, and spent the day keeping warm while watching the brush burn.

With large circles of white ash polka-dotting the field from the burned brush, the field was ready to be plowed. Again I obtained the help of one of the Revis boys and their tractor and watched as rich black dirt emerged from the back of the shiny steel plows, taking the place of grass and brambles and filling the air with the musky scent of loam. But with the field plowed and disked, my work in turning it into a cornfield had just begun. As soon as the weather was warm enough, and after the last frost, the field had to be worked again, had to be loosened up. All this had to be done by hand, since the ground was so rough that no walk-behind tiller would have been able to do anything with the large clods left from the plowing and disking. Facing the daunting task of breaking up the half-acre field, I went to work with an oversized hoe blade I had bought from the farm supply store in Hendersonville and for which I had fashioned a hefty sourwood handle. For a couple weeks, day after day you could find me down in the would-be cornfield busting clods and loosening soil with my hoe. To say that my back was sore and that my arms ached would be a gross understatement. But finally the day came when I had finished with my hoeing, and the field was ready to plant.

Meanwhile, I had planted the peas and hearty green leafy vegetables and tubers, such as collards, kale, spinach and mustard greens, cabbage, onions, leeks, garlic, parsnips, potatoes, radishes, beets, turnips, Jerusalem artichokes, and kohlrabi—all of which could go into the ground before the final frost, which that first year came at the end of April. That year, luckily, there had been no late frost, so everything was in and up before even the first kernel of seed corn went into the ground. As soon as the ground was good and warm and was going to stay that way for the remainder of the growing season, the more fragile crops were planted—corn (sweet and grinding varieties), squash (summer and winter), tomatoes, Swiss chard, sweet potatoes, lettuce, peppers, beans, okra, pumpkins, cucumbers, carrots, and Brussels sprouts. But first, the seed corn for grinding had to go in while the soil was still loose and could be hilled. Easier said than done. Even digging rows to plant the white seed corn I'd bought at the farm supply store was a chore. And after the rows were furrowed out and lined with seed, the business of covering the rows was even rougher work. The field there by the drovers' inn had been left untilled and unworked for many years, and it was going to take more than a single plowing and a single season to loosen it up and make it pliant for continual use.

I found this out the hard way, when many weeks later I had to hill up the rows and lay the corn by, and I found that grass and bush sprouts had already begun coming back in an attempt to reclaim the field. Then again in June, when I went to cultivate the corn, working between the rows, the realities of breaking in a new field came only too prominently to light. With my heavy-bladed hoe—now an inch or more shorter from repeated filings (which were done to keep the blade knife-sharp, therefore making it easier to penetrate the sod-solid soil)—I worked the entire cornfield that year. A year that remains imprinted so vividly, even now, that I doubt it will ever be erased from either mind or muscle-memory. Even so, the happy ending to this story is that I got enough corn that first year to grind a couple fifty-pound bags of meal, with enough seed left over for planting the following year's crop. Since then, even with some years being better than others, I can proudly say that I've never been without cornmeal for my daily pone of corn bread in all the time I've been living here in the woods.

The Season

"For everything there is a season, and a time to every purpose under heaven: a time to be born, and a time to die; a time to plant, and a time to pluck up that which is planted," says Ecclesiastes. This is particularly true with regard to a gardener and his garden. Each season here in the mountains—winter, spring, summer, and fall—presents a new schedule and a new set of challenges, often different from the previous year's. At no time and during no season of the year is there not something that needs to be done, either physically or mentally, pertaining to the garden. In the winter it's the business of recovery—letting the body rest for a few months, following nine months of constant labor—and of planning the various strategies for the coming year. These strategies invariably include the plotting of an outline for the next season's planting. A map of what goes where and when. Something that is put down on paper that serves the dual purposes of being a point of reference and a historical record. This includes, perhaps first and foremost, the business of crop rotation—the moving of certain crops from one place to another in order to keep from working a plot of ground to death from continually covering it, year after year, with the same crop.

After crop rotation (quality control) has been considered, I need to think about quantity and the number of different crops I plan to grow. Despite my transfinite ambitions, a finite amount of space will nourish and sustain only so much vegetable matter. So decisions have to be made as to precisely what I want to grow in any given year. Some years, for considerations of nitrogen fixation, for instance, I may decide to move the bean crop over to where I grew sweet corn the year before. Or I may want to put potatoes in the place where, last year,

I had tomatoes. Or I may want to move the bed of greens over to where, the previous year, I had grown squash—making change an important aspect of the dynamic of my yearly plan and a part of the map of the "how much of the what goes where."

Aside from the more cerebral work of garden planning, other winter work includes caretaking and sharpening one's tools, occasionally turning compost, repairing old trellis wires and posts in grape arbors, pruning fruit trees and vines (which often includes burning webworm nests in late March or early April), maintaining spring beds and spring boxes (one must always be thinking ahead about water supply), sewing clothes (including coveralls and socks), and reading up on organic gardening techniques and practices.

In spring things begin in earnest. In his beautiful book *Flowering Earth*, published in 1939, Donald Culross Peattie says: "A million million of springs, and many million more, have come as they promised to come. And gone again. On this day I first felt regret that spring must always go, and that when I am gone it will forever return." Perfect sentiments for the lone woodsman or gardener, these, as each spring comes with hope, promise, yet also with a sense of dread, even foreboding. But mainly, with the first signs of the colorful budding of trees, the greening of the grasses, and the warm winds, one is energized and elated with the return of the spring season. I know that I am, as I can't wait to be outside again and to get my hands and feet into the dirt and to work in the sun. To feel sweat on my brow and wind in my hair. Spring! Also a time of human blossom and bloom after lying fallow, dormant for a seemingly long winter.

First there are the preparations: the tilling, the turning, the tinkering and transforming. Then the planting: making rows, adding composted soil and cottonseed meal to line the rows, planting seed, covering seed, mulching, and watering. By the end of spring, what had been a flat, receptive plane of brown earth is a veritable collage of textures in various shades of green. At this point creativity turns to maintenance, and one finds oneself working double duty as custodian and caretaker to keep everything healthy and productive. Tomatoes are staked, potatoes are mulched, bean rows are hilled up, and the corn is laid by.

With everything in the "oven," the summer months are spent in the baking heat. In this tropical rain-forest climate, crops sit in the sun's sauna and cook. The gardener's task: to quench their thirst and keep the weeds and pests away. Long hours of picking insects and eggs from plant leaves with fingers yellowed from bug blood, and wielding a hoe with blistered hands. While there is wearisome work to be done, there are paydays during the first weeks of summer, when one can harvest early vegetables (the mainstay of the garden harvest comes at the far end of summer, after plants have been through long weeks soaking up sun and rain)—summer squash, early sweet corn, new potatoes, tomatoes, and beans. While many of the root crops such as turnips, beets, and carrots may be ready to harvest by the end of summer, if not before, they can be efficiently and safely stored by simply being left in the ground—some are even able to make it through the fall and winter without being removed from their earthy abode.

With the bristling of the air and the descent of leaves in fall, one begins the business of storing food for the rest of autumn and for winter. With a cover crop of buckwheat blooming and bees buzzing in the garden field, apples and grapes are picked, jams and jellies are made, and perhaps a few bottles of wine are put away in the root cellar for a special meal, an occasion with unexpected guests, or to chase the blues away. Beans, tomatoes, and applesauce are canned; corn is milled into cornmeal; and potatoes, apples, and a second crop of onions are tucked away. With these things done and with the cool, clear air of autumn ripe in the nostrils and lungs, my blood and body activated, the desire to write, to read, do research, and be creative, comes over me and continues until the pink and jade tints ravage the redbuds and poplars in the spring.

The Signs

The people who refer to themselves as natives here in the mountains of western North Carolina often do their planting, harvesting, and other garden-related activities by the signs. By "signs" I mean doing garden work in direct correspondence with the phases of the moon and the signs of the zodiac—the constellations in the sky. Many of these folks get their inspiration and information for this practice from the Book of Genesis in the Bible and a publication that is called Grier's *Almanac*. In Genesis, one finds the lines: "Let there be lights in the firmament of the heaven to divide the day from the night; and let them be for signs, and for seasons, and for days, and years." According to Grier's *Almanac* (which has been published annually since the early 1800s, and which is something of a secondary bible to farmers here in these mountains), going back as far as 1000 BC there are charts and records of the evenly spaced positions of the constellations in the firmament and of the monthly path of the moon. These observations were recorded and then divided into twelve parts or signs. Each sign was named for an animal and a corresponding part of the human body. Early astrologers used these charts in creating horoscopes and in the arcane art of soothsaying. This tradition has been carried down through the ages, and with the help of the *Almanac* it has become a source of direction in the daily routines of people who consult it as a forecaster of weather and as a guide for good planting and fishing days. They even turn to the *Almanac* to determine when it is favorable to do such things as cut hair, kill weeds, and pull teeth. There are those I've encountered here in the mountains who consult the *Almanac* daily before they do almost everything, as it is set up to be easily understood and used as a tool for divination.

Zoro introduced me to the *Almanac* and to the idea of planting by the signs. Since it seemed to work for him, I got a copy from Pace's store and studied it, hoping to learn not only about its origins but also about the secret to its apparent success. Over the past three years, I have tried this method of farming with varying degrees of success, and in the end I'm not sure that I understand it or believe in it any more than I did when I first attempted planting, cultivating, and harvesting in this manner. For instance, having derived from the *Almanac* that the best time to plant is in one of the dry signs and when a dry day falls on both an ideal sign and an ideal phase of the moon, one year I planted my potatoes on a moonless night in March when the signs were not in the feet—the feet, bowels, and head not being particularly positive signs at this time of the year. While I did get a good crop of potatoes that year, it was not the best crop I'd grown and, in fact, was not as good as the crop I had the year before, when I just planted them when it was convenient and the weather was good.

I've had similar mixed results with tomatoes—which are always a persnickety crop to grow. I dug my tomato holes according to the proper signs as indicated in the *Almanac* (in the "new" of the moon, the first quarter), waited a goodly amount of time until the signs were propitious for planting the tomato slips that I had started from seed in my makeshift greenhouse on the south-facing side of the field, and planted them when the signs were in the hands—which predicted that there would be more flowers and less vine and therefore a greater yield. That year I got the best crop of tomatoes I'd ever had—larger and with less blight. Well, the next year I did exactly the same thing, using all the same signs in the same way at the same time, and, in comparison, got almost nothing for my efforts. And then this year I planted without consulting the signs and got another good crop.

My first year, Zoro told me to plant my corn when the signs were in the arms. "And whatever you do," he added, "don't plant any corn when the signs are in the bowels." His reasoning for this was: when the signs were in the bowels, the seeds would rot in the ground or be infected with impurities—just as food gets when passing through the body, from mouth to bowels. I did what Zoro said, and I got a good corn crop that year. But then the next year it rained all during the time when the signs were right and so I planted my corn late. Even so, I got an equally good crop that year. So I'm still on the fence where this business of farming by the signs is concerned. Sometimes it works, and sometimes it doesn't. And sometimes it doesn't seem to make any difference. But since I'm here living in a culture that largely embraces such a belief, I figure I'll do it this way, since it's tried and seems true for those from whom I am here to learn. What have I got to lose? Truth is I've got a lot to lose living as close to the edge of things as I do. But I'm game for trying new things and am susceptible to that which is odd, mysterious, or downright *quar*.

Aesthetic Gardening

While on the subject of arcane farming practices, I've developed a rather peculiar (or at least Zoro thinks so) approach to my gardening since I've been here. I use a technique I call "aesthetic gardening." While my elder mountain friends put a lot of stock in faithful following of the *Almanac*, I have come to place an equal faith in organizing my garden and my surrounds by certain principles of aesthetics. While the signs methodology is precise, ordered, organized, and in a word, rational, my methods are more intangible and intuitive. I have come to let my organic sense of beauty and the process of intuition and spontaneity largely determine what goes where, when, and why in my garden. I have made the general assumption that if it is pleasing to the eye, then it must also be pleasing to the plants and therefore good for them. Zoro thinks this line of reasoning suspect at best. He prefers a little more pure science in the occult aspects of his life. Me, I'm wide open, and with a short attention span am capable of going in almost any direction on a whim or a change in the wind. A little of this, a dab of that . . . following the lead of my curiosity and my interests is the way I have lived my life. This irrational nonphilosophy of mine has inspired more than one naysayer to describe my lifestyle sarcastically as the Follow Your Bliss Syndrome. And it's true, I'm blissed-out on beauty. Keats's "beauty is truth, truth beauty" pretty much describes my life's philosophy as well as the bottom line for what would be any spiritual credo.

Here's the deal: If it's beautiful, it works. If I like the configuration of potato plants running parallel with the corn rows, and if it pleases my eye this aesthetic is going to work in behalf of benefiting the companionship aspects that nurture both crops. If a backdrop of staked tomato plants fronted by the broadleaf blooming of zucchini squash, side-dressed with green and purple cabbage, paints a pretty picture, then I'm ready to believe that because it looks good it's good for the health and productivity of all three crops. I try to organize my garden on paper like an artist might sketch something out before attacking canvas with paint—trying to imagine how things will look when color and proper dimension sprout and bloom in the real-life span and spacing of the plants. Then, as I am actually in the garden in spring, and planting, I allow for changes in my on-paper design that may occur spontaneously. Sometimes I will plant seeds heavily in one area and in another give space to rows of the same crop. Sometimes crops that are planted in rows or in densely planted intensive beds will be designed in a geometric fashion. Very linear. In other areas the shapes of plantings may be nonlinear, nongeometric, curvaceous. Every year Zoro's field is an empty canvas, which I paint pliantly with plants and the creative use of empty space. Sometimes I will leave an area open, for no reason other than it appeals to my eye that it should be done so. In this way I order and organize my garden. Adding, I imagine, sustenance to beauty in the blink of an eye.

The philosophy is thus: The care and the energy the gardener puts into his garden in an aesthetic way compensate for, or more precisely dovetail with, any scientific considerations and knowledge, yielding the same result. For in his tenderness and in approaching his every care-full step of preparing, planting, and harvesting his crops, he is at the same time actually subconsciously aware and knowledgeable of the more chemical, biological, and practical aspects of farming know-how. With the love of one's work comes the specific knowledge of that work. In the end the plants are well taken care of and thrive!

I approach my work in the environs around the garden in the same way I do within the garden itself. Using a kind of intuitive Feng Shui, I have determined the design and placement of certain things—the woodshed, the compost pit, the drying barn and solar greenhouse, the grape arbor and rhubarb patch, gourd trellises, rooting box, berry terraces and onion patch, beehives and sweat lodge—so that someone stepping into Zoro's field is struck with the beauty in the placement of each individual thing as a part of the whole. Each separate thing working wonderfully in its own place yet adding to the overall look and feel of the home-place in general. In this way I have made for myself a place that is pleasing to the eye (looks natural) and pleasurable to the body (feels natural). By doing this, I have created for myself a healthy atmosphere and environment in which to live and work. I have been here for three years. In that time I have not spent one day ill from colds or flu. Have not spent one moment depressed or sad. Have been productive and had energy left over to be reflective and creative. If you ask me, I'm going to tell you that my theory of aesthetic gardening and living works.

Foundations

On the more practical side of things, a few commonsense observations that I have made these past three years exist at the very foundations of growing a good garden. First of all, a farmer needs to pay attention to the soil. Since the field here by the cabin had been unused in over a generation, I needed to get an analysis, a reading, of the health of the field. In those first weeks of winter during the first year, I took soil samples and sent them off to Raleigh for the Agricultural Extension office to analyze so that I would know what the soil's deficiencies and strengths were. The dark loamy soil in the field, which drained from both the northeast and southwest, was pretty healthy, but the sample studies showed a low pH, meaning that the soil was too acidic. To counter that, during the winter of the first year, I bought (when I still had a little money) some lime from the farm supply store in Hendersonville and spread it judiciously over the whole field. Assuming that the balance was achieved after putting on the lime (I have never sent another sample to the Ag Extension Service), I began the work of creating a large compost pile (enclosed with railroad ties that were being given away by the Southern RR, which was replacing old ties with newer ones in the section of track that ran through downtown Saluda), hoping that it would not only enrich the soil with a variety of nutrients but would help to loosen up and aerate the soil if done extensively.

Over the years, my compost pile has been a hodgepodge of all kinds of biodegradable materials (biomass). Hay (from threshing the tall grass in the untilled portion of the field), pine needles (from the pine trees on the north side of the field), decomposing vegetable matter and organic matter from rotted or poor-quality produce (including table scraps and spoiled canned vegetables—of which there was, thankfully, very little), rich dirt, sand (from a sandbank along the dirt road a short distance from the garden), leaves (in the fall), and essentially anything that was biodegradable and organic. Over time my compost pile expanded to become quite large, demanding that the work to sustain it also increase.

Another thing I've done to help strengthen my soil is to plant cover crops during the months when the ground would, otherwise, lie fal-

low. Although I've tried winter rye and clover, my cover crop of pref-
erence is buckwheat. Not only is it a gentle crop, easy to sow (by
just scattering the seeds on the top of the ground) and easy to till
in the spring, but it is beautiful when fully in bloom with its prolific
white blossoms and jade-colored stems. On top of this, the bees love
it! When it's in full bloom, the bees from my hives, and their kin
from who knows how far away, cover the field, pulling pollen from
the flowers and singing all the while. The composition of subtly different tones and pitches from thousands of honeybees, bumblebees, yellow jackets, hornets, and wasps is truly symphonic. I can plop myself
down in the blooming buckwheat field in the middle of the day when
the sun is shining and it's warm, and the bees won't pay any more
attention to me than if I wasn't even there, so busy are they gathering pollen and sucking nectar. I can sit and listen to the sound rising
up out of the field and feel the buzzing energy of the bees at work.
There's nothing else in nature like it. It's music for the soul!

One of the biggest surprises or epiphanies that I've had through
three complete seasons of growing a garden here in Zoro's field has
to do with the element of water. Moving to a region that has been
described as a deciduous rain forest, I never gave the issue of water much thought until I began living and gardening here full-time
as a means of sustenance and sustainability. For the most part, there
has been plenty of water, especially during the growing season, with
regular summer thunderstorms in the late afternoons during July and
August. But last year we went through a period of drought during the
crucial weeks of early growth for the garden plants. With the combined heat and dryness my plants were struggling. So, I had to begin
bringing water up from the spring—carrying plastic milk jugs (seven
at a time on a short rope) and five-gallon buckets full of water from
the little spring below the cabin to keep the plants alive.

That summer I had to do everything I could to trap water and to
create cisterns that were on higher ground than the garden, so that I
could run irrigation channels or hoses downhill to water the plants.
To do this I borrowed anything that was convex, conical, or cylindrical
from Mac or other friends and neighbors in order to catch rainwater.
In the end, and with a little help each day from the morning dew, the
garden made it, although I didn't produce as much, in quantity or

quality, as I had the year before or as I have since. The most profound thing that I learned from the experience of this summer drought was that springwater or well water (I had carried some from the well overflow spigot at the McHughs' as it was easier to fill the jugs and buckets there even though it was a longer distance to travel), while it does keep the plants alive during a dry spell, doesn't give them enough water-based oxygen and nitrogen to allow them to grow. So, during the dry spells that summer, the plants would just sit there in the field in a kind of wait-and-see mode. Then, when it would finally rain, immediately you could see the difference, as the plants would shoot up, put on more green matter, begin to bloom or increase the size of the already existing fruit. The epiphany: the plants need rainwater. There is something (a mysterious ingredient, and no one seems to know what exactly this mystery ingredient is!) that the plants get from water falling from the sky that they don't get from water issuing from the earth.

Zoro, too, has of course noticed this phenomenon and seemed a little surprised that I was so ecstatic about my discovery. "Lord, everyone knows that," he responded to my naive declaration. "Been common knowledge for as long as people have been growing gardens in these parts. Thing is, no one knows just why the *sass* and such like the rainwater so much more than they do *fotch* water or every other kind. My guess is that it's the warmth of the water coming from the sky. The plants can sop it up a whole lot easier than they can that cold springwater. If it ain't that, then I don't know what it is that makes the *differ*. You tell me if'n you figure it out." So far I haven't been able to come up with anything to tell Zoro that he doesn't already know.

Preservation

Almost all garden work is done with a single goal in mind: the preservation and storage of food. Food enough to carry me through the fall, winter, and early spring, when there is little, domestic or wild, that can be harvested or foraged for sustenance, such as nontoxic mushrooms, grapes or berries, wild greens or cresses, nuts or mast. Like many animals who work diligently in the fall to fill larder or bury foodstuffs, I set to work in the latter part of summer and continue into the month of September canning, drying, and storing various foods for the long, cold months ahead. My priorities and my focus reside on those crops that will sustain me and that I will be able to store, living as I do without nonnatural refrigeration. Potatoes are stored in wire and wooden crates in the root cellar. Winter squash (butternut, acorn, and buttercup) are stored, also in the cellar, in piles of straw. Apples are dried during the sun-bright, warm days of late September, outdoors, and then brought indoors and stored near the woodstove, where they will be kept warm and dry. Beans, tomatoes, and applesauce are all canned in quart mason jars (which I've bartered for and gathered over the years) and stored on the shelves in the cellar. The long-keeper apples that I have culled from Mac's orchard, or over in the old orchard on the ridge road, are bedded in straw and kept in another of the wire-and-wood boxes in the cellar. Sweet potatoes are stored in burlap sacks behind the woodstove. Cornmeal is stored in anything I can find that will keep out the bugs and the damp. Jams, jellies, and honey (what the mountain folks call "sweetnin'") are canned in smaller glass jars and reside, too, in the cellar on their own shelf, like the aristocracy of all canned foods. Hearty cabbage, beets, turnips, and Jerusalem artichokes are left in the ground and covered in mulch, or sometimes stored in the root cellar if I can come up with some kind of container that will keep out pests and also allow the vegetables to breathe.

This assortment of vegetables and fruits is my larder, and from this meager list of foods I make my diet. A diet that is only as diverse as the list is long. But as repetitive as my eating habits are, they are also of the highest quality. One could even say gourmet. Gourmet in the sense that everything is more tasty and fresh than anything you could get in the grocery stores in town. And safer too. No noxious chemicals have tainted this food, as I have grown everything organically. I never tire of potatoes and green beans for dinner. Never tire of cornmeal grits and honey for breakfast. Never tire of an apple and a piece of corn bread for lunch. Despite the repetition, each meal, like each new day, is a fresh start and a new experience for the palate. When writing about his garden and the food he ate in his cabin at Walden Pond, Thoreau penned philosophically: "Not that food which entereth into the mouth defileth a man, but the appetite with which it is eaten. It is neither the quality nor the quantity, but the devotion to sensual savors. I have been thrilled to think that I owed a mental perception to the commonly gross sense of taste, that I have been inspired through the palate, that some berries which I had eaten on a hillside had fed my genius." While not able to write as eloquently as Thoreau about my meager larder, I would wager that I don't enjoy the fruits of my annual labor any less.

My organic and mainly vegetarian diet, supplemented occasionally with rabbit, squirrel (or other pilfering varmints that might try and fail at raiding my garden), fish from either the river or Johnson's Pond, and an occasional rattlesnake, has served me well these years. And I find that I don't suffer from any lack of protein manifesting in the form of waning energy or insufficient strength. I'm fit, strong, and well fed despite what some folks might think of as a dull diet. The dullness in my diet is what has allowed me to spend time doing the other necessary things that sustain me and my lifestyle here in Zoro's field. If things were any more complicated, I wouldn't have had time to chop wood and carry water, as the Buddhists would say.

In a simple diet it is a challenge to come up with new combinations, new recipes, to treat my palate from time to time. "How many ways can you cook a potato?" someone once asked me during a conversation about my eating habits. "I'm only as limited as my imagination. And I've got a good imagination. You've got to have a good imagination and a good sense of humor, living out in the woods alone. Need these to keep yourself entertained, if not fed," I replied. And it's true. We are limited only by our lack of imagination. I look forward each night to my plate of potatoes and beans. They not only keep me alive, but they are welcome company and companions to my hunger at the end of the day. The fact that I appreciate them all the more because I have grown them adds to their inherent dignity and wonderful taste.

The topper for any woodland meal is a good glass of mountain springwater. I suppose I drink at least a gallon of fresh springwater each day. During the summer months probably two gallons a day. A large glass of water with my midday meal or with my supper in the evening is as complementary as it is copacetic. One of Mac's favorite sayings in regard to the preservation of food from the garden is: "Nothing less than first-class!" By this he means that if it isn't a prime specimen of any fruit or crop, it won't be canned, stored, or eaten. Only the best parts of the apple are used for applesauce. Only untainted tomatoes are sliced to go into the pot for fixing stewed tomatoes. Only first-class carrots go into the stew. And water is the fine wine of the mountain recluse and aesthete. I would take to task anyone who might insinuate that "water is the poor man's wine." This is much too slanderous, for the flavor of good mountain springwater is every bit as engaging as any other drink you could find in a store. I haven't had a soft drink or any other sugared drink in over three years, and I can't say I've ever felt deprived. Vendors of popular and fast foods would have a hard time convincing me that what they sell is anywhere close to being as good as the water that comes up from the ground in the holler beneath my field.

Blue Ribbons

Using Mac's credo as a catalyst, this year I've taken the notion of first-class food a little further and in a much different direction than in years past. Instead of taking pride and pleasure in my harvested and canned food only in ways that come naturally and of necessity, I decided out of curiosity to take my best-of-the-best to the county fair. To see how my produce stacked up against that of folks living in the fast-paced world with their many modern conveniences. This impulse was as much a lark as anything else. Something bordering more on mischief than on a desire for recognition and accolade. I did it in order to play a Walt Johnson kind of prank on Mac. Since no monetary prizes were given for winners at the county fair, profit was certainly not the motive for my conduct. It was just that I'd gotten good at growing things and going first class here in the woods, and I was ready to take the sharp hook of my learning curve in the woods and drop it into the lake of the outside world and see what I could catch.

The largest agricultural fair in western North Carolina is held each year just outside of Hendersonville and represents the far-western counties of the state. By entering my produce I'd be competing with farmers and suburban gardeners from ten counties. To say that I had no illusions about winning anything is an understatement. I simply wanted (for some reason unknown even to myself) to have my work there as part of the best of what the western part of the state had to offer, regardless of the outcome. "It's the journey that matters, not the arrival." So says the sixteenth-century French essayist Montaigne. And it has been rephrased by many others in centuries since as koan or coda for how best to live the journey of one's life. For me, with regard to the Western North Carolina Agricultural Fair, it was the entering, not the winning, that mattered. Or at least this was what I was leading myself to believe.

I figured that if I was going to take the trouble to do it at all, I might as well do it big. In the end, and as the punch line for my prank, I made labels for the canned goods I was entering that read: McHugh Farms. Mac would have never authorized such an action, but I took the liberty and caught a ride to Hendersonville with Saluda native Paul Rhodes, who had come out to see how my bees were doing. Not only did I take samples of my canned applesauce, green beans, tomatoes, and some passion fruit jelly, but I also took a couple of sunflowers that had just come into full bloom, gourds, and my largest acorn squash. I had a tote sack plumb full, as Zoro would say, and I felt a little like Dorothy departing for Oz.

Two weeks later I returned to the fairground and came home with a slightly less bulging tote sack but with a handful of ribbons. When Paul let me out of the truck on the old ridge road, instead of heading over the hill toward the cabin, I went straight up the hill in the direction of the McHugh farm. On the big table on the back porch I put the canned goods with their McHugh Farms labels. Next to each of the winners I placed a ribbon. For the green beans: yellow (second place). For the applesauce: blue (first place). For the canned tomatoes: white (third place). For the passion fruit jelly: blue (first place). For the wildflower honey: blue (first place). As well as ribbons for my canned entries, I had also won a first premium blue ribbon for my sunflowers as part of the flower show and a second premium yellow ribbon for a couple of unusual Dinosaur gourds that I'd raised from seeds given to me by an elder over on the Cherokee reservation.

I laid the ribbons out on the table and quietly slipped off the porch and walked back down the hill and across the road and over another hill to the cabin. When I returned to the McHugh porch later in the day — when I knew Mac would be there having his end-of-day scotch and water—he greeted me not with an expression of displeasure for having used his name in vain, as it were, on the labels of the canned vegetables and jellies, but rather with a large smile. He said nothing. Just smiled. I think that, although he didn't say it, he was just as pleased as I was that we'd run the table at the WNC Fair with food and flowers grown on his land. Even now, some months later, the string of ribbons won at the fair is hanging up like hunting trophies in his canning kitchen in the old converted barn, where he can see them whenever he passes by.

PLANTING CORN

When the moon
beds warm and silver in the sky, and
the signs are in the hands:

it's time to plant corn!

When crow starts
in spring with his breakfast songs
and cotton meal lies golden in the row:

it's time to plant corn!

As the bluebird feeds
its first batch of young and
the sky takes earth in hand,
and I dance in the darkness of
a moonlit field where spring now rules the land
to the tune of Kanati's horn:

plant corn!

THE PACIFIST
AND THE HUNTER

Every good hunter is uneasy in the depths of his conscience.

JOSÉ ORTEGA Y GASSET

Alone far in the wilds and mountains, I hunt . . .

WALT WHITMAN
"Song of Myself"

When I came into the woods to live a self-sufficient life, I thought of myself as a pacifist. I had lived for thirty years without killing, intentionally, another living thing other than ants, spiders, and a few snakes — which were acts of unconsciousness during my youth. Years later, I became a conscientious objector during the Vietnam War and went on to protest nonviolently against that war. All this was based on my belief in the kind of pacifism that was exhibited by Gandhi — who, interestingly enough, got his ideas on civil disobedience and nonviolence from reading Emerson and Thoreau. I came to the woods fairly naive and as a virgin where knowledge of living off the land was concerned.

While being one of the gentlest and most thoughtful of people, Zoro smiled at me as I espoused my pacifist ideals and delivered my animal rights monologue during one of our earliest encounters. I haven't forgotten his silent sarcasm concerning my self-possessed prattle, and it wasn't long after that conversation that I was confronted face to face with my own idealistic beliefs. As I stared down the barrel of my twenty-gauge shotgun at a rogue squirrel who had been pillaging my fruit crop that year and was threatening to lay waste to another apple from my old limbertwig apple tree, my pacifistic worldview changed forever. With a single squeeze of the trigger, I lost my virginity as a member of the benevolent race. While it was one of the harder things I've ever had to do, it was done with full knowledge that it was the right thing to do, in that there really was no reasonable alternative to save my fruit.

I was faced with the same choice a short time later, when the raccoons threatened to plunder my sweet corn. I had tried everything from scarecrows to pie tins banging in the breeze, to urinating in the rows, to voodoo . . . but nothing worked. Even Havahart traps were only a temporary deterrent to the predations of the coons and other scavenging animals like woodchucks, skunks, chipmunks, squirrels, and mice, as all of these critters always find their way back home. The only thing left to do was to shoot. Something I do now without shame yet with reluctant aim and a certain reverence, as I still am not comfortable with the taking of life. But sometimes necessity takes precedence over theology or philosophy.

The whole question of owning and using a gun to kill other living things, while it's not much of an issue here in my community of born-and-bred mountain folks with long histories of self-sufficiency, is nevertheless an emotional issue in the outside world. First, there are animal rights groups and supporters, who embrace an inflexible ethic of thou shalt not kill anything, anywhere, anytime. That is, if it's an animal. Hypocritically, these same people may have opposite views on issues such as the death penalty, waging war, and killing human beings. And then there are religious groups such as the Quakers in this country and the Jains in India—both of whom embrace their own particular doctrine of pacifism. While the Quakers believe in a deep pacifism that forbids not only participation in war but also the resolution of human conflict by means of any sort of violence, the Jains take their pacifistic stance even further, by outlawing aggression or violence toward *any* living thing, be it insect, animal, or human. While this may be good food for intellectual or spiritual debate in the meetinghouse or temple, I defy the practitioners of these faiths to defend their crops from raccoons with their peaceful ethic, lest they find themselves being offered up, unwillingly, to the gods of malnutrition as a sacrifice.

While in principle I agree with the tenets of pacifism (as strategy, for example, of social nonviolent protest and for purposes of commonsense negotiations of disagreements among individuals, groups, or governments), in reality, after having lived the kind of life I have for these past few years, I have come to see the argument as little more than an indulgence perpetrated by those who have the luxury of not having to fight for their survival. Few of us would, I am convinced, play possum rather than defend ourselves or our loved ones if violently threatened, just as few of us would starve to death rather than kill an animal or eat meat. Total pacifism, much like the notion of political and social anarchy, is the product of prosperous times, middle-class lifestyles, and a naively liberal, intellectual mindset. It is, perhaps, a great thing to aspire to (were all people spiritually advanced to a much loftier plane of awareness and behavior), but given the right (should I say wrong?) situation, for most people pacifism is a next to impossible ethic to put into practice. And I have learned this the hard way, as I have had to kill to survive.

The Spanish philosopher and writer José Ortega y Gasset has written in his essay "Meditations on Hunting": "There is no animal, pure animal, other than the wild one, and the relationship with him is the hunt. It should also be noticed that only by hunting can man *be* in the country." I can honestly say that without my hand-me-down single-barrel shotgun, I would never have lasted in the woods this long. Despite its good-ole-boy stigma, its brutish appearance, and its jolting bark, the beauty of this piece of equipment is, in having one, the absoluteness of its advantage. An advantage that has leveled the playing field for this soft-skinned, enlarged-brained mammal and allowed him to survive amongst much keener and stronger, street-smart critters. This has allowed me the luxury of a learning curve and an insight into nature that I would have otherwise never been privy to.

The gun is a definitive answer to roving scavengers who would decimate the better part of a garden in a single night's debauch. It is an instrument like no other for evening the odds in an environment where one is in a state of constant combat with the elements and Nature's offspring. While a gun can also be a helpmate for bringing in game as a necessary source of food, it can also be a deterrent to any neighbor or outsider who might wish you ill. The known fact that I keep a gun in my house gives pause to humans and critters alike before they cause any damage to my crops or harm to my body or possessions. Word of mouth travels fast in a community such as this, as neighbors within earshot hear the cannonlike explosions every now and again coming from the vicinity of my woods and know that the hermit up on the hill is not without means of protection and persuasion—and seems to be a pretty good shot to boot. These facts are passed down the line to family members and friends and out into the community at large.

But primarily the gun is for hunting and for eradicating garden pests that can't otherwise be curtailed. In my case, I don't go out of my way to hunt for meat (and I wouldn't have to go far, as there are easy pickings provided by roving families of deer that unabashedly, and yet with full permission, come into the orchard to feed on the drops from the early and late fall apple trees, as well as a solitary flock of wild turkeys that occasionally wanders into my garden field to feed off the seed and cracked corn I put out for the birds during the winter months), as my diet consists primarily of what I can grow. But when the local rabbit population exceeds the carrying capacity of the neighborhood, or the squirrels have not enough mast to feed themselves or their spring crop of young and start making forays into my garden, arbors, and orchard, robbing me of food that will for the next several months keep me alive, there is no moral dilemma. It's simply and clearly a case of them or me.

Being that I am here and aim to survive, I use the gun to thin out those thieving rascals I find amongst the bean rows, the strawberries, the apples, and the corn—turning the dynamic upside down by making them a part of *my* menu for some future evening's meal. In the name of independence and survival, I have rationalized my right to carry and use a gun. Yet I have at the same time maintained the hunter's time-honored code of always eating what I kill. Also, particularly in the case of rabbit and squirrel, the skins can be dried and cured for certain practical uses. In this way I use as much of the animal as possible so as not to be guilty of greed or waste.

During the last three years, I have shot woodchuck, raccoon, rabbit, squirrel, and snake. In every case have I used and/or eaten that which I have killed, except for the raccoons, which I feed to a flock of turkey vultures that roost in a grove of pine trees on a bluff overlooking the Green River Gorge. In doing so, I have kept the raccoons from decimating my corn crop; managed to keep the woodchucks from eating the beans; kept the rabbits away from all leafy greens; and the squirrels (who seem to exploit my fruit crops more for spite and play than from actual hunger—taking only single wasteful bites from an apple, plum, or strawberry before moving on to the next ripe opportunity) from the fruit. If I weren't using a modern firearm, I'd have to be killing these critters with another kind of weapon. The gun is easier and more accurate and has saved me hours upon hours of crudely creative plotting trying to rid myself of various garden pests.

Lest anyone get the impression that I consider myself to be ethically elevated along with being an accomplished marksman or to be anything resembling the stereotype of the great white hunter, let me come clean by telling a story on myself that will put things into perspective and set the record straight. For, if intention were the issue, I am certainly not without sin.

During my second year here in the woods, I decided that in order to become a complete woodsman, I needed to become a hunter. Being reluctant to do so, I opted for the most benign method of hunting as my vehicle to procure game for my winter larder: the bow and arrow. My reasoning in choosing this weapon rather than the gun was that it gave the animals a fair chance, considering my nonexistent skills, and that it would satisfy my fascination with more primitive technology coming from centuries past. With all this in mind, I began the process of mental and physical training in preparation for the hunting season that would come around in the fall of the year, several months hence.

I began by teaching myself how to use a bow that I'd borrowed from a neighbor and that had belonged to and been discarded by their adolescent son. While neither the bow nor the arrows were state-of-the-art hunting equipment, they were good enough to allow me to begin to hone my skills as an archer. I set up for myself a disciplined schedule of practice and an archery range that consisted of a bale of straw into which I ran four rather thick tree branches for legs, and a couple of leaf-adorned end-branches to represent head and antlers—creating a somewhat surreal imitation of a white-tailed deer. This crude attempt at concrete art served as my target. I set the straw-bale deer up in the northwest corner of Zoro's field about twenty-five yards out from the first row of pines and huckleberry bushes.

My custom and my practice regimen for the next few months was to station myself in various positions up in the woods between trees and shrubs and to try hitting the straw-bale deer. By trying to simulate real hunting situations, I figured I would get the best possible training for the day when I would go into the deeper woods with the intention of taking my first turkey or deer. With this in mind I was diligent in my practice and was getting to be a pretty good shot—able to hit my improvised target with increasing regularity despite all the interference from having to shoot my arrows from twenty yards or so up in the woods and around and through all manner of trunks, brush, and foliage.

To make a short story even shorter, all my efforts at perfecting my skills as a would-be archer went unrequited, as I would never actually take my new-found skills as an archer into the woods in search of the deer I had fantasized about with every draw of the bowstring and every release of an arrow. At the last minute, as bow season arrived coincidentally that year with the falling of leaves from the trees, I made an emotional decision not to become a hunter, based on the epiphany that I didn't need to add meat to my diet as a regular staple and that I didn't want to alter the benevolent relationship I had with certain animals. As a result, my hot date on a cold day with a dead deer or turkey would go unconsummated. The balance and behavior of my larger woodland friends went unchanged and unscathed. They still come into my garden field and into the orchard unalarmed by my presence. I don't intend to alter this dynamic, as I value my natural neighbors more as friends than as food. So far necessity hasn't intervened to destroy this relatively elevated ethic. But who knows how long it would last if I were pushed closer to the edge of self-sufficiency as a result of drought or a devastatingly poor year of yield from the garden. Each year is certainly different from the last, and one never knows and cannot predict what Nature has up her sleeve. With this in mind, while enjoying the company of my forest friends in relative harmony I never say never, as "never" is only one letter longer than "ever" and only one degree removed from "always." It's a small world here in the woods, where nothing is certain and nothing stays the same.

LICENSE TO KILL

"Shoot," he said.
And the orders were to kill.
A gust of wind
didn't stand a chance against
the aim of my bow—
searching the darkness for
the faintest flash of light.

Was there anything there
that would put more food on my table
than meat?
To be moral with this hunger
rolling around in my gut
is a joke.
When I have been sentenced to a life
I clutch like a gun.

Having said "no" to meat,
the deer and the wild birds
still come to my field to dance.
To feed on what I have decided
and that which I have not done.
Wanting to be friend,
not foe.
Saying "Please stay.
Don't go."

FISHING

The river rises in a deep cleft or gorge in the mountains, the scenery
of which is of the wildest and ruggedest character. For a mile
or more there is barely room for the river at the bottom of the
chasm. On either hand the mountains, interrupted by shelving, overhanging precipices, rise abruptly to a great height.

JOHN BURROUGHS
Preface to *Pepacton*

I awake from a sound spring sleep to the noise of knocking at my
cabin door. It's still dark outside. In my half-conscious state, my mind
immediately leaps to Poe's poem "The Raven": "While I nodded,
nearly napping, suddenly there came a tapping, / As of some one
gently rapping, rapping at my chamber door." I am slow to move,
and the knocking comes again before I pull myself out of bed and
ramble over cold wood floors to the door. Opening it, I see Horace
Pace standing out in the dooryard. "I'm goin' down to the river to fish.
Thought you might want to come along," is all he says, slightly smiling. My mind still moving slowly, I try to make sense of the situation
in order to come up with some sort of intelligent response. All I am
able to mutter is: "Fish?" My mind finally engaging, I remember that I
was going to spend the day working on the little barn I'm building on
the east side of the field, and check the bees—do a first housecleaning
after a long winter. "Sure," I say, still half asleep and without thinking,
with Horace still standing in the doorway waiting for my response.
"Give me a minute and let me get on some clothes."

Horace Pace lives in Saluda and enjoys a healthy reputation as a
consummate woodsman. For the past three years he has been teaching me to fish for trout in the Green River. This isn't the first time
he has shown up unexpectedly at my door before dawn. Because
he likes to fish down in what the locals refer to as Rocky Mountain
Cove—maybe the roughest part of the whole river—he likes to go
with a partner in case something should go wrong. On days when
he can't get anyone else to go, he comes by here on his way down to
the end of the road at Johnson's Pond, where he parks his truck and

85

where there is an old logging road, downhill, that gives easy access to the river.

During the first year of my new life here in the woods, I was an aggressive student, seeking out those who could teach me the skills of self-sufficiency. Needing some kind of supplement to my mostly vegetarian diet, and with the river nearby, I thought of fish as an obvious answer. When I asked folks in town who would be the best person from whom to learn to fish, the immediate response was: Horace Pace. I eventually met Horace one day over at Mac's place, where he was high up in a tulip poplar trimming out limbs that were hanging over the house. After he had finished pruning the tree and had returned to the ground, I helped him drag the branches into the woods—a good icebreaker for questions I had about fishing the Green River. He was quick to pick up the conversation and was off and running on the subject, which we continued over iced tea on the McHughs' back porch. It wasn't much more than a couple of weeks before Horace made his first appearance at my cabin door—much like this morning, unannounced and before daylight.

Those first trips to the river to fish for trout were little more than a comedy of errors. While I had done a minimal amount of pond, lake, and even ocean fishing, I was a true greenhorn on rivers, and especially on such a wild white-water river as the Green roaring through Rocky Mountain Cove with a vengeance. At the end of those early trips, I would usually emerge from the river and the woods wet and covered in loamy dirt and leaves—looking like the legendary Green Man as recorded in Irish mythology. And rarely with any fish. I can only imagine the kinds of tales that were told in town at my expense. But learning from my mistakes, I became a better fisherman, more knowledgeable of both river and woods. In Horace Pace, I had a learned and patient teacher.

It's still early in the spring and the bees can wait another day, I think to myself as I rummage around the cabin looking for appropriate fishing clothes. The breeze that had blown in through the door as I opened it to find Horace standing there in the dark felt unseasonably warm. A perfect day to waste down on the river, I rationalize. I load myself, my five-foot graphite fishing rod, and some walnuts and corn bread for lunch into Horace's old workhorse of a truck and ride to the bottom of the hill where the dirt road ends down at the old Johnson home-place. From there it is a short walk to the other side of the little lake, then about a twenty-minute walk downhill, on an old logging trail, to the river at the upper end of Rocky Mountain Cove.

By the time we reach the far end of the lake and the old logging trail, the sun is showing signs of coming up in the east. The woods are dark, but not so dark, now, that we can't see where we are going along a rough and uncertain path. Birds are beginning to stir, and I can hear the early-morning calls of a cardinal and the high-pitched *see dee, see dee* of a chickadee not far away as a crow carps loudly in the further distance. The path is still wet with dew and so we slip and slide our way down through stands of hemlock, glades of poplar, and ravines of rhododendron—a little spring branch running quickly, yet Zenlike, over beds of mica and fool's gold alongside the path—until we finally reach a small, flat, sandy beach that borders the river to the west. By now the sun is up and we can see clearly the high granite cliffs on the opposite side of the river, as well as the river itself, tumbling willfully into Rocky Mountain Cove.

Rocky Mountain Cove got its name largely because of the sheer rock cliffs and huge boulders that have fallen into and on both sides of the river. Steep slopes of rock and rhododendron thickets define the western side of the river while a smooth granite face outlines the river to the east, both banks of the river merely anchors for the high mountain ridges overhead—hence Rocky Mountain Cove. But we are here to fish, not sightsee, and so we collect our gear and divvy up the night crawlers and crickets Horace dug up that morning before arriving at my door, and make our way over the sandbar and onto the boulders that lead, like stepping stones for the mythic Cherokee giant Judaculla, downstream.

Whenever we fished together, Horace would pick certain pools and eddies in the stream and cast his line into the dark water that flowed back in and under the large rocks. I would follow suit, following him and fishing another angle of the hole, all the while watching his methods of approaching the holes, his casting techniques, and his general manner around the fast-moving stream. We would take turns fishing any given hole, until Horace was convinced that there were either no fish or no fish biting in this place, and then move on to the next likely spot. We would continue this routine for an hour or so, which constituted the teaching segment of our expeditions together. At some point, about midmorning, Horace would bring his line in from fishing a hole we'd exhausted and say, "I'm going ahead. I'll meet you at the pools beneath the Narrows," which meant: "I've taught you all I can teach you today, and I'm going ahead to fish certain spots I know about that I'm not going to tell you about, where I am pretty sure there are some fish." And he would disappear into the laurel thicket and be gone. At this point I was on my own and had to fend for myself.

On this day I reel my line back in, sans worm, and follow his trail through the steep and slippery banks of the laurel hell, thinking I'll catch up with him at the next pool. When I get there, as usual Horace is nowhere to be found. I decide to stop here anyway and try my luck in a large pool bordered by giant boulders, despite knowing that this is a spot where I've never gotten as much as a nibble before.

The most important thing I've learned from Horace over the years is the idea that to fish for native trout you have to learn to think like the fish you are fishing for. In other words, become the fish. Where would a trout hide? What kind of food would it go for at this time of day? Would it be lethargic or active? In the three years I have fished this river with Horace and on my own, I've learned a great deal about trout and their habits. As when living in the woods you must be in touch with the habits of the plants and animals, you need to know the water world and its inhabitants if you are going to go home with a mess of fish. I've gotten good at making my way over and around the rocks, through the laurel and rhododendron without snagging my pole, and casting low enough not to get my line tangled in the overhanging trees. Technically, I have become efficient enough, but there is more to fishing than athleticism; there are also the elements of instinct and luck.

As I fish the big pool just above the Narrows, I know that Horace has made his way well down the river ahead of me. The Narrows is a part of the river that funnels into a little canyon where the river is only about ten feet wide, creating a sluice of white water that is loud and powerful as it descends a shoot of water-whittled rock into a pool some one hundred feet below. The local lore pertaining to the

Narrows is as long as the river itself and includes stories of young people who have been foolish enough to try to jump the river, only to fail and be washed down the slim shoot of rapids to their death. As I approach the Narrows, these tales fill my head, and I step cautiously in the wet leaves and on the slippery stones, taking note of new-leafing ginseng and trillium. Since there is nowhere to fish the sluice, I make my way around the roaring white water as it hurls itself downstream, coming finally to a large pool at the bottom of the shoot adjacent to a grove of new-growth poplars and oaks. Here there are several spots where the water eddies up quietly, near abandoned beaver lodges, into calmer dark areas that are a perfect habitat for the trout. On previous trips I have had some luck fishing this hole, and so I figure that realistically I can expect to catch a fish or two. With that thought in the back of my mind and the sound of a grouse drumming in the woods, and with two green darner dragonflies strafing the shoreline, I bait my hook with a big fat night crawler and cast my line in under a large rock at the south end of the pool.

By now it's late in the morning and warm enough that if there are any trout to be had, they should be hungry and willing to move out from their hiding places to snatch my menu of worm or cricket. Casting upstream and not finding any takers under the rock at the bottom of the large pool, I crawl around a slick rock with deep potholes where the footing is a bit treacherous and get into a position to fish another spot where I can cast from a more inconspicuous downstream angle. I can see that Horace has been here ahead of me, as his footprints are clearly etched into the wet moss on the rock. As I wonder if he's had any luck in this spot and if he's left me anything to catch, a kingfisher flies up into a birch on the other side of the river and sits there, unfazed by my presence, watching a small snake wriggle its way out of the water and onto a sunny rock. This is a good sign, I think to myself as I bait my hook with a small young cricket. The kingfisher wouldn't have stopped at this place unless he'd had success here before. I try to think like the big blue bird and to get a read on what part of the pool he's watching. There is already a glare on the water from the sun overhead, making it difficult to discern the deep from the shallow water. Regardless, I pick my spot and toss my line into the water about twenty feet from where I am standing. Almost immediately I get a tug that becomes a bite, and my line goes taut. I can tell from the pull and the action on the other end of the line that I've got something of good size. I pull, it pulls back. I pull harder still, it pulls even harder. Each of us trying to outguess and outmaneuver the other. But I'm winning this tug-of-war, and I've soon got the fish near the shore where it finally breaks water and I can see its green-gray skin shining in the noonday sun. Sixty seconds later and I've got the fifteen-inch native trout in my hands and am taking the hook out of its mouth.

Not having a basket, a proper satchel, or even a stringer to secure the fish, I lay the trout down on a sandy spot above the water and break a branch off a dogwood sapling and break it a second time so that it takes the shape of a large, long-handled fishhook. I slip the short end of the stick through the gills and out the mouth of the fish, giving me a means of transporting it for the rest of the day. After a few more casts into various spots in the pool and not having any further success, I pick up my "fishstick" and make my way farther downstream. Here the banks are not so steep and the water is calmer, making it easier to move from one spot to another. I make out deer tracks in the soft dirt. From the looks of the tracks, they must have been here drinking earlier in the day. In no time I have found another of Horace's pools. Where I am standing, a bottombush limb inhabited by a treehopper has recently been snapped. Feeling lucky, and since it worked for me before, I bait my hook with another cricket and cast it into a place where the water swirls back upstream in a quiet little pool under the overhanging branches of a young chinaberry tree. Immediately I get a bite and jerk my line to set the hook. But my line goes limp, and I reel it in, the hook empty. I put another cricket on and toss a line into the same hole, scattering water striders as the bait hits the surface, hoping that whatever fish took the first cricket will be hungry enough to want more. I make two or three casts into the same spot before I get the second tug. This one's even bigger, and I've hooked it this time. After a long fight I land the fish—another fourteen- or fifteen-inch native trout—and thread it onto my forked carrying stick.

After several hours of fish psychology, climbing boulders, negotiating laurel thickets and leafy embankments, I'm beginning to think of home. Two trophy-sized trout seem enough for bragging rights, as well as a substantial meal, and so I put my gear in order, pick up my fishstick, and turn to make my way downstream hoping to catch up with Horace near a spot where we can hike back on another old logging trail that follows a ridgeline that will take us back to the truck. No sooner have I taken the first step on the mossy rock around the pool where I caught the second fish, than the next thing I know I'm waist-deep in the river, thrashing around to keep my balance and not get any wetter than I already am. As I finally recover and make my way out of the water, holding my rod in one hand and the forked stick in the other, I notice that what I am bringing out of the water in my left hand is an empty stick. My two native trout, and all the bragging rights that go with them, have slipped off the end of the stick and disappeared into the river. I'm sure Horace must hear my cursing downstream, as I stand on the bank of the river letting fly with all manner of expletives. "Sure, you did," I can already hear him saying. Wet, tired, and embarrassed, I begin walking downriver toward wherever Horace and inevitable humiliation await.

When I finally catch up with Horace, he is sitting in the sun on a small sandbar eating a meatloaf sandwich he'd packed in his fishing vest. As I approach, checking my pockets to find only soggy corn bread, he pulls his fish basket out of the water, opens the lip, revealing five large native trout. "You have any luck?" he asks.

"Not much. Caught a couple small ones upstream near the big pool at the bottom of the Narrows, but threw them back. They were less than twelve inches," I say, not wanting to make a fool of myself with the story of the lost fish.

"Looks like you got wet," he says, glancing up from his sandwich. "You'll have better luck next time." I could see him checking out my dripping pants and the crooked stick I was still carrying unconsciously in my hand. He smiles, gives me a knowing wink, and goes back to eating his sandwich, not pushing me for the rest of the story that is written all over my face and clothes.

I had potatoes, corn bread, and applesauce, as usual, for dinner that night. All of which tasted like those two large native trout that got away.

FISHING THE GREEN RIVER

Like the legs of giants
the poplars stand in these woods.
Warblers whistling at the
rising sun.
Acrobatic water leaping
through heavy air
to the trout pools
below.

Here, there is nothing
but the voice of water
and the memory of rock.
As I rough my way downstream,
I dream of fish.
Carry on a conversation
with my boots.
Where the water quiets
behind boulders big as houses,
I cast a line into the pool.
A big blue bird
watches from branches,
above,
as I try to think like the fish
I want to catch
who waits in the darkest part
of the river
for its last meal.

HOMEBREW

Alchemy prepared the greatest attack on the divine order
of the universe which mankind has ever dared.

CARL JUNG

*W*hile the subject of distilled liquids is well documented here
in the southern Appalachians, everyone has their own story when it
comes to the devil's drink. And what stories they are! I could probably fill these pages with nothing other than the tall tales I have heard
about local moonshiners and their product—which might be a more
entertaining read than what I am writing about my solitary life in the
woods. In fact these woods reek of fermented corn and the smoke of
gunpowder from bygone days. And barrel rings, old steel drums, and
remnants of copper stills can even now be found in treacherous laurel
hells and along small spring branches almost anywhere in these hills.

While moonshine and corn liquor are preferred beverages and a
primary topic of conversation where people congregate, and while it
is still readily available, I have kept my palate seasoned these past few
years by making my own beer, or "homebrew," as it is more casually
called. My homebrew has helped in keeping mind and body warm,
on edge, and just loose enough as not to become loony (or a little
"queer," as the old folk would put it) from too much time spent only
with myself. I also consider my stash of homebrew a source of medicinal comfort. While it doesn't have the overt healing properties that
whiskey has (moonshine was, and still is, used in naturopathic and
home remedies in the treatment of many maladies—such as arthritis,
rheumatism, colds, coughs, dysentery, gall bladder infections, head-
aches, pneumonia, and even spider bites—and as a tonic and cure-all),
it is a pleasant sedative that I like to believe wards off potential illness,
including ill states of mind.

But maybe the best and most honest reason for my having made
homebrew is that it is cheap and easy to make, and it quenches my
ever-present thirst. And with its relatively low alcohol content, it
is much less likely than whiskey to get me into trouble. In a short
amount of time and with few materials and little effort, I can throw

93

off a batch of brew that can rival, if not surpass, anything that can be found on tap in any town or city in this country. In fact I've begun to take a certain amount of pride in the quality of my homemade beer, always striving to raise the standard with each new batch, as for the past two years or so I've always had at least a little homebrew stored in my root cellar in old clay jugs.

Before beginning to make my own beer, I made a trip to the Hendersonville library and checked out a couple of seminal books on the subject. Reading up on the history of beermaking, I found that beer is one of the earliest alcoholic drinks ever to be produced worldwide. Records of drinks made from various grains are recorded in Egypt as far back as 3000 BC. And in Europe, many countries claim it as their national drink, with honey being used instead of sugar in earlier times. The first breweries were apparently started in monasteries as early as the eleventh century. These small early breweries were, not unlike the moonshine stills of modern-day Appalachia, built next to pristine water sources, and it wasn't long before everyone in the village where these monasteries and bodies of unspoiled freshwater were located was brewing their own beer. Most of the early beers were what is called "porter," or dark beer, which was an offshoot of the early honey ales, or "mead."

Being as I am near a spring that provides wonderfully clean and savory water, and being that I have beehives that produce all the honey I would ever need, I already have two of the primary ingredients for quality beer production right here at hand, and with no outlay of cash. The ingredients that I don't have I get in Saluda in trade for some of my wildflower honey. The needed ingredients include malt extract syrup (the Blue Ribbon brand makes, I found, the best-tasting beer), hops, yeast, and a little flaked oatmeal, which gives the beer a stouter consistency and taste. Since I don't make great quantities at a time, I keep the outlay of money and materials at a minimum, and I can do my brewing in a small space.

My first batch of homebrew was made with Mac over in the basement of his barn. He was in the mood for some good homemade beer and agreed to work with me in bringing off my first batch. Using a five-gallon ceramic pickling crock that he had in the barn for pickling beans and sauerkraut, we began our bit of alchemy underneath the floorboards of the barn. To a base of about three and a half gallons of pure springwater, we added a couple of large cans of Blue Ribbon malt and about three ounces of hops—all into two large pots we had sitting on top of an old woodstove that we'd fired up very hot. When the mixture in the pots came to a boil, we began stirring it, and did so continually for almost an hour. After boiling, the wort in the pots was poured through a large sieve into the crock and left to cool overnight. The next morning the sediment in the bottom of the crock was filtered through porous paper, and more springwater and honey were added to bring the amount back up to about four gallons. To this new concoction, I added the contents of a bottle of yeast starter we had made up the day before.

For the next three days I checked and stirred the crock until, on the fourth day, I skimmed off the layer of top fermenting yeast and stirred the mixture again thoroughly. Fermentation continued for a couple more days. When there was no longer any clear evidence of fermentation activity, all yeast was skimmed off the top of the liquid, and the beer was transferred into a five-gallon demijohn that was capped with a tight-fitting tube and airlock cork. I let the beer sit in the demijohn for another day to make sure the fermentation process had finished off fully. Then I emptied the beer into the ceramic crock, washed out the demijohn, and returned the beer to the plugged glass container, letting it sit for three more days, after which time Mac and I siphoned off the excess sediment and poured the beer into five old one-gallon clay jugs, adding a teaspoon of sugar into each jug, filling them not quite to the top. Again we let the jugs sit for about three days in a warm place until the beer began to build up gas and some pressure. When there was finally sufficient evidence of gas in the jugs, we put them in a wheelbarrow and transported them to my root cellar, where they would be kept at a constant temperature of around fifty-five degrees.

To ensure drinkability, as well as to increase the level of alcoholic content, I left the ceramic jugs in my root cellar for almost two months. While I could have drunk from the jugs almost immediately, I pushed my more-than-moderate level of patience to the limit and didn't touch the jugs until eight weeks had passed. On D-Day (Drink Day), I went down into the root cellar and brought out the oldest of the clay jugs Mac had loaned me — a little brown jug that was stereo-typically hillbilly. After carrying it, cautiously, up the root-cellar steps and handling it like the antique that it was as I walked back around to the front door of the cabin and inside, I set it down on the kitchen table next to my almost-matching brown ceramic mug, which was waiting there as if for a long-lost friend.

For me this was a ceremonial moment. Celebrating the first taste of beer I had made from scratch. Regretting that Mac couldn't be present to share in the ceremony or in that first tasting, I wasn't able to wait, and I uncorked the little brown jug. The light honey-brown liquid that poured from the jug into the mug was a wonderful sight. And the aroma that wafted up from the open jug into my nose was akin to musky perfume. "If the taste is anything like the smell, I have produced something of truly alchemic proportions," I thought as I watched the foamy head form and spill over the edge of the mug. When the foam had settled, I picked up the large brown mug and put it to my lips, taking a healthy dram of the dense, dark liquid. A big smile came to my face as the potent brew slid down my gullet, creat-ing a warm sensation in my belly and a little tingle in my brain. "First-class!" I exclaimed, while wasting no time moving the mug again in the direction of my eager mouth. With the second gulp of beer, I knew I'd brewed something special. The second taste was even richer than the first, and the rush of alcohol went straight to the business of killing brain cells and exploding warmly in my ears. This was hooch! Even if it was only beer. Mac would be proud of our efforts, which in my mind, and with each additional swig of beer, could almost qualify as 'shine. I was guessing, after the third or fourth swallow, that the level of alcohol in the beer was around 10 percent, if not higher. My head was light and my soul was flying! Even if it was beginner's luck, I'd done myself proud. God knows, I'd drunk enough beer in my young life to know what was what. And what this was was good!

With the golden mead going down like water, it wasn't long before I was, as they say, in my cups, and was singing a rather raucous version of "Little Brown Jug" to the curvaceous kerosene lamp, which cast surreal shadows on the walls of the cabin as I choreographed my a cappella incantations with arms akimbo and feet attempting an inebriated buck dance. With my little brown jug only half full, I went to bed that night in a dive. Dreaming of half-human, half-animal bacchanals and sleeping till after daylight the next day.

A lot of wort, sediment, and good beer has gone over the dam in the last couple of years, as there are always corked clay jugs in the root cellar, aging. In hindsight, however, I think that first batch of hooch was something extraordinary. Like the myth that one's first sexual experience is always the best, such was the case with my first batch of beer. Never since have I been able to achieve that elusive combination of great taste and texture and high level of alcohol. While that first batch lasted me a long time (a little of the high-octane beer went a long way), I've gone through subsequent batches rather quickly, which means that there is almost always a new batch in the works to quench my thirst or to give me a slightly enlightened perspective on a gone world.

While beer has been my first love as an intoxicating extracurricular drink, I have also tried my hand at making wine. Although it is a very similar process and uses similar equipment, winemaking is a more delicate aqueous art form. Results are dubious, if rarely duplicated. Aside from making one good batch of muscadine wine and an acceptable batch of blackberry wine, my efforts at winemaking (despite my years of having worked in premier wineries in both California and the Bordeaux region of southern France) have been disappointing, if not downright dismal. When visitors appear, albeit infrequently, at my cabin door in the latter part of the day, I offer them some homebrew rather than taking a chance on the wine. Almost always my guests have come back for a second mug of beer. As for hard liquor, I've left that undertaking to the realm of legacy and legend, rarely stepping into the high-shot world of 100-proof hooch, much less having tried to make it myself. While I've usually got a quart jar hidden out in an old stump about a hundred yards from the cabin, from which I will take a snort from time to time for the sake of sheer excess, I choose not to go down the well-traveled road of alcoholic indulgence. My 7 percent beer and occasional glass of sweet wine are plenty to give my life here in the woods something spicy and spectral.

GOOD WINE

When the moon
  is in the morning wine:
    delicious

BEES

By the bee's example taught, enrich thy mind,
Improve kind nature's gift, by sense refin'd;
Be thou the honeycomb—in whom may dwell
Each mental sweet, nor leave one vacant cell.

from Eva Crane's *The Archaeology of Beekeeping*

*S*tanding in the middle of Zoro's field, covered from head to toe
with bees, I thought I was having a heart attack. I had been up at
the edge of the field working the hives. Checking for new honey. In
trying to lift the uppermost super gently off the top of the hive, I had
inadvertently lifted not only the top super but the lower one as well,
as the bees had sealed the two supers and the queen excluder divider
with wax. The lower super stayed glued to the upper super for only
a second before it came loose and went crashing down on top of the
brood chamber, which together with the lower super housed the majority of the bees. Thinking that they were under attack, the hive of
wild black bees (the most aggressive of all honeybees) came out in a
great swarm, covering me within seconds. As the first wave of bees
attacked with stingers activated, I took off running. By the time I had
reached the middle of the field, I was covered in thousands of bees.
Luckily I had dressed for the occasion—with bee veil and cap, gloves,
coveralls, and high-top boots. By now the bees were so thick on the
upper part of my body that I couldn't see through my veil. Not able
to see where I was going and therefore not able to retreat farther, I
stopped amidst the blooming buckwheat and began flailing my arms
like a misaligned windmill, swatting at bees I could no longer see.

I had been besieged by what must have been almost a whole hive
of bees and was in a state of pure panic, with my arms waving, my
legs kicking, and my heart racing to such an extent that I could hear
its beating in my ears and feel a growing pain in my chest. I had already been stung by a few bees whose stingers were able to penetrate
my heavy denim jeans. Feeling the stings, I feared that I'd soon suffer
hundreds, if not thousands, of stings and would be stung to death—a

thought that, combined with my frantic movements, had caused my heart to start racing out of control.

Just when I thought I had taken my last breath, and with the collective and resounding buzz of a couple thousand bees in my ears, I experienced an unexpected moment of clarity. In that moment a voice within me said: "If you don't calm down, you are going to die." Knowing that the voice was right, I immediately began to calm myself. I stopped my flailing and my dancing and stood still, letting the bees do what they would. I then began to concentrate on my heartbeat and my breath—breathing more slowly, hoping to lower the flow of adrenaline and quiet my heartbeat. As, in increments, I became calmer, there came a kind of lucidity, and I also became more aware of the bees and their activity. It was as if everything was happening in slow motion. Within a very short time (that felt like a very long time under the circumstances) I could feel my heart rate decreasing and my whole state of mind shifting to a place of acceptance and balance, rather than a state of hysteria and flight. With this shift of consciousness and behavior, a most amazing thing happened.

As soon as I began to shift my attitude and behavior and to become calmer, I noticed that simultaneously the loud buzzing made collectively by the bees blanketing my body began to subside. Also I was noticing that the energy of the bees wasn't as vicious and aggressive. A few of the bees that covered the veil in front of my face actually flew away, so that for the first time in what felt like hours, I could see a little bit of the field in which I was standing. Getting my bearings a little better, I was able to progress with my meditative ritual even further, until finally my heart rate was almost normal. The bees must have somehow picked up on my sense of quiet and calm, for as I stood there in the middle of the field breathing quietly and thinking thoughts like "Bees, you can go back to the hive now, you've nothing to fear from me," gradually, bee by bee, the swarm began to lift off my clothing and fly away. And it wasn't long before I was standing in the center of the field amongst blooming buckwheat and singing sparrows, free of bees as if nothing had happened.

When Mac was teaching me to work the bees during my first year in the woods, he had reiterated over and over that when you work around bees you have to move slowly and deliberately and not make sudden or awkward movements. "Stay calm," he said. "Think calm thoughts, and above all, don't project fear. The bees respond to your calm demeanor, but also to your fearful thoughts." I wasn't sure I believed the bees could read my mind, but the slow, deliberate work ethic around the hives seemed to make sense. As I stood in the middle of Zoro's field after I was free of bees and had given a mental, if not literal, sigh of relief, I was struck with the thought that the honeybees had indeed responded directly to my shift in behavior and state of mind. As soon as I began to think positive thoughts and to calm down physically, they had in fact reciprocated by calming down themselves and eventually vacating my body. I was as stunned by this fact as I was by the experience of being stormed by an entire hive of bees and the fear of the possibility of being stung to death. I had experienced, firsthand, direct communication with the bees! In the past I had been respectful and curious about bee life and behavior when working around the hives, but now things had gotten personal and the communication was more direct. I had told the bees that I didn't mean them harm and asked them to spare my life, and they had responded benevolently, en masse, by buzzing more softly and by flying away. Who says we humans are an isolate species and that we can't talk to the insects, the animals, and the trees?

Since my close encounter, things have mainly gone smoothly in my dealings with the bees. That is, except for a few occasions when I was standing in the far rows of the garden hilling up the potatoes and was attacked by a lone honeybee. Since I was far from the hive, it seemed odd that a single bee would go out of its way to attack me. And for it to happen three different times and in the same spot made these incidents even more perplexing. All three times it was a wild black bee that had stung me, and all three times it stung me around my head. Because each situation had a similar dynamic, I figured I was dealing with a renegade bee who had it in for me. Not being able to come up with any other explanation for these bizarre occurrences, I began to take the whole thing personally, thinking that this psycho-killer bee was obsessed with me. This was during my first year in the woods and my first garden season. It wasn't until later in the fall, after I'd been stung for the third time and after I had dug my potatoes and taken them from the field, that I finally figured the whole thing out.

I was up on the far side of the field late one afternoon working with my compost pile and was taking a rest, leaning on my pitchfork and looking over the field to the west, when I saw one of the wild honeybees fly down into the field from the trees to the south. I could see the small bee in the late afternoon light come from the treetops and into the field and over to the hive. Almost immediately my eyes picked up the flight of another bee coming along the same path—down from the treetops and across the field to the hive. My eyes, now accustomed to the light as well as to the flight of the bees, allowed me to witness the approach of bee after bee returning to the hive at the end of the day. While this was all interesting enough, the lesson lay in the fact that I was also noticing that each bee was making the exact same landing procedure and was taking the exact same path across the length of the field and into the hive. It dawned on me that the reason I had been stung while hoeing my potato rows and minding my own business was that I had been standing directly in the flight pattern of the honeybees as they made their approach to home. Loaded with a heavy cargo of pollen and having made this approach and landing hundreds of times before, they had a strict and familiar flight pattern and couldn't make sudden evasive moves to miss a lumbering object in the middle of their runway. Rather than take evasive action, they had simply flown into me and, pissed off, had let me know their displeasure by stinging me, maybe hoping I'd get the message and stay out of their way in the future. Having figured out the mystery of the aggressive honeybees, I have since tried to stay clear of the direct path of the bees and am happy to say that while I've had a few close calls, I've managed to avoid being stung by the low-flying craft.

The following spring the black bees in the hive swarmed and flew off into the woods, lighting in a mature cottonwood tree too high up and too far away for me to be able to bring them back to the hive. Being as they were wild bees, it was probably time for them to find wilder quarters. I compensated by bringing in a couple of new communities of Italian bees that I got in trade from an elderly beekeeper in Saluda for helping him with the work of extracting honey from his hives. He told me he had more hives than he needed and seemed glad to have someone my age turning the crank of his homemade extractor while he siphoned off and jarred up the honey. The Italian bees, I found, were much more docile and user-friendly and not as apt to become alarmed with a beekeeper's awkward move or slip. And they seemed to like their suburban digs in the hives at the far end of Zoro's field, with the long, open runway for approach, and were able to avoid me and my potato rows without future incident. On top of all this good news, with the new bees I was able to expand the neighborhood by two more hives—making three in all—which was plenty for all the honey I would need for myself as well as some to trade.

I began working with bees for the first time almost immediately upon moving to the woods. Mac had entrusted me with the care of a single hive that had not done particularly well in his orchard, thinking that it might do better over in my field. So we struck a deal and became partners, agreeing to share equally in any honey taken from the hive. On top of that, I had cleaned up some old and unused brood chamber boxes and a couple of supers and wax frames that Mac had given to me. I soon got a second hive of bees from a swarm that appeared on the edge of the field one morning, not far from the original hive. After putting foundation wax in the brood box and super frames, and with Mac standing nearby coaching me, I went about the business of capturing the wild swarm. Since the bees had lit in a young dogwood, it would be an easy climb up the tree to where they were. Clad in my beekeeping gear and looking like an alien astronaut, I climbed up the tree. Once I reached the branch where the swarm was attached, I had to work quickly, yet carefully and methodically so as to not alarm the swarm and cause it to fly off. I got in a comfortable position in the tree with the bulbous branch of bees right at eye level and began gently sawing the small limb with a pruning saw Mac had brought over from his toolshed. As I made the last pass of the saw to sever the limb from the trunk of the tree, I firmly grasped the limb with my other hand so that there would be no sudden jerk or untoward movement causing the limb to fall and me to lose the swarm.

With the branch in one hand and holding firmly to the trunk of the tree with the other, I shinnied down as the bees began to buzz loudly.

Upon reaching the ground, I immediately went over to the empty set of boxes I had placed close to the existing hive, where Mac was waiting for me. "Now, gently shake the branch down onto the front of the hive," Mac said to me with his most patriarchal teaching voice. "Start shaking the bees off onto the front of the hive before they take a notion to fly away. Be gentle, but be firm. They will want to come off the branch and will go onto the nearest thing, to safety. We want them to go into the hive and accept it." I did as I was instructed. Just as Mac had said, the bees began dropping off the branch onto the runway entrance and flying a short distance onto the face of the brood box. In only minutes the whole swarm had recongregated on the face of the bottom box and all over the entryway. And within ten to twenty minutes they had almost all disappeared, making their way inside the box to where there were wax frames waiting for them to make cells and create a colony to protect their queen. I had successfully captured my first swarm and now had a colony of bees that I could call my own.

I nurtured the two healthy and active hives for almost a year until the swarming and departure of one hive made it necessary to bring in the two new hives of Italian bees, which then gave me three in all. For that first year, and before expanding my operation, I worked alongside Mac and watched as he gently tended our hives. I watched as he would take his smoker and blow a fog into the entrance at the bottom of the brood box and in from the top of the opened super to get the workers inside the hive to think there was fire and imminent danger, which would set them all to gorging themselves with honey in preparation to leave the endangered hive. With the bees too busy to be bothered with a couple of hovering humans, we could go into the supers and brood box to see if the bees were making honey in excess of what they would need for themselves, as well as to see if they were healthy and free from disease and invasive predators and mites. These impromptu inspections were all good practice in preparing me for the main event: the actual extraction of honey from the hives.

Several days before stealing honey from the hives that first time, with Mac's coaching I placed what is called a "bee escape" into the hive. A bee escape is a thin board that covers the entire area between the super and the brood box. In the center of the board there is an exit hole that allows the workers to leave the super and go down into the brood box from above but is too small for them to return to the box where the excess honey is being stored. As soon as the super is free of worker bees, the beekeeper captures his prize. In my case, everything worked according to plan, and a few days after inserting the bee escape I robbed my first hive.

My first experience with extraction was fairly primitive and routine, as I simply took the honey-filled frames from the supers, cut out the wax portion of the frames, removing wax and honey from wood, and then cut out large chunks of honey and comb and put them into pint jars. I've since found that while this process is simple, it is unsatisfactory in that I didn't care for the comb honey and having to chew and digest all the attached wax. That being the case, the next time I robbed my hives, I borrowed a cylindrical extractor from my old beekeeper friend in Saluda and learned how to sling the honey from the frames—getting a purer honey devoid of wax.

The process of extracting honey using an extractor is an ingenious one. By simply placing the wooden frame of combed honey into a device built with an arm on the inside of a barrel the size of a thirty-gallon drum, and after cutting off the tops of all the filled cells in the frame with a hot knife, one uses a hand crank on the outside of the drum to spin the frames round and round inside the drum—slinging, by centrifugal force, the honey out from the wax cells in the frames and onto the inner wall of the drum. The honey then runs down and fills the bottom of the barrel. From a spigot or opening on the outside near the floor of the drum, one empties the pure, clean honey into smaller, more manageable containers, such as quart mason jars, for storage.

Depending upon when Mac and I would rob our hives, we would get a variety of kinds of honey. The honey year has four seasons here in the mountains: locust, tulip poplar, clover or "wild honey," and sourwood. With the early spring profusion of white locust tree blossoms, the honey year begins, followed later in the spring by the blooming of the tulip poplars. With the synchronous burst of clover and other prolific flowering plants and trees comes the third crop. Then the year is topped off with the perennial favorite: honey that comes from the blooming of the sourwood trees. All during the spring and summer, the bees are busy in the hives making new cells for the incubation of larvae and busy outside the hives gathering pollen and nectar that will go into the cells in the supers as honey.

I'm now into my third season of working with bees. Thus far I've been able to gather only mixed honey from the hives, as the bees for whatever reasons have not been able to make enough honey quickly enough for me to rob them at the turn of each of the four blossom times. So I'm getting a combination, later in the summer, of locust, poplar, clover, sourwood, and, from apple orchards here in western North Carolina, some apple blossom honey. Despite the "mixed blood" of my honey crop, the result is pure. Delicious! And I've been able all these years to sock away plenty of amber-gold honey as sweet-nin' to go on my corn bread and grits.

Honey and beekeeping have been a part of human life for over ten thousand years and probably go back further than that. In paintings in caves in Spain from eight thousand years ago, there are pictorial references to the robbing of hives and the extraction of honey. The ancient Sumerians and Babylonians wrote poems about honey as the nectar of the gods. The same is true in ancient Egyptian hieroglyphs and in tombs where pharaohs were embalmed in concoctions of honey and wax. In many cultures throughout recorded time, bees and the production of honey appear in history and in myths. From the time I have spent with the bees here in my "bee-loud glade," as Yeats put it in "The Lake Isle of Innisfree," I have not only extracted and eaten my share of honey, but in the process have become fascinated with the social structure and behavior of bees.

The bees in my hives at the upper edge of Zoro's field work, I've discovered, in an amazingly well organized and clearly defined caste system that is almost, you could say, governmental in the ways duties are designed and carried out. The workers gather pollen and make combs and honey and are the farmers and laborers of bee society. Sitting at the entrance of the hive on the hottest days of the summer, these bees can even be seen fanning their wings in unison, creating air-conditioning to cool the hives and keep the honeycomb from melting as well as to accommodate the aristocratic desires of the queen. The division of labor amongst the worker bees, which make up the majority of the hive, is exacting and efficient. There are those who do most of their work out-of-doors, and there are those who do the more domestic chores within the hive.

Then there are the drones. The ne'er-do-wells. The bon vivants. The men about town. Few in number but with a life span of an entire year (compared to the four- to six-month maximum for workers), drones can be seen hanging out on the front stoop or in the throne room waiting for an audience with the queen. Should they be one of the select few chosen to mate with the queen, they will be given invitations to a regal, ritualistic ball followed by an orgy. However, after the ritual and bacchanal comes a brutal denouement in which they are jealously assassinated by other members of the hive and their corpses thrown out the front door into the street.

At the epicenter of the social world of the bee is the queen. The matriarch and director of hive operations, the queen has the principal role of making babies, at which she is amazingly prolific. In a single mating ritual that occurs mainly in the air, she is impregnated with enough sperm cells (millions) to last her entire life (as long as four years) and to create enough bees to see a single hive through several seasons. In the matrilineal hegemony of the hive, everyone knows their place and their job, and does it unfalteringly upon threat of expulsion or death.

The bee's work year in the mountains of western North Carolina is from spring and the beginning of warm weather until autumn and the onset of cold nights and chilly days. During the warm months the bees are constantly active, caring for unhatched larvae in the cells of the brood chamber or out gathering nectar and pollen. At both the beginning and the end of the year, I have learned that the bees need to be fed, as there is little for them to forage on, and I don't want them to begin eating up their store of honey that is neatly contained in cells in the supers and brood box. To accomplish this feeding, a combination of sugar and water is just the thing. A properly designed feeding jar placed at the hive entrance gives everyone access to both water and something sweet and gets them through those lean weeks that come during late fall and early spring.

During the winter the bees go into a semidormant state, coming out of the hive only on those rare days when the temperature might reach into the sixties—with a small portion of the total population looking for the few things that, at this time of year, will yield sweet nectar or pollen. Otherwise the whole colony is holed up inside for the duration of winter. To help them through the worst months, I wrap plastic and insulation around the hives, making it easier for the bees inside to generate enough steady heat to survive the terribly cold snaps that occur on occasion here in the mountains.

While for the most part the bees don't need my help, both they and I benefit from the little I have learned to do to make their lives more comfortable and regular. If I do my job, their lives are easier, and they are healthier and so produce more honey. I scratch their backs (gently) and they scratch mine (more gently). In this sense I am part of their social structure, part of the hive. Interacting with their government gives my reclusive, renegade life a semblance of structure. While I don't much cotton to the social structures devised by humans, I quite enjoy being part of the workings and the hierarchy of the hive. Things are accomplished through action and a kind of psychic understanding. I like the bees' company. They benefit by mine. Life goes on, harmonious and humming here in my bee-loud glade.

IN SECRET TIME

In secret time a flower
looks like velvet could
become corduroy
Could cry or clutch at
light wanting to be bone
Be nectar shining on skin
Sky fishing for honey
in a drink of stars

See how the old petals fall
from the head of wild ghosts?
Here, even weeds would eye the grass
Blush in the embrace of pollen
tasting like fire

The touch of trees
And the nectar-drunk hum of the bees . . .

In secret time
I break fast with bread of corn
Make song with something sweet
Beg only for night
in a light that looks like dawn
breaking from behind the hills
Where summer is somewhere where
winter would never want to be
Burned by the frost in heat
Like God-food wrapped in sweet skin
of watched wildflowers
Or love cradled in the palm of a hand
Where the heart opens as rain comes down
And the woods are a liquid land

NEIGHBORS

Some of our neighbors fished for pickerel through the ice in midwin-
ter. They usually drove a wagon out on the lake, set a large number
of lines baited with live minnows, hung a loop of the lines over a
small bush planted at the side of each hole, and watched to
see the loops pulled off when a fish had taken the bait.

JOHN MUIR
The Story of My Boyhood and Youth

*P*eople like to talk. And people like to talk about each other. Such
is the case in a small mountain community. If the adage "everyone
knows what everyone else is doing" ever applied, it applies to the bor-
ough of Saluda and its environs. In a part of the world where the oral
tradition and the art of storytelling is still prevalent, some of the best
tales, of course, are true stories. And in a land where truth is indeed
stranger than fiction, yarns and rumors abound.

Over time some tales find their way into the realm of oral history
and myth. Figures who in their day may have been considered quite
common can, in the span of a generation or two, become larger than
life. And then there are certain people who by their very nature exude
mythic status whether it results in condescension or praise. Here in
my neighborhood (a term I use loosely, since it generally implies an
urban environment) there are and have been many such characters. I
would be reluctant to write about them here except for the fact that
they are so often the focus of uninhibited conversation amongst others. And being that gossip is an essential aspect of human interaction,
and since the characters here are of such glowing colors, I will shed
shyness in favor of my proclivity to gab and will talk about my neighbors—those who live here still, as well as the ghosts of neighbors
from the past who live on in stories smartly, if not often, told.

By way of the road, about a mile from my cabin is the home of
an old mountain family. What makes these neighbors the subject of
community conversation is the fact that so little is known about them.
They maintain such a low profile that it is rare to see them outside the
confines of their house. By being so reclusive they have, much against

their intentions, I'm sure, created such a mystique that speculation has filled the void where fact leaves off. In short, curiosity has become the current and currency of conversation where these quiet folk are concerned. And not knowing only exaggerates the speculation about that which is not known.

"Oh, if I could only be a fly on the wall of that house," Mac said to me one day recently when we were pruning apple trees in his orchard. Mac had been their nearby neighbor for more than twenty-five years, and he was fascinated by what he did and did not know about this quiet family. And Walt Johnson had almost prided himself on the fact that his family and theirs had lived close to each other for so long and had rarely, if ever, spoken. In the case of Walt, I feel sure the sentiment and behavior were more feudlike than simply contrary, as everything with Walt was either black or white. Where people were concerned, they were either friend or foe. Walt was a burner of bridges—if not figuratively, then literally. After all, was it not he who had burned his family home-place to the ground in a fit of rage over a pittance of money? Walt didn't have anything good to say about the family down the road—but his tales were suspect owing to his biased perspective if not to his coyote-like personality. But in the end I think Walt knew no more than the rest of us about these old mountain folks—all of us hog-tied by our ignorance and fit to be tied by the tall tales told.

Of course, Walt Johnson himself was one of the most colorful characters of all. As my friend, if not an actual neighbor during the early days of our acquaintance, I often thought of him as a classic character for a southern roman à clef. "Faulkner would have loved this guy!" I would think as I watched or listened to Walt in action. A kind of hillbilly Charlie Chaplin, Walt engendered such sentiments about himself. In a way, he was his own worst enemy and at the same time his own best friend. Aside from his big, baggy bloodhound Mac, Walt was pretty much friendless despite the fact that he was very social. A kind of God's oddlin', people suffered him because of his prickly wit and his devilish sense of mischief but were wary of him at the same time. If Walt took a notion to covet something you had, he would try every angle in the book to get it. I know, as he had taken a liking to a 1949 Chevrolet pickup truck I had bought and fixed up after finishing school and had brought to the mountains on one of my visits before embarking on a yearlong sojourn in France in 1972.

Walt saw dollar signs all over that vehicle the minute I drove into the field. I hadn't been there fifteen minutes before he was grilling me as to how much I'd take for the truck. When I told him I'd paid only five hundred dollars for it, that was the clincher. It didn't matter that I'd already made plans to store it in a friend's barn while I was away. Walt quickly talked me into leaving it with him, telling me he'd look out for it—even crank it up and drive it once in a while to keep it fit. Of course, when I returned from my year in France, Walt had sold the truck and was only too happy to hand over the five hundred dollars I'd paid for it, as he (or so I was told later by a reliable source) had sold it locally for the sum of fifteen hundred—making a thousand dollars on the deal. This was Walt Johnson. I could tell a hundred stories like it, either experienced firsthand or heard from others who suffered a similar plight. While he was devilish and even insincere, that too was part of his charm, as he could bamboozle the skin off a hissing snake or talk a naive college boy into eating a hot pepper thinking it was red okra.

While Walt gained his notoriety by being conniving and colloquial, by being "torn-down" (mischievous) and a "bull-ragger" (a tease), his older brother was a genuine genius. "Local," as he was called by his family and friends (short for Local Freight Johnson, the name given him by his mother because the one thing she remembered about his delivery was the whistle of the freight train making its way down the Saluda Grade), was a self-taught reader who had never spent a day in public school. His knowledge of history and nature lore was legendary. There was virtually no subject he couldn't discuss with authority and amplitude, or so I was told by Mac, who knew Local in his prime and loved to reminisce about him and sing his praises.

In addition to his acumen, Local Freight Johnson was one of the most celebrated moonshiners in these parts. Mac's stories about Local and his reputation as a distiller extraordinaire of corn liquor seemed to have no end. From his own experience Mac could vouch for the superior quality of Local's likker, saying, in his best rendition of southern Appalachian dialect: "Hit's got a whang to it I like." But, as in many good stories and many good characters, there is a fatal flaw. Local's Achilles' heel was his love for his own whiskey. His binges were as legendary as the liquid itself. After running off a batch or two of 'shine, it was not unusual for Local to disappear for weeks, maybe several months, before showing up again on the streets of Saluda. For a long time folks thought Local had wanderlust and would make enough money selling his "Straight Creek" to take off and travel around for a while—coming back when his money ran out to make another batch of mash and save up before taking off yet again. But Mac knew different, as he'd seen Local in the throes of his binges. Having not eaten anything for a couple weeks, Local would appear like a specter in Mac's front yard, "so drunk he couldn't hit the ground with his hat," looking for his stash, not remembering where he had hidden it. Mac told me one story over and over about giving Local a glass of homebrew to steady his nerves and taking him over the hill from the old Guice farmhouse to search for some mythic tree stump where Local had supposedly hidden a hundred dollars' worth of moonshine bottled in quart jars. Mac said this scene was played out many times over the years, but they never found the 'shine-filled stump—that is, not until years after Local had died from drinking one dram too many of a quickly stilled batch of 'shine that had turned bad. Mac had finally stumbled on a large stump filled with "dead soldiers" (empty mason jars) that at one time held Local Freight's best hooch. The fact . that Local died unintentionally by his own hand is not only ironic but somewhat tragic in light of his lofty reputation as a master of stilling up corn liquor. Mac talked affectionately and respectfully, almost in awe, of Local Freight Johnson, by whose death he had lost not only a good friend and brother but also a kindred spirit.

Maybe the most interesting story that comes from my immediate neighborhood is the story of Zackey Dorton. Zackey Dorton was in his early thirties at the advent of the Civil War. In the western North Carolina mountains, loyalties to the armies of the North and South were often divided within communities and, in fact, among members of the same household—with one brother enlisting in the army of the Confederacy while another would leave home to fight for the North under General Grant. So communities and families were often split, sometimes violently, with local "Home Guard" militias, representing both sides of the conflict, ever on the prowl for deserters and turncoats. Zackey Dorton had done the unthinkable and decided that he would remain neutral, and he refused to enlist on either side. Since this stance was unpopular as well as illegal, Zackey was obliged to find a place to hide from the Home Guard and from members of the community who may have taken offense from his pacifistic stance.

Zackey ended up living in a cave, which was little more than a rock overhang, surrounded by a laurel thicket on a precipitous north-side embankment overlooking the Narrows on the Green River. In such steep, rugged, and camouflaging terrain, Zackey's cave was not only unapproachable from almost any direction but also invisible. "Zackey Dorton's cave," as it is now called by Saluda natives, was on a wooded section of the Johnsons' property, and it was the Johnson family who offered Zackey refuge there. The long and short of it is that Zackey Dorton hid out under this rock overhang for the duration of the war till such time as it was safe for him to come out and show his face.

For four years the Johnsons fed Zackey from their larder—food that was taken to him by Walt and Local's granduncles and other kin. Zackey's secret was so well kept that he was able to go undetected by the local police, the Home Guard, and marauding raiders, which were prevalent during the war years. In fact, so well was the secret kept from the community that when Zackey did finally emerge from the Green River cave, he had hardly been missed by those who might have taken offense at his conscientious resistance. To be on the safe side, though, he moved to Henderson County after coming out—to avoid unpleasantries if not official persecution.

Walt told me this story years ago when I was first getting to know him. In those early days of our friendship he gave me directions to the cave but, because it was located in such rough terrain, never actually took me there. I eventually, after several tries, found it. I have been to Zackey Dorton's cave on numerous occasions since. I sit under the huge overhanging rock during thunderstorms or simply rest there after a long walk to the river or in the woods. The little cave is as amazingly cool in hot weather as it is surprisingly warm in cold weather. I can see how Zackey could have survived here, albeit wildly.

These days I still go down the path along the little spring branch to

Johnson's Pond and then to the far end and down an old logging trail till I get to an almost undetectable animal trail that leads into the ivy. After about five minutes of scrambling uphill on a forty-five degree slope, I reach one of the oldest and densest patches of rhododendron and mountain laurel you'll see anywhere in these mountains. On this steep upper north side of the mountain, which has never been logged, the laurel hell has vines thick as a man's leg, the path disappearing at the edge of a hillside of shimmering green leaves and light brown limbs. Scrambling through the thicket is like I imagine it must be for a wasp or fly entangled in a spider's web. All efforts become focused on merely getting out. In my case, I'm trying to get through the web of vine and leaf into the clear air of the cave.

Once inside the cave, usually my first inclination is to scour the dirt floor with my eyes—looking for tracks and signs. Recently I've seen signs of bobcat, chipmunk, what look to be paw prints of a larger cat (cougar?), slithery traces of snake, skunk, and the presence of crow. From the front of the cave I can see the river almost a thousand feet below, yet from down along the river I have never been able to see the cave. A wonderful front porch is created by the lip of the cave, offering a great view, as real estate hawkers might say. The prominent and steady sound of the river below makes a meditative drone that soothes and calms. Here, where there is no hint of mechanical intervention or human life, you know you're in nature. It is easy to feel wild, like the bobcat or the snake, sitting in the open air at the front of the cave—as I imagine Zackey Dorton did often and for long periods of time, contemplating the wild world around him as he became more and more at one with himself and his natural surroundings.

Besides the neighbors I know personally or have known through the experiences of others, a few members of the Saluda community who don't live literally in my neighborhood come by on occasion in a neighborly sort of way to visit. One such occasional neighbor, and one of the few people I come into contact with who is of my own age, is Paul Rhodes. Paul is a fifth-generation native of Polk County and a member of the Fork Creek Rhodes clan. He comes from a community that lies beautifully in the bottoms of a valley a few miles southeast of Saluda. Paul is among the few people of my generation who exude, in speech and in practice, the dignities of the disappearing southern Appalachian culture. Not a throwback exactly, he has one foot in each world—the old-style mountain life and the modern, dominant culture (he got his college education at Western Carolina University over in Jackson County). He moves with ease in and out of both. This ability, combined with his extraordinary skill as a natural-born storyteller, makes him one of the most interesting and sought-after members of the Saluda community.

Being around Paul Rhodes always brings to mind the stories I have heard Mac tell of Local Freight Johnson. I imagine Local must have been in many ways like Paul—a clear genius with plenty of character and panache. Not one for chewing the cud, and having a photographic memory and a particular love for the history of the South, Paul Rhodes is a walking encyclopedia of human history—able to roll off names, dates, and minutiae from world events going back to the beginning of recorded time. Locally he is considered by many to be the unofficial oral historian of Polk County—centuries of the area's history filed neatly in his head. Along with his knack for human history, Paul is one of the savviest woodsmen I have met in the three years I have been living here. His considerable knowledge of the natural world is based on personal experience rather than on book smarts. Stories of his experiences in the wild could fill volumes. They are rich with detail, drama, and mountain dialect. In fact, the unself-conscious dialect of his speech is one of the things that attracts me most to Paul Rhodes and is, I think, the source of the bond between us: our love of language. Turns of phrase and idioms slide off his tongue like sourwood honey from a slice of corn bread on a hot day.

Paul will show up unexpectedly (but usually on days when the weather is too sorry for outdoor work), and I'll get into his duotone green Ford pickup truck, and we'll ride the back roads of Polk County as he recites an oral history to the visual accompaniment I am seeing through the windows. And when we're not talking local history, we're talking literature. Paul is not only one of the best-informed people I've met during my stay in Polk County, but one of the best-read. And not just on the subject of history. In addition to his wealth of knowledge of nonfictional subject matter, he's up on contemporary novelists and poets, American and international literary figures and titles alike. "I've always loved to read," he has told me more than once. "I guess I've got a curiosity that's larger than just these mountains. Seems like there's always room in my mind for a tad more than just Polk County." That's putting it mildly, as our conversation during an afternoon traversing the roads of Polk County runs the gamut of everything from *One Hundred Years of Solitude* by Gabriel García Márquez to theoretical physics and quantum mechanics. "You ever notice that your beard grows faster during a new moon?" he asked me one day recently, after we'd spent the better part of an hour discussing the economic theories of Karl Marx. These kinds of leaps of mind in conversation are comparable for me to what happens in the best poems. What the long jump is to a track athlete, ideas and images are to a poet. In Paul Rhodes, rapid-fire associations are made in thought and are vocalized in speech patterns that are a wonderful union of past, present, and future. From Boris Spassky and international chess matches to bee balm and booby owls in a heartbeat. From supercolliders to sass patches in the blink of an eye.

CHORES

Where will they go
these men and women of earth?
This man whose sweat
waters grain.
This woman
whose milk is the strength in human bone.
As the seeds they have saved
from great grandparents to be given
to children not yet born
are eaten by the fiery incinerators of banks.

How can they replace the pain
of what their bodies have become:
this farm
that feeds those who rule to crush
this land.

A million years of digging in dirt,
now passed on as the nightmare
of empty hands.
Who will separate, now,
the wheat from the chaff?

Now there will be nothing
but tears that go into the rows
that once furrowed their dreams.
What kind of food can be grown from
the water in salt?
From the lonely song of a dry desert air.

Friends, think of the music gone from
the symphony of those fields.
The dance of breakfast
being born there for the human race.

Life out of balance.
Lost like the homeless in city streets.
Like walking suicide.
Deprived of their chores.

CONNEMARA

When will men know what birds know?

CARL SANDBURG

*R*eturning to these mountains three years ago, I immediately took up the literature that was created here and marks the place: Horace Kephart (*Our Southern Highlanders*), William Bartram (*Travels*), James Mooney (*Myths and Sacred Formulas of the Cherokee*), Thomas Wolfe (*Look Homeward, Angel* and *You Can't Go Home Again*). In Kephart one passage in particular spoke to me and my new life here in the woods:

> I came to dwell in the wilderness, not as one fleeing or hiding, but that I might realize, in a mature age, a dream of youth. Here, in the wild wood, I have found peace, cleanliness, health of body and mind. Here I can live the natural life, unfettered and unindebted. Here duty itself is pliant to any breath of fancy that may stir the buds and foliage of thought.

While these words have given me courage and something of a challenge, the words of Thomas Wolfe have had a slightly different effect. Reading Wolfe's sequel to *Look Homeward, Angel* and hearing his anguished cry that "you can't go home again," I found myself reacting instinctively and vocally: "you *must* go home again!"

This impulsive utterance reflects a bioregional ethic that I can trace back to my years in California and my work with what was referred to as the "Bioregional Movement" there, and it represents my personal conviction. It also presents a tangible philosophical problem for those who are not living, as I do, deep in place. Collectively Americans these days are hunter-gatherers of sorts and are a mobile, migratory people. Only the game we hunt is different. Instead of moving with the seasons, with the herds, as did the original inhabitants of this continent, we now hunt for material goods, for jobs, for more comfortable and economically advanced lifestyles. In this sense "home" is a relative term used to describe migration routes along which we have spent little time in any one place. But even migrating animals come back to familiar territory—to the range that defines the borders of their home and habitat. Since this story of migration has become our modern mythos (except for those rare souls who have remained in one place over the course of a lifetime), we are forced to identify with places where we have become transplants and where we try to live consciously and with empathy.

I'm thinking specifically of Carl Sandburg, who, had I come here fifteen years earlier, would have been my neighbor. Not literally, as his adopted home in Flat Rock is some ten miles from here, but close enough for me to imagine time and distance to be only a minor impediment to such a notion. Sandburg's relationship with Connemara, as his farm is named, and the western North Carolina mountains was such that one might easily imagine him having lived there his whole life. His soulful *embrassade* of place was complete. It included the necessary surrender, the deep grounding, and the rest and serenity that is indicative of how one, ideally, evolves after "returning home." From 1945, when he moved to Flat Rock, until he died in 1967, this was truly Sandburg's home. The farm had everything he and his family needed—plenty of pasture for his wife's goat breeding operation and plenty of seclusion for Carl, including the four things that he said were all he needed in life: "to be out of jail, to eat regular, to get what I write printed, and a little love at home and a little outside."

The 240-acre Connemara (named by Sandburg for County Connemara on the west coast of Ireland, a landscape reminiscent of the rolling green hills of western North Carolina) was then and is now divided roughly into half woodlands and half cleared pasture. The balance between woodlands and open space couldn't have been better for Sandburg's poetic soul, and here his soul took root while his farm and family flourished, giving rise to one of my favorite of his poems, "Instructions to Whatever Gardens"—a song in praise of beauty, nature, being, and staying in place.

In recent days the Sandburg place and its former owner and I have become more than a little friendly, as my connection with Connemara goes deep. At least as deep as the six inches of sawdust and goat droppings that form the floor of the goat barns. Once a month I've been going over to clean out the stalls and bring the rich organic fertilizer home to dump in Zoro's field. Through a barter with one of my neighbors, I arranged to use his dump truck to haul off the goat droppings and sawdust, which will become compost in my own gardens. I got this job through a bit of serendipity and by making friends with the National Park Service employee who is in charge of the goat herd. I met the goatherd during my first tour of Connemara soon after my arrival from the West Coast. Now, three years later, I'm working as something of a subcontractor for the Sandburg farm.

Besides the fact that I get paid a small fee (enough to cover my expenses for using my neighbor's truck) for hauling off the potent fertilizer—which goes into my gardens, enhancing their productivity—other bonuses have come with this job. Since the goats need to be fed and tended, even on days when the rest of the staff is taking a day off, I've worked it out to come with my borrowed truck to clean out the barns on those closed-to-the-public days. After I've finished cleaning the barns, and if it's not too late, I'm often allowed into Sandburg's study in the attic of the house, where I carefully and respectfully look through his files, papers, and books, which are as he left them in 1967. I have spent many hours up in that attic room snooping—wearing Sandburg's print-shop visor, hoping some of his unused poetic lines will filter into my mind—and reading everything within reach. The ambience of his words and work as well as the memorabilia (such as a notepad that lies open on the nightstand beside the little bed he used for catnapping, and a well-used pencil with the inscription "half the pressure, twice the speed"—a kind of koan, if not a magical spell, that I imagine fortified and fed Sandburg's late-night revelations and poems) includes, on occasion, what I perceive as his ghostly presence, a presence that appears as an abstract specter in the sunlight coming through the attic window and filtering through swirling dust.

From working over on the Connemara farm this past year and from my time up in Sandburg's roost, I've come to appreciate him as a poet of place as well as a poet of the people. Although he adopted western North Carolina as his home late in life, he quickly became both a homeboy and homebody at Connemara, where he was protective of both place and privacy. A good story provides some manner of proof for these claims I've made for him—one I heard recently from talking to an older black woman who was Sandburg's housekeeper and unofficial bodyguard during the Connemara years.

In the spring of 1964, a twenty-three-year-old poet named Bob Dylan arrived on the Connemara property unannounced. Standing on the front porch, Dylan introduced himself to the housekeeper: "I am a poet, my name is Robert Dylan, and I would like to see Mr. Sandburg. I'm a great admirer of his." After a lengthy wait Sandburg appeared, somewhat disheveled in his plaid shirt and baggy trousers, which were his normal writing attire. He took one look at Dylan and said: "You certainly look like a very intense young man. You look like you are ready for anything!" According to the housekeeper's eyewitness report, Sandburg and Dylan visited for about twenty minutes on the front porch and talked about poetry and folk music, which Sandburg said he regarded as kindred arts. Dylan at some point handed Sandburg a copy of his newest album *The Times They Are A-Changin'* and reiterated that he too was a poet—which, according to Sandburg's housekeeper, got the elder poet's attention, and he promised to listen to the record Dylan had brought him as a gift and literary offering.

Despite their age difference Sandburg and Dylan had much in common. Both were born of immigrants in the Midwest, and both were admirers of Walt Whitman and Woody Guthrie and were collectors of folk songs. However, Sandburg cut the visit short by saying that he was in the midst of working when Dylan arrived and that he had to return to his study to finish his day's writing, giving the young celebrity what amounted to little more than a nod and a handshake in order to preserve the sanctity of his cherished seclusion and his regimen.

So when I go up to the Sandburg farm these days, I'm in good company — my goatkeeper friend, the goats, Sandburg's ghost, and the ghosts of the famous friends and admirers who visited him there. What rubs off on me mostly, however, is the sense of calm and stability the old place exudes. "The goats, the gardens, and the peace," as Sandburg referred to it. Of all the places Sandburg lived during his lifetime, I think in the end it was Connemara that he thought of as home.

And the place is beginning to feel that way to me too. As beneficiary of my monthly visits to purge the barns of their pungency, I've come to think of it almost as an upscale extension of my little shack in the woods.

Thinking of Sandburg's ordered and balanced life at Connemara and at the same time seeing how out of plumb (as the older generation here in the mountains might refer to it) the world has become these days, it seems all the more clear to me that we *must* go home again! Take the knowledge, the experience, and the strength gained from all the years of wandering, searching, working, and plant this in the soil of our adopted or native homes—whether the west coast of Ireland or the mountains of western North Carolina—wherever they may be.

AFTER READING HAN-SHAN

How much alike are the wise man
and the drunk!
The wise man sees the light in the cloud,
the one who drinks: the cloud in the light.
Each seeing the same thing.

How I love the way Han-Shan laughs when he speaks!
And in laughing, the way he cries—
His dreams are like mine: full
of maidens in cloaks of crimson silk.

Wondering today the direction in
which my life will go, the *I Ching* says:
"Where disorder develops, words are the first steps."
No word this time of crossing the great water.
But a message of keeping still.

So tonight I have made myself a cup of tea
and sit with my friends: all the words I know.

Having taken the first step toward tomorrow,
I make a bold stroke with my pen
that in this dim light looks like one
of those court maidens Han-Shan and I know so well.
I sit for a moment in the trance of another world.
Far away from here. But like this small shack in the woods,
still home.

NEW NATIVE

In a distinct, diverse and interdependent part of the planetary
biosphere that deserves a unique social, political and cultural identity
to match its natural endowment, it would be possible for us to
deliberately put a renewed culture into harmony with the natural
flows of energy and life—in a process that could be
called reinhabitation. We can become natives.

PETER BERG

The Planet Drum Review, summer 1981

Reinhabitation

*W*ith rain coming down in snarelike drumbeats on the tin roof of
my cabin, I'm holed up this afternoon inside. Sitting here in my sheep-
skin-lined nineteenth-century rocker held together with twine, grape-
vines, and Elmer's glue, reading Donald Culross Peattie's *Flowering
Earth* and thinking deeply about the time I spent in Gary Snyder's
community up along the San Juan Ridge north of Nevada City in the
Sierra foothills. In his book Peattie writes: "For every man there is
some spot on earth, I think, which he has pledged himself to return
to, some day, because he was so happy there once." This has certainly
been true in my case, for I remember the years of my youth in the
Smokies as being not only informative but also happy. And perhaps
that same happiness accounts for why I am here now.

Most of the folks inhabiting the Ridge were living what we referred
to as a "bioregional lifestyle," largely manifested by escaping from
the city, cultivating a small vegetable garden, participating in periodic
seasonal community ceremonies and rituals, and studying and partly
adhering to Buddhist and Native American religious and social ideology and practice. In those days Gary had defined "bioregionalism"
as a reference to "the tiny number of persons who come out of the
industrial societies and then start to turn back to the land, to place.
This comes for some with the rational and scientific realization of
interconnectedness, and planetary limits. But the actual demands of a

life committed to a place, and living somewhat by the sunshine green plant energy that is concentrated in that spot, are so physically and intellectually intense, that it is a moral and spiritual choice as well."

This newborn bioregional movement, in which I participated during the late 1970s, also included ideas of reinhabitation, ecological awareness, and giving constitutional-type rights to nonhuman species; and it was manifest in the establishment of the *Planet Drum Review*, the Reinhabitory Theatre, the Primitive Arts Institute, and the All Species Day Parade, as well as in the creation of an alternative school and an enthusiastic volunteer fire department. All these undertakings and much more were based on the belief that the well-being of the Earth depends upon our understanding the importance of biological diversity and correct relationship to place—place viewed in both its microcosmic and macrocosmic incarnations as it dovetails with our day-to-day lives and stewardship of the place we call home. It is here at home, I believe, that "the real work," as Gary Snyder calls it, begins. And that real work these days must begin with rediscovering and establishing intimacy with the natural world. In fact I would go so far as to say that only this kind of intimacy can save us from the current megamaniacal plundering of the natural world—which we are clearly, consciously or unconsciously, carrying out, while at the same time causing the extinction of hundreds, if not thousands, of animal and plant species every year.

Most of us have come to live where we do as uninvited guests from other places, other cultures. Many, maybe most, of the people who have moved into the mountains of western North Carolina from the outside have come here oblivious to and unconcerned about what has culturally preceded them. Unaware of biology, geology, geography, genealogy, and the historical and cultural balances built into natural and social systems that have coexisted and cohabited in relative harmony for untold generations prior to the arrival of the latest wave of incoming migrants.

Planet Drum founder Peter Berg implies in one of the early issues of the *Planet Drum Review* that by changing our perspective and practices regarding where we live we can become "natives." I would like to propose another term to identify those of us who have made our way back to a land-based lifestyle as stewards and apprentices of self-sufficiency: "new natives." By "new native" I mean those persons who have come to live in a place, either physically or mentally, for the first time and yet feel it is truly home. New natives are caretakers of the old as well as heralds of the new. They come into a place (in my case the mountains of western North Carolina, what some are calling the Katuah Bioregion after a village and spiritual center of the Cherokee nation) with a sense of reverence and responsibility, recognizing that it is their inherent duty to respect the past, enjoy the present, and safeguard the future.

I returned home to these Smoky Mountains—after a sojourn away that lasted almost twenty years—to embark upon a life of relative isolation and self-sufficiency. My world here in Zoro's field is very different from the world on the other side of these woods, with its shopping malls, its computers, its consumer-driven media, its TV . . . Despite my attempts at monkishness and anonymity, word of my Thoreau-like lifestyle here in the Green River woodlands has leaked out beyond the protective borders of trees and water. Recently I have been approached by outsiders to become involved in activities and organizations—such as a project to identify and protect Native American sacred sites in the southern Appalachians and to help create a bioregional journal in the Southeast. All this attention is attributable, I assume, to my farming experience, as well as to my current wilderness lifestyle coming on the heels of my former life with the Planet Drum folks on the West Coast.

So I guess my roving and ruckus-raising over the years has proven to be useful in that it has allowed me to bring home some of the goods and the good news acquired in the process. Whether or not I'll become deeply involved in these projects remains to be seen—as I am reluctant to compromise the pristine nature of my privacy and risk the schizophrenia of living here while trying to work with people on the outside with their "civilized" values and notions. Maybe I can figure out a way to work from my "bee-loud glade" as a consultant, not having to partake of life amidst the madding crowds. At the same time, because of my West Coast experience, I feel obligated to do my part in spreading the word.

To my way of thinking, and at the core of the ideals of the new native, there is an understanding that what the modern world has given us, has offered up as "progress," is not healthy, healing, meaningful, or good for either individual or planet, and that the patriarchy and the subterfuge-aggressiveness manifested in the accumulation of wealth and power (and further manifested as the psychosis that leads to nationalism and constant war) will fall back eventually, like sand, into the sea of a repetitive and fruitless history. In my experience both on the West Coast and in Zoro's field, when living with the mind-set and focus of reinhabitation it becomes possible for realities such as extended family, for instance, to reestablish themselves as part of our living culture. It becomes possible for clans and stewardship communities to be started or revived and then to survive within the framework of sustainable local economies based on meaningful work and social structures that are, in turn, based on fraternal intercourse rather than on economic, racial, and religious feuding. The new native ideal advocates an even more finely tuned sensitivity to reinhabitation, incorporating not only the notion of the collective unconscious but a transfiguration of one's psyche into a more spiritual and sense-liberated whole. Hypothetically, it produces total beings whose values and sociosexual politics are more in harmony with the psychosexual balance of their watershed-ecosystem and with the planet and the universe.

While the role models for my reinhabitory life in the Green River watershed are the myriad species of animals that have lived, ranged, and procreated here for millennia, our true cultural ancestors and exemplars for living with a sense of place here in western North Carolina (and in North America generally) are the American Indians. Even at this late juncture, I don't think it's preposterous to suggest that we of European descent still owe a rather large karmic debt for our genocidal relationship with the original human inhabitants of this continent. With respect to this would-be debt, I think a good place to begin resolution and settlement would be through bio-centered, region-centered education and, further, through the incorporation of the knowledge, sensibilities, and traditional wisdom of these peoples into our own consciousness, culture, and lifestyle.

I am not advocating that we become carbon copies of the Native Americans of the past. Being a new native entails, rather, embracing, without guilt, a consciousness that learns from the cultures that have been here longest and therefore know the place best. With this education and awareness gained, new rituals, celebrations, and lifestyles may be conceived and carried out, compatible with the past but reflections of an ongoing sustainable present. The next step will be redefining and reinhabiting the place in which we live and thereby becoming truly modern. Not modern in a postindustrial sense, but modern in reference to the creative ways we manifest new designs of living that make us participants with rather than competitors against the natural world. These thoughts are echoed for me in lines from Ruth Beebe Hill's book *Hanta Yo*:

> But the truly wonderful things, the great mysteries, move quietly.
> Who will hear the sun climb the sky, hear the grasses push up?

Indeed, who will be the visionaries, the mythic ministers, of our postindustrial period (what Thomas Berry calls the Ecozoic Era)? The quiet ones who are living at the pace of nature, at the speed of life, who can hear the sun climbing the sky, the grass pushing up through decaying leaves in the spring? Will there even be a wilderness in that future? And who, if any of us, will live in it? And how? Thomas Berry is full of profound thoughts on the future of humanity in the natural world. "In the end," he says, "it is the land that is the most sacred element of our lives." To my way of thinking, if we don't hold the earth and all its life as sacred and worthy of reverence, we are undermining our own well-being. Without a healthy environment, we humans, like all other life forms, cannot hope to live a healthy, mentally balanced life. One thing predetermines the other. Without breathable air and potable water where would we be? Without a diverse and expansive range of plants and animals where would we be? Without the flowers and bees, the pine nuts and squirrels, the berries and bears . . . where would we be? Where will we be when all this is altered, compromised, or gone? I, for one, am clear about this idea of diversity and my relationship with other species. I don't want to live in a world absent of elephants and whales.

Community

"I am a storyteller, and I think stories communicate. When a community starts to get a story, it becomes a community. People are freak-ing out because they can't fit themselves into a local story, or into any story. If you don't have one you have to make it up, and if there is no local culture, you have to make it," says Gurney Norman in *Simple Living* magazine in the fall of 1976. Thinking about Norman's quote and possible futures for humankind calls up my own past. I can remember how isolated it felt growing up as a boy in the deep mountains of Graham County. Winters tended to be more severe than they are today, and there were sometimes long stretches when folks couldn't get in or out of the little town of Robbinsville, which intensified the kind of tribal feeling that occurred during bad weather. The community ethos was a warm one, and I remember feeling secure, knowing that in hard times we could take care of one another and that life somehow would continue as it always had.

Those were formative years for me. Years that instilled in me an idealistic picture of community and at the same time gave me a strong sense of independence and self. These memories include the congregation of great groups of kids at elder persons' homes to crack burlap pokes (sacks) full of walnuts, and neighborhood workdays to help someone pick tobacco or to build or repair barns. It's true I was just a boy and so hadn't experienced the kinds of antagonistic things that adults can do to each other, breaking or at least disturbing community relations, but the idea and experience of community I enjoyed as a boy has stayed with me through the years.

As they say, those were the good old days, and those days and those kinds of sentiments have faded. Even in small towns like Saluda here in rural Polk County the word "community" is rarely used. Old buildings that have served as community centers and general stores outside of the town proper are used rarely and are often in disrepair. Almost all the roads have been paved and are busy with continuous traffic night and day. These days one is more likely to catch up on news and local gossip in the housewares sections of the new superstores near Asheville than at a community center potluck or from friends casually dropping in — as they used to do with regularity in former times.

The American Heritage Dictionary of the English Language defines "community" as "a group of plants and animals living in a specific region under relatively similar conditions; ecology; fellowship." This is a good place to start, as the idea of community, according to this definition, encompasses not only human life but plants and animals also—and the term "ecology" helps put things in a more complete and proper perspective. Not only are intercourse and interaction implied but also stewardship and education—both of which in the old days might have been considered essential to the well-being of the community. And let's not forget the fellowship that in those days was a regular and continuous conversation among those whose paths would cross in the barbershop, the feed store, or the general store as the years and generations passed . . . These days we barely know our neighbors and are more likely to spend extensive time with TV sitcom families than with our own. Times have changed, and in my more insecure moments I find that I miss the old days of my boyhood in the Milltown neighborhood of Robbinsville along Snowbird Creek—the naive innocence, the prepubescent camaraderie, the woods and the creeks as places to play.

"Most important," the Kentucky poet and farmer Wendell Berry writes, "a community must be generally loved and competently cared for by its people, who, individually, identify their own interest with the interest of their neighbors. This notion of community began to vanish in America after World War II. Our small towns have never been worse off than they are now." Everywhere I look on the subject of community, I find references to fellowship and sustainable economy. Among his writings on global cultures and ecology, Thomas Berry (no relation to Wendell Berry) has written this on the subject of community: "We have lost immense areas of intimate knowledge carried in traditional craft and in farming skills, knowledge that provides a relationship between the human community and the natural world that is immensely more bountiful and less destructive than that of large-scale business projects." As our communities have broken down and been replaced with sundry technologies and corporations, the skills that fostered neighborliness have been lost in a single generation. Today community has more to do with consumerism than with conservation and commonality. And with regard to the ecology side of the coin Thomas Berry adds: "The well-being of each component part [of the community] is intimately related to the well-being of the other parts and to the well-being of the whole."

I have been taken aback by this solitary and monkish thinker Thomas Berry. My notebooks are filled with his words. An apostle of the great French eco-philosopher Pierre Teilhard de Chardin, Berry has carried the torch of planetary and personal wisdom higher on the mountain of enlightenment and leadership. From my notebook I read: "Every mode of being has inherent rights to their place in the single community that is the Earth community, rights that come by existence itself. The intimacy of humans with the other components of the planet is the fulfillment of each in the other and all within the single Earth community. It is a spiritual fulfillment as well as a mutual support. It is a commitment, not simply a way of survival."

Living in the woods I am beginning to understand these words. My community includes as much (and maybe more) the plant and animal life as it does the human. Living as we do in proximity with each other, it is necessary that we live harmoniously and with mutual respect. And in terms of interdependence, I see clearly that the plants and animals are far less dependent upon me than I upon them. It is no accident that almost all creation stories and myths of indigenous peoples on this and other continents include animals and plants at their origin, in some cases humans being derivative of one or another animal species. Early peoples saw how inextricable human life is from the natural world. This can be seen most dramatically, perhaps, in the fact that people were often given the names of animals and plants, and they bore them with honor. Humans once knew the importance of interdependence and cohabitation with the plant and animal kingdoms. Today with industry and technology removing us further and further from our former relationships with the natural world, we take our animal neighbors for granted at best, and we slaughter them into extinction at worst.

While I don't live a town life anymore, and much prefer my own company or that of my animal friends to human social gatherings, I still think with compassion of the vast majority of people who cannot escape constant human interaction and conflict. I have read some of the new future-primitive prophets who speak of a rural future for the planet, predicting that we are entering an era when small towns will be valued again and that out of necessity we will reinvent social economies using local assets and resources. While this kind of talk is inviting, it seems foolish to think that humanity will, at this late date, literally go back to the "good old days." However, we may in increments be able to move forward to the "good new ways"—which might include essential and traditional aspects of the old, such as embracing the reinhabitory idea of community. Communities that operate with greater degrees of social, cultural, and governmental autonomy and where currencies are circulated and recycled—filtering money back into local receptacles to benefit those who have come upon hard times and been forced to live on less. These new communities, as I envision them, would be based on the self-realized merits of each of their members, where every person has a place and finds appropriate and meaningful work. In this paradigm, work is generated, barter is encouraged, and community members do not have to leave home in order to survive, as they often do in the rural communities of western North Carolina today. Community becomes a place of "continuous harmony," as Wendell Berry has called it, a place that functions simply and therefore well.

Thinking on this I am reminded of Occam's Razor, an axiom that proposes that the simplest and most direct way to do anything is always the best. This implies that, as E. F. Schumacher says in his book by the same title, "small is beautiful." Community is, for me here in the woods, a much smaller paradigm than for those who live in towns or in cities like Asheville. And small, as far as I can see—through the windows of my cabin to the pine grove on the far side of Zoro's field—is the only way that works.

Native Tongue

Love of place and love of language go hand in hand. Or as Zoro has said, "Who you are is all about where you are from." As a boy in Graham County my first language was what has been called Southern Mountain Speech—a complex blend of Scots, traces of Chaucerian and Elizabethan English, elements of the speech of seventeenth-century immigrants from the British Isles, a witty Irish lyricism, and numerous other forebears. This Appalachian dialect was rich with poetic idioms and colloquialisms, lyrical inflections and rhythms, making it unique as well as almost incomprehensible to any outsider. I can still remember a rainy Saturday in the Snowbird Supply General Store in Robbinsville and an old fella calling the summer thunderstorm that had me and my buddies holed up inside drinking RC Colas and eating Moon Pies a "sizzly sod-soaker," and later during those years hearing references to such "thundery weather" as a "Devil's footwasher" and a "nubbin' stretcher." There was no lack of colorful speech. Surrounded by such language, it's no wonder that as early as the third grade I became interested in poetry and by the fourth grade was attempting to write my own.

But during the summer of 1962, my parents moved our family out of Milltown in Robbinsville to the northern end of the Blue Ridge Parkway just west of Charlottesville, Virginia—thus separating me from the culture and the language I had grown up with. Moving away from the place where I had consciously begun to identify and know myself was my own trail of tears. As I said my good-byes to my Cherokee and Scots-Irish friends and to my life along Snowbird Creek in Graham County and the particular, if not peculiar, culture there, little did I know that I was also saying good-bye to the way I linguistically viewed the world.

As my father uprooted our family time and time again in a march of migration farther and farther north, I lost more and more of my contact and association with my cultural roots. By the time I finished high school in the steel town of Bethlehem, Pennsylvania, I had become little more than the proverbial rolling stone—one that had not had time enough in any one place to gather moss. As years went by and I moved myself farther and farther west on my own, I learned to distance myself from any semblance of a southern accent—so strong were the prejudices I encountered in other parts of the country against southern speech. Tired of being castigated and denigrated, I taught myself a generic American speech that was without dialect and therefore without character—a final act of acculturation.

Even though I continued to write poetry, it had become a poetry whose language was unaffected by place. Instead of the organic lyrical and idiomatic poetry that might have come easily had I remained in Graham County, I was, by the time I was twenty-five, writing in rhetorical rhythms a kind of message-based poetry more influenced by Russia and France than by the Appalachian South. People who met me were astonished that I had come from the South, so well had I hidden my past in my newly formed speech. Only once can I recall slipping and falling back into grace—when I was living an apprentice's life in San Francisco surrounded by many of my Beat generation idols—on the occasion of meeting in a North Beach cafe a young musician named Wayde Blair from Berea, Kentucky. Because of his strong southern drawl, I reverted to old speech patterns that had become buried in my subconscious but broke ground upon hearing his voice and the familiar language. I would, I was told (for I was unaware of the shift), lapse into dialect and even old Appalachian metaphoric idioms when I ran into Wayde and we talked casually about home and the past. Aside from these few San Francisco slips, I remained dialect free.

Now that I am back in western North Carolina many years after leaving the region as a young teenager I find that the cultural life, as well as the language, is dying out, as more and more of my generation have moved to larger towns in the region or farther to search for prosperity. One can hear good old Southern Mountain Speech only from the elderly, who decrease in number each year. This being the case, upon returning to the western North Carolina mountains I found myself gravitating toward elders: Zoro and Bessie Guice, Mose Bradley, Mac . . . But now, in my early thirties, my recall of my native tongue is faulty, almost nonexistent. I taught myself too well, over the years while I was gone, how to speak sans dialect. And no matter how hard I try to converse on an equal basis with my septuagenarian and octogenarian friends, I am able to give only lip service to my former language.

Here in my cabin at Zoro's field I have been moved to try to return to my cultural and linguistic roots and to incorporate these back into my daily speech as well as into my writing. Since moving to Polk County, I have continued my habit of spending time with the elder generation as well as the remaining few of my own age who have held tight to traditions, culture, and speech harkening back to the past. In addition to conversations I've had with my Saluda neighbors, there have been many memorable conversations with characters such as the now deceased Cherokee medicine man Amoneeta Sequoyah and the historian and arts dealer Tom Underwood over on the Qualla Boundary. I remember a conversation that took place on the back porch of an old mountain sawmill shack looking out into the woods, not long after I had arrived in Polk County fresh from the West Coast. The talk was about gardening, mountain farming, and the old days—of garden sass and wild greens, bird's toe, fiddleheads, speckled dick and lamb's-quarter, mouse's ear, blue root, hen pepper, and wooly breeches. Of cans and pokes. Of sour sop, chitlins, churn rags, and clabber. Of pawpaws, mayapples, wildfish, and ramps. Of coal oil and coal-of-fire. Of broom corn and blackstrap. Of bedbugs and rapscallions, rounders, swap slobbers, and swangs. I've had many colorful conversations over the years with younger generation yarn-spinners such as Paul Rhodes, whose lickety cut mind and quick wit, coupled with his mountain drawl, have caused me to rar back in my boots with laughter.

Since the beginning of my sojourn in the Green River cabin I've worked to reestablish my identity, my sense of belonging to a particular place and culture, by utilizing Southern Mountain Speech as much as I can, mainly through my writing. While it may be true, metaphorically and metaphysically, that you can't go home again, the fact is that I have come home again and am finding that I can call up the past in bits and pieces and bring it into the present-day voice in which I write. Can pull up Chaucer-era canticles—the triple negatives, the likes of "don't make no nevermind" and "not nary a any"—to grace the images of my poems and fictions.

During the winter months, when I have concentrated time and energy to read and write at length, in poems with titles such as "A Beatnik Wanders into Appalachia and Learns the Language of Earth and Sky," "Crack-Light," and "Who-Shot-John," I've been able to relive the past as well as to bring it to light (life) and into the present for myself. When I write "Dig the Big-Eyed Bird in swag or hollow / of locust and locked wood" (which when translated means: "you can see God in nature"), I am back in Graham County on the mountain behind my family's house in the Milltown community along Snowbird Creek, and, at the same time, I am here in Zoro's field experiencing a kind of time travel generated by language. A leap of more than twenty years. Or when I write, "couldn't hold a candle to this wick of words" or "where in tarnation," I can feel strength and satisfaction coming from the heart. In these moments it seems as if I've got the best of both worlds: past and present.

As a gardener of both legumes and language, I know that a time will come when I'll have to lay down my hoe, and my pen, forever. But until that day comes I aim to keep on diggin'. Harvesting the bounty afforded me by good organic food and this beautiful Southern Mountain Speech.

A BEATNIK WANDERS INTO APPALACHIA AND LEARNS THE LANGUAGE OF THE EARTH AND SKY

Climbing cold streams' wet weave of root
& rock   a warm murmur breathes beneath
a pool of song where water and wilt shine
on green tendrils moist with deep moss
        and dew.

Dig the dance of vine
climbing circle of stone.

Dig the blue bloom of rose
cut to caress torrents of rotting soil.

Dig the ripe wave of evening that touches flame
& breaks blood's slow boil of mulch & rain.

Walking green trees' coppered limbs of stairs
& canopy   a thrush of whistles rises in
a swoon of sunlight when thunder slaps and
color arcs in clouds' turbid mood of limber logs and leaves.

Dig the skiff of snow that preeks soft
near the rabbit's lair.

Dig the Big-Eyed Bird in swag or hollow
of locust and locked wood.

Dig the heave of new ground and the golden comb
of honey with winter rye.

Dig the dogtick and the rowan tree.
Dig the sky!

CHEROKEE

Far away from the main-traveled road of modern progress, the
Cherokee priest still treasures the legends and repeats the mystic
rituals handed down from his ancestors. It is among these
Kitu'hwa elders that the ancient things have been preserved.

JAMES MOONEY

Myths and Sacred Formulas of the Cherokee

What Is Sacred

*W*hen visiting Cherokee people I have come to know over on
the Qualla Boundary, as well as Snowbird Cherokee whom I know
going back to my boyhood in Graham County, I've taken time to listen intently and have learned a lot about people, their cultures, and
how one goes about living in the natural world. The Cherokee and
the Scots-Irish settlers have dwelled side by side here in these mountains for generations, and while being similar in that both embrace
clanlike social systems, pagan spiritual beliefs, and a fiercely independent self-sufficiency, they differ noticeably in perspective, mind-set,
and attitude. I've found that the descendants of Europeans are more
pragmatic and linear in their thinking about life and the world around
them, while the Cherokee are more holistic, using cyclical-circular
constructs as metaphorical or symbolic models to illustrate their spiritual beliefs and social practices. The white folk tend to think of the
land and life around them as something that has been placed there
specifically for their personal use—theirs for the taking—a skewed
view of independence stemming from outdated European thought
constructs and from their Protestant religions' self-serving interpreta-
tions of the Bible. The Cherokee, in contrast, tend to see themselves
as part of a larger whole that includes all forms of life. When viewed
from this more animistic perspective, life and all life-forms inherently
demand respect, even reverence. Contrary to the Christian beliefs of
the mountaineers who see the land and what lives on it as merely
convenient fodder for their sense of manifest destiny, the traditional

Cherokee worship the life that surrounds them and sustains them. A profound disparity exists between these two paradigms, which have been at odds with each other since the first Europeans landed on this continent. The disparity and conflict continue to this day, the gap ever widening with population growth and with increasing emphasis on personal material wealth and free-market capitalism.

The traditional Native American peoples have believed for thousands of years that the earth itself is sacred, a gift from, and a covenant with, the Creator. Would we here in the heart of the Bible Belt dare to curse in or to desecrate in any way our houses of worship? If not, why then would we show less respect for the earth itself? The earth which gives us our sustenance, our life, without which we could not and would not exist?

In my garden here in Zoro's field I try to perform my work with a sense of reverence. I am grateful for the blessing of rich loamy soil and of clean water nearby. I grow my crops organically without the easy assisting chemicals—pesticides, herbicides, and fertilizers. I do this out of respect for myself, for my own health, and for the well-being of the land—that others who come after me may benefit from my labors by inheriting a place from which they too may harvest healthy food. It has taken me a long while to begin replacing European utilitarian ideas of dominance, division, and manifest destiny with the more harmonious values of my Cherokee neighbors, who see things interdependently and from a holistic perspective of sustainability. But I'm making progress. I've still got a way to go, I know, as I work toward seeing the bigger picture that comes so easily to my Cherokee friends, who tell me that we are all related and that everything is sacred.

Sacred Sites

During the past three years, I have on occasion snuck out of my hermit's hideaway and made my way west into the deeper mountains to spend time with certain elder Cherokee traditionalists and traditionalist-activists. During recent visits there has been talk of starting a project to identify and protect Native American sacred sites. In conjunction with these discussions I have sometimes been taken (having promised not to violate confidence) to these sites, which were to the uninitiated eye just places in the woods. Thereby have I spent time in places that exude a numinous energy or exhibit a personality of presiding divinity that is not only physically noticeable but also entirely remarkable. There is a consistency, I have noticed, in where these kinds of places are found. Geographically, aspects of these landscapes are typical and readily identifiable—bends in rivers, waterfalls, groves of trees, springs, mountain peaks, rock cliffs—characteristics that when chanced upon during my own forays into the woods along the Green River give me cause to slow down, pay attention, and take note.

I have become fascinated by these "power places." Noticing my enthusiasm, one of my elder friends recently gave me a little dressing down. "To the Cherokee," he said, "all things, all places, are sacred. The rivers, streams, and springs are all sacred. The bottomlands, hills, and mountains are all sacred. The creatures that live in these places are all sacred. This is the basis of our beliefs and how we live our lives. To the Cherokee way of thinking, there is no separation, no segregation, between things in this world. The separation of things is the white man's idea. To us, everything is connected. Everything is sacred."

The implications of these beliefs are far-reaching. Embracing them, how can we justify any emotion other than horror concerning the pollution of our rivers, the fouling of our air, the clear-cutting of our woodlands, the strip-mining of minerals? In fact, how can we justify even the taken-for-granted practice of owning land?

While honoring the idea that everything and all places are sacred, it must be acknowledged that in nature some places are pristine and powerful in ways that other places are not. During my walks in the woods I've come across spots that took hold of me and captured my imagination. I find that I go back to these spots again and again because of their beauty or the kind of energy I experience there. It may be a solitary grove of old pines tucked away in a cove. It may be a place like the natural spring that issues from under a poplar tree in a grotto surrounded by a laurel thicket near the site of what was once the drovers' inn. It may be a section of river that strikes me as especially beautiful one morning as I walk along the bank fishing for trout.

Or it may be like the moist, mossy area I found last year inhabited by a colony of what the Cherokee call "painted-lady" turtles. A place that turtles also come to die, as evidenced by their shells scattered throughout the site. I come here not only to be with the turtles but also to find the empty shells, from which I make rattles to trade for things I need, as well as to give my Cherokee and culturally inquisitive white friends.

One place I especially like to visit, where I go more often during the summer months than in the winter, is a pool close to a poplar grove way back in the woods where Camp Creek falls into a natural black-granite box that is perfectly sculpted in a rectangular shape. There the water stills, creating a deep pool that is perfect for cooling off or bathing. I've lightheartedly named the place Kanati's Tub after the god of the hunt found in Cherokee mythology, as it seems the kind of place a larger-than-life entity would use to bathe or to cool off on hot summer days.

Many wonderful places in the woods beckon and inspire, and I love to find new spots as much as I love revisiting the known ones. While it's true that they are part of the Whole, they also have their own personalities and are therefore appropriate for certain kinds of use. This random discovery of places must also be how indigenous peoples found and designated sites for special usage. And herein lies the essence of the notion of "sacred sites" and the reason for carrying out the sacred sites project to identify and preserve them for future generations as part of an ongoing and living native religious tradition.

I was attracted to becoming involved in this project because of the possibility of visiting known Native American hot spots, but I was reminded again by my Cherokee friends that while this was a legitimate desire, I should think beyond myself. "Even if you don't do anything else but go sit on one of these spots," I was told early in my visits to the Qualla Boundary, "the earth will be a better place. But when you do that, think of the rest of us. Send a little of that place our way — so that it's not just a receiving thing, but a sending thing too."

In those first meetings, I expressed my concern about identifying places that maybe shouldn't be made known to the general public. "I've already done that by not telling you everything, not telling you about every place—so that you won't be responsible," I remember one of the elders saying. I understood perfectly, knowing there are places still being used that the Cherokee don't want the white man to know of—in order to keep them secret and therefore safe.

As things have progressed toward the creation of a sacred sites project these past months, the traditionalists have developed an outline of the kinds of places that concern them, as well as a list of actual sites. These include mountains connected with mythology or having actual usage as power places for fasting, healing, or visions; water places—creeks, rivers, waterfalls, and springs—used for purification rituals, fasting, and gathering medicinal plants; mythic and historic sites such as burial mounds and villages; and ceremonial sites used for fasting, initiation, healing, tribal ceremonies, and vision quests.

With an initial list of some fifty places, the work of gathering information about the sites has begun. The project intends to produce a body of information that can be used for understanding and protecting the sites. Field-workers use forms created for on-site notation, with space for recording the following information about specific locations: directions for reaching the site; Cherokee and English names for the site; physical description, including soil, rocks, plants, animals; elevation and other features; traditional use of the site if known; frequency with which the site is currently used; present condition; potential impacts on the site; current owner's name and address; and associated myths, other oral accounts, and bibliographic references.

Among the sites being looked at is Alarka Falls in Macon County, which was and is a water place used for fasting and purification. Over in Transylvania County there's a large rock outcropping named by white settlers Devil's Courthouse but used by the native peoples as a place of prayer, fasting, initiation, and vision-questing. The Nikwasi mound, also in Macon County, was part of the ceremonial village that was there before the incursionary development of the town of Franklin. It's also a place where the "spirit people," or *nunnehi*, are said to exist—an incorporeal race of indigenous people living in another dimension and on a higher spiritual plane. Another Macon County site is Raven Place, a sheer rock mountainside where dark, or evil, spirits are sent. These spirits are embedded in the rock at Raven Place, isolated from everyone and everything, unable to interact darkly with the world—a kind of jail for evil spirits. In Jackson County there is a place up Betty's Creek Road where a major pre-Cherokee ceremonial site is located. This is one of the most powerful places of any I have ever visited. My visits to the Betty's Creek site always result in a rapid heartbeat, extreme neuroelectric reactions bordering on anxiety attacks while on the site, and vivid dreams and visions during the following night.

This sacred sites work is being done under the auspices of the American Indian Religious Freedom Act of 1978 out of a perceived need to raise the level of awareness of the dominant culture concerning sacred land areas and the traditional values of Native American peoples and to preserve them in definitive ways. One of the primary goals of this work will be for the U.S. Forest Service to negotiate a written statement to include in their land use planning documents, guaranteeing the Cherokee and other native peoples access to federal land for religious and cultural usage without disturbance or harassment, and to set up a formal link between tribal elders and Forest Service representatives to ensure that Forest Service land will not be logged before Cherokee elders are consulted, thus minimizing damage to religious and cultural sites. While all this work is linear and task-oriented, the greater model the volunteers are working from is a holistic one, a perspective of which I am always reminded when meeting with my Indian friends—the bigger picture. There is always talk of "the Web," as exemplified by a story that was shared with me only this past week.

My grandfather told me that the English translation of the Cherokee words for "medicine people" is "the sacred fire burns inside of them." He also told me that at the Katuah village there was a sacred fire that was the central fire for the whole Cherokee nation. It was kept alive with the sacred wood of sourwood, hickory, cedar, locust, yellow pine, white oak, and sweet birch. Once a year, at the time of the Green Corn Ceremony, all the fires in the whole Cherokee territory were put out. The sacred fire at the mother village was then relit by a specially designated firekeeper, and runners would take the fire from the central fire to all the villages in the Cherokee Nation.

The old people used to say that the fire was the bond that kept the tribe together. It did not matter that the people were members of different clans and spoke different dialects. It did not matter that we might have different enemies and different friends. The fire was the same. Wherever our village was, we all cooked over the same fire and heated our lodges with the same fire. It was the central fire that held us together, and was a constant reminder that we are all One.

What the Elders Say

My visits with Cherokee elders are often long notetaking sessions. Coming from the perspective of an oral tradition that has served them well for thousands of years, my elder friends think me a little strange as I scramble to record, in my improvised shorthand, everything being said on the subjects of sustainability and spirituality—which, from what I've experienced these past few years living in the woods, are concepts that, by way of actual practice, are essentially inseparable. On one of my initial excursions away from the Green River woods and into the deep mountains near the borders of Georgia and Tennessee, I ended up sitting around a small fire and recording the following recitation—as the words flowed effortlessly and eloquently from the lips of one of my Indian friends.

We have been told that there is a purpose for every individual being. And that we are all caretakers. Just by the fact of our being conscious, that responsibility is placed upon us. Individually and in groups we must take a stand against the injustices of the world. At times like the solstice, when we are empowered by the forces of the earth and the heavens, we can stand together collectively, and powerfully make a difference.

We have been told that the most balanced way to be is found by following the examples of the natural forces within and around us. The way of water, for example. We have been told that the river is *yunwigunahita*, "the Long Human Being." We have been told that the function of water is flowing. And that the flowing brings cleansing, purification, healing, and change. If we are in need of healing, we go to water—to that sacred place where the shallow water touches the bank—and offer gratitude and thanks to the water in the form of offerings and prayer. We are told to then plunge underwater seven times, giving thanks to the water with each plunge. In this way, healing will come.

We are told these are the oldest mountains upon the earth. That life has been here longer than anyplace else on the Great Mother. We are told that this is one of the few places upon the earth where spirit still dwells—in the deep rich coves where the ginseng grows and the voices of water still talk. We are told it is the Giver-of-Breath's plan that we may have differences. All of the Giver-of-Breath's creation lives in harmony and peace with one another with the exception of man. Now, during the "time of great rest"—when trees lose their leaves and evergreens get greener—let's listen to the message that the mountains and the streams give to us. During these days we should strive to pull our communities together, to work together, even with our differences, to preserve this beautiful place—the land upon which we live. The land lives its own life and provides for us all. It cannot be bought or sold or won in war like trade beads or moccasins.

Saying it somewhat differently and from a feminine perspective, my new Cherokee friend Marilou Awiakta shared similar sentiments:

In order for us to restore reverence for the Web of Life in time to save our planet and ourselves, people need to understand the Web and how their lives weave into it. They need to tap into and remember what they already know deep down: all life is interconnected. To survive, we're going to have to change our ways. Science is demonstrating what Native Americans have always taught as a physical and spiritual truth: everything in the universe is one family. We are all relatives. Science uses detached language to speak of this. But Native Americans speak with words of deep attachment: Mother Earth, Father Sky. Brother, sister, grandmother, grandfather are used not only for biological family, but to refer to other things as kin. The concept of interconnectedness itself is expressed as the Web of Life or the Sacred Circle.

My parents taught me about the Web in everyday ways. As a child I loved to pick blackberries. But snakes also love to nestle in blackberry bushes. Daddy said, "Remember you're going into the snake's home.

Be respectful. Be courteous. Take a stick and rustle the bushes. Give the snake time to keep his privacy. Surprise him and he'll strike you." People are the same way. Nobody likes being slipped up on. I've never gotten crosswise with a snake or with many people either. Except the ones that slip up on me. Being mindful of the Web is a way of living in the world.

Western thought uses as its model an emphasis on the individual over the communal, and the part separate from the whole. To me the Western model looks like a series of boxes stacked up on top of one another. Together they may make a whole, of sorts, but they don't interconnect like a web does.

In Cherokee tradition, woman embodies continuance; man embodies change and transitoriness. Together they make a whole that generates life. Like many other tribes, the Cherokee see woman as the center of the home and the center of the Nation. Because of her regenerative qualities, physical and spiritual, she was the force of continuance for the people and carried the strength of sacred Mother Earth. As a result, Cherokee women had a powerful voice on the council and in spiritual matters. But nurturing and assertiveness were instilled in both genders, and this translates as living in harmony with each other and with the earth.

Looking at the effect of acid rain on the trees on Clingman's Dome here in the Smokies I wrote this little poem called "Dying Back."

On the mountain
the standing people are dying back—
hemlock, spruce, and pine
turn brown in the head.
The hardwood shrivels in new leaf.
Unnatural death
from acid greed
that takes the form of rain
and fog and cloud.

In the valley
the walking people are blank-eyed.
Youth grow spindly, wan

from sap too drugged to rise.
Pushers drain it off —
sap is gold to them.
The walking people are dying back
as all species do
that kill their own seed.

Maybe we will wake up in time to repair the shreds of the Web of Life. It takes grit and gumption to keep working quietly where you are with whatever threads of the Web are at hand. But energies fuse. This is a law of physics. And so do spirits, which follow the same law. I follow one of the oldest traditions for all Appalachian people, regardless of race. If you need something useful—a quilt, rocker, basket, blowgun—you use the native material around you and make it. We're going to have to apply this kind of thought and action regarding the natural world if we are going to protect it and bring things back into balance.

One of the older people I've been spending time with over on the Qualla Boundary is a traditional medicine man named Amoneeta Sequoyah. A direct descendent of the same Sequoyah who created the Cherokee syllabary and written language, Amoneeta has been working with me on a manuscript of his life story that I hope will make its way into an as-told-to biography. We've spent hours and days in conversation—with him doing most of the talking and me sitting in a chair and writing as fast as I can in my improvised shorthand in order to keep pace. When we're not sitting on the porch of his old mobile home in Big Cove talking, we're out in the woods on the reservation gathering plants he uses to make his medicines.

While not nearly finished with the book, in recent months we've made good headway, between his bouts of ill health. As he approaches his eightieth birthday, he is becoming more and more contemplative about the past ("the old ways," as he refers to them) and about prospects for the future. His story as one of the last initiated medicine men in the Eastern Band of the Cherokee is a fascinating history of not only his own life, but of a way of life that has all but disappeared from these mountains. Along with his fascinating life story is his wisdom concerning the environment and the natural world.

A small, thin man in an oversized Western hat with an eagle plume stuck loosely in its band, he sits on the porch of his trailer and speaks.

> Finally the day came for me to be born and my father, my mother, and I started out over the mountain to my grandparents so I could come out safely into the world of light. When the birth pangs hit my mother right about the top of the mountain, my father ran to fetch my grandmother. But I was in a great hurry to see what was going on in the wide world outside. We stopped beside a big old chestnut tree in the cool shade, and by the time my father and grandmother returned, I had already jumped out. I was the last of my people to be born like a wild Indian—out in the woods.
>
> Some of my fondest memories of when I was a boy are of walks with my grandfather—who was also an elder in the medicine fraternity—in the woods around the reservation. On these walks I learned much of his knowledge of herbs, their locations, their identifying factors, their medicinal qualities, and the proper combinations in which they were to be mixed and used. By the time I had been initiated into manhood I already had much of his knowledge of herbal lore. From when I was about eight years old, up to about fifteen years, I doctored people for toothaches, earaches, and such as that, without any medicine. I used my hands. And later, I found I could stop blood, even if someone was bleeding very badly. And that too I did only with my hands.

My talks with Amoneeta include stories of his years growing up here in the mountains when cougars got in the hog pens and dragged off the livestock; of a reservation full of bear, deer, fox, and eagle and creeks and streams full of native trout; of a time when travel was done primarily on foot or on horseback; of a time when, as he put it, "there were still men alive who had the power of *ada'wehi'*—great spiritual healers, magicians who could change into animals and then back, who could make a turtle from a rock, a snake from a stick"—men he managed to spend time with and learn from.

But all those kind of medicine men are gone now. None left anywhere now. The last ones died about forty or fifty years ago—those that had that kind of power.

I've learned all of the over six-hundred plants and herbs used in conjunction with modern and native medicines—in their English names as well as their Cherokee names. Each herb must be collected at the proper time, and a medicine man's got to know the time and manner as to how to gather the herbs just as much as he knows how to mix and use them. You got to know the right season for each one. If you get 'em at the wrong time, they won't be no good. I always get enough to last just a year. After that they lose their strength. Mostly, it's the herbs, roots, and berries like crowfoot, snakeroot, star-root, ginseng, goldenseal, white walnut, prickly ash, red elder, he-balsam and she-balsam, and hickory that I use to cure folks.

As for the problems we're facing, all I know is that we all have to do something. We've never, in all the years people have been on earth, seen such dying, disease, and destruction. Nature is being taken away from us. Some of the plants and animals are disappearing. I think we're going to have to go back to the old ways, y'know. Yes, we're going to have to go back to the old ways.

Listening to Amoneeta talk about plants, medicine, healing, and ritual not only has been an education for me, but has inspired my own life here in the woods. From Amoneeta and from my elder mountaineer neighbors of European heritage, I've learned to identify certain wild plants for which I forage as part of my diet, as well as herbs that I use as medicines—such as mullein, bloodroot, ginseng, and jewelweed. I can identify, for example, the edible wild greens that appear in early spring and can be used for salads and for cooking, such as miner's lettuce, creasy greens, ramps, cress, cliff onions, poke, dandelion, plantain, fiddleheads . . . And then as the season progresses, morels, puffballs, and meadow mushrooms magically appear.

Soon after moving to the woods I began doing small personal rituals in conjunction with important work-related activity and in recognition of auspicious seasonal moments. On full moon nights, for example, I sometimes drum out in the field with a hollow red oak log and a couple of sourwood sticks. The acoustics in the field at night, especially during the full moon, are heightened, enlivened. With the sound of sticks against wood echoing off the pines on the other side of the field, it could be a dozen drummers laying down perfectly synchronized improvisational rhythms. The overall effect can be marvelously powerful. Sometimes these sounds, this drumming, can even produce altered states of awareness.

For the past couple of years I've also been doing small rituals of thanksgiving after planting my crops. When I'm finished planting my corn and potatoes, for example, I bend down on one knee and, along with reciting an invocation, sprinkle some of the excess corn seed on the ground there in the corn rows. Or maybe I'll take some bee pollen out of my pocket (which I keep there and use as an energy booster on days when my strength wanes during particularly heavy work) and mix it with a handful of rich black dirt while saying a short improvised prayer of thanksgiving and asking for a healthy yield from the seeds I have just planted. And I do similar, albeit more elaborate, things on the days or nights marking the equinoxes in spring and fall and the solstices in summer and winter. These are things that have come to mean much to me as I intuitively search for symbolic and mythic meaning here in my home amidst the natural world. Spontaneously I have identified certain moments during the natural cycle of seasons as appropriate times to renew my connection with the earth, living things, and the stars and planets in the sky — all of which I have come to see as sacred, as part of a larger Whole.

Then there are totally unrehearsed rituals I might do when I'm in the midst of discovery or revelry in a certain place or activity unrelated to the normal cycles of work and seasonal observance. In those moments, no matter where I am or what I am doing, I will stop and spontaneously do whatever seems to move me, as a way of giving thanks or as a celebration of grace or epiphany. What I have discovered and manifested on my own regarding ritual, I have found is synchronous and in line with what I have heard and learned about ritual and ceremony from my Indian friends, leading me to believe that these sorts of things have been done and shared universally for millennia as a manifestation of human consciousness and spiritual impulse and that this animistic behavior is part of our genetic coding—a healthy and necessary part of our material and spiritual lives as we interact with the natural world.

IN PERMANENCE
for Marilou Awiakta

Tired of traveling
the path of the always traveled and never putting down,
I come to this place.
A small home in the woods.
And although there are no neighbors
or no women for miles, I set down my bags.

Here, at the end of all roads,
there is nothing but wilderness as far as the eye can see.
A rich black earth.
And the saddest of deep blue sky . . .

I think it's the quiet
has brought me here. Or
maybe the special green color of the pines.
Who other than God could know?
Yet, I'm beginning to see
myself in the balance of all things.
The family way of the bees.
And the silent language of trees.

The sidewalks and the cul-de-sacs of noise
are as far from me now as Space.
It's been too long. And
I doubt that I'll ever go back.
Away from these gardens.
Away from these mountain streams.
The small roots already beginning to grow

from the bottoms of my feet
are holding me to this fertile soil.
And soon I will be held here.
Held without hands.
In permanence.

Woven into the Web of Life.

THE NEW NATURALISTS

Here is his library, but his study is out of doors.

WILLIAM WORDSWORTH'S MAID
from Henry David Thoreau's *Journals*

Overpopulation

*W*hen I returned to western North Carolina in 1979 after being gone for almost twenty years, on the surface things looked about the same as they had when I left. With the exception of a few new interstate roads, the countryside, the towns, the rivers, the wilderness that I enjoyed as a boy growing up in Graham County at first glance seemed to have survived intact. I reveled in this misperception as I began setting up house beside Zoro's field. Living wild and self-sufficiently and far from the "real world," I allowed this illusion of an undisturbed environment to continue for some time. But recently I have begun to awake from the Rip Van Winkle sleep that has sheltered me from the storms of capitalist commerce and ideology, but has also kept from me the truth that all around me these mountains have been changing and are full of "hostile tribes." More to the point: the Smokies have been discovered and are up for sale. And if this weren't enough, there is evidence of air pollution and acid rain on Mount Mitchell, and a tough fight between environmentalists and the owners of Champion Paper Company is erupting over the pollution of the Pigeon River. Among other modern-day prophets, Bob Dylan was right when he wrote: "the times they are a-changin'."

"I'm holding on to most of my land here in Polk County," said a middle-aged man down at Pace's General Store when I was in there last week trading for kerosene for my oil lamps. "I'm holding out for the big boom that's comin'. It won't be long before Polk County will be discovered by the same people who are moving into Brevard, Cashiers, and Highlands. They've got the big money, and that money's gonna make its way down the mountain into Saluda. I'm certain of that." I remember thinking at the time that the fella had gone a little over the top with his dreams of Florida and New York money making its way into the quiet Green River community out Macedonia and Howard Gap roads.

I studied on the ambitious landowner's predictions during the five-mile walk home down the winding dirt road from town. By the time I got to the edge of my field I pretty much agreed with him. I'd passed three for-sale signs hawking big tracts of rugged mountain land. I also considered the two sold stickers I'd seen up Old Macedonia Road, the first quarter mile of which has recently been paved. Telltale signs, I thought to myself as I sat in my rocker that evening pondering the future. "I sure hope that landowner fella doesn't turn out to be some sort of Nostradamus, dragging his apocalyptic dreams down into Polk County," I said out loud, yet oh so quietly, lest some baleful spirit hear and get ideas of its own.

The word down at the Saluda barbershop is that along the mountain bluffs and ridges, beside the rivers, and in pastures of old farmland, trailer parks are appearing and new homes going up, just as in almost every other county in western North Carolina. Add to this the fact that the Great Smoky Mountains National Park is one of the most visited wilderness and recreation areas in the country, and the writing is indeed on the wall. The "good ole days" are being replaced by a tidal wave of "good ole American progress" stemming from the recent onset of a booming economy. But more importantly, and more devastatingly, here in Polk County, as in other of the region's rural counties, is the advent of overpopulation.

After all this town talk, and the thinking that I did afterward on the subject, I walked all the way down Macedonia Road and stuck out my thumb on Route 176, headed for Hendersonville and the county library. There I found reference books full of statistics on the global population explosion. After a couple of hours of reading and notetaking, I noticed through the windows on the far side of the room that the sun was going down and it was time for me to get back on the road in an attempt to make it home before dark. I quickly wrote down my impressions and these words to finish off my afternoon's research:

What we have been hearing for years on the nightly news, from our politicians, from our educators, from our "experts" . . . concerning the current distressed state of the world, are only the peripheral symptoms, the residual camouflage of the cause of these symptoms: OVERPOPULATION. At the end-of-millennium root of all our social, cultural, medical, psychological, pathological, and environmental ills is the fact that the Earth has been too crowded for some time. There are too many people and not enough space, not enough food, not enough money, not enough (clean) air, not enough organized wisdom to approach any sort of human balance whereas the environment and our individual or collective lives are concerned. The issue of Overpopulation has been always avoided. Never addressed. In order to even attempt setting things back into a state of balance, both regionally here in western North Carolina, or worldwide, the CAUSE of our problems needs to be addressed. Space is running out, as is time, and the issue of whether or not we will learn to recognize and curtail our indulgences before we infest the entire planet like a plague of locusts, needs attention now. By everyone.

Worldwide the human population is growing at the rate of 300,000 a day (more than 100 million a year). An average of 5.5 children are born to every procreating female, and less than 10 percent of married couples use birth control. A result of all these factors is that the total population of the planet is expected to double in the next half century. Does it not follow that at least some of this escalating wave of humanity should be spilling over onto the ridgelines of the southern Appalachians? Add to this an increasing abundance of carcinogens (CO_2 and SO_2 emissions and dioxins from industrial waste), higher levels of PCBs in plants and animals, the breakdown of the earth's ozone, and the warming of the planet's surface and oceans. If these statistics are correct, then things are much bleaker than I wanted to believe.

And if our clairvoyant landowner is correct and the Green River watershed is going to be swamped in the great tidal wave of humanity that is headed this way, how will this all play out? For one thing, to state the obvious, the more people there are, the less there is going to be for everyone. (And in "everyone" I include plant and animal wildlife.) Less space, less land, less food, less clean air and water. Fewer farms, fewer jobs, less meaningful work, and not nearly as much peace and quiet. And along with the less, we can also expect the more: more noise, more pollution, more crowding, more traffic, more taxes, more corruption, more illness (including mental illness).

The bottom line here seems to be what I heard referred to as "carrying capacity" during my northern California days. Carrying capacity is the measure of how much or how little a particular ecosystem or environmental community is able to sustain. The Katuah Bioregion does not have enough carrying capacity to support much influx of humanity. So small an area with such rugged terrain, and its elemental, floral, faunal, and human diversity, cannot carry the incoming load of humanity it will be asked to. In short, after a certain point there will not be enough of everything to go around.

When a human being is ill, we see symptoms—fever, nausea, weakness, paleness—and we seek a physician, someone who is trained to help us put our bodies back into a state of balance, health. When the ecology of the environment is out of sorts ("anti-godlin," as my mountain neighbors might say, referring to anything that is out of balance or out of plumb or that goes against God and the laws of nature), we also see symptoms: changes in weather conditions, wider foraging ranges for predatory and grazing animals, smaller game populations for animal and human consumption, a decrease in animal and plant species, polluted air and water, an increase in antisocial behavior in all species, pandemic disease, less wilderness and oxygen-generating forests . . . What doctors can cure the illnesses producing these kinds of symptoms? What schools will educate those needed to put an end to an epidemic of overpopulation?

When I go to town and look through the plastic windows of the newspaper boxes, what I see in the headlines these days is the kind of thing I used to read about developing countries on the other side of the planet: potential EPA Superfund cleanup sites; the pollution index in the Smokies going higher and higher; evergreens dying off by the thousands because of acid rain; ponds and lakes testing high for airborne pollutants, and the fish in them dying; crime rates higher than ever even in small towns and communities like Saluda, where for generations folks have never locked their doors; wildlife populations and habitats seriously declining as the endangered species list soars . . .

At this point I'm already thinking about solutions. I remember first being introduced to the work of ecologian Thomas Berry, and I remember his words: "It will take a conversion experience deep in the psychic structure of the human to get things back on track and moving toward finding ourselves in a state of balance with the natural world and the universe." While this prognostication seemed daunting at the time, it resonated deeply with me, and rang true. I remember thinking that if Berry is right, then we have a lot of work ahead of us—building bridges between human and nonhuman life-forms, as these life-forms are essential to our very survival and must stay healthy and abundant if we are going to remain healthy and abundant. To manifest this kind of healing paradigm it seems obvious that, while not everyone can be expected to live as I am living, we do need to be more intimate with our natural surroundings and begin relating to the Earth as a respected and living *object* rather than an inanimate *subject*, something to be conquered and possessed.

The question I am now asking myself is: how much longer will this old mountain farm I am living on, surrounded as it is by natural springs, woods, and the Green River and populated by all kinds of wildlife and native plants, remain the way it is? How long will it be before the woodlands full of foxes, wild turkeys, and deer are replaced by trailers, summer homes, and condominiums? How long before the indigenous quiet and the solace of rural sounds I so enjoy turn into human and machine-made noise? How long before the wildlife that comes freely into Zoro's field will not feel comfortable here and thus will disappear—along with myself soon thereafter?

The New Naturalists

With issues such as development, zoning and land-use legislation, toxic waste, and air pollution almost constantly on the lips of my neighbors these days, I've been thinking further about the desecration of the environment and who might be able to lead us out of the self-destructive paradigm that was set into motion with the Industrial Revolution and that has continued to gather momentum in the last century and a half with the rise of free-market capitalism. "Where are the dirt doctors, the earth healers?" I keep asking myself. Where are the great charismatic voices in government that might begin the work of turning things around? And if not in government, then in the culture in general? When you look in all the obvious places, you find no one addressing the most pressing questions of our day: overpopulation, development, preservation, free-trade capitalism.

In retrospect it seems to me that it has always been the naturalists who have led the way toward more progressive thinking about questions of balance and sustainability. Nature writers have often positioned themselves on the front lines of the myriad battles to save and preserve the environment. Through their writing, seeds have been sown that have sprouted as ecological movements, private foundations, and governmental programs focused on the long view of the country's and the planet's natural landscape. I think of nature's emissaries of the late 1800s and early 1900s, such as John Burroughs, John Muir, Ralph Waldo Emerson, and Henry David Thoreau—the pantheon of nature writers who not only set the stage, but set the standards for those who followed in their footsteps—the likes of Aldo Leopold, Rachel Carson, and Loren Eiseley in midcentury and Gary Snyder, Wendell Berry, and Thomas Berry in the succeeding generation. These writers and others over the past hundred years have made an indelible impression on human consciousness and the American landscape. As Loren Eiseley wrote: "If we turn the pages of the great nature essayists we may perceive once more the role which the gifted writer and thinker plays in the life of man—pure observation giving way to awe, and the obscure sense of the holy." In Eiseley, as in Thomas Berry, I hear the call for a necessary spiritual conversion experience as the organic solution to the tangible ills of the environment.

During the winter months these past three years, I've spent a great deal of time wedded to my old flea-market rocker, reading the work of America's nature writers. I have reread much of the Riverside Press edition of John Burroughs's writings—twelve books in all, most of which he wrote in the barn of his rural home in the Catskills. His *Indoor Studies*, *Breath of Life*, *Under the Apple-Trees*, and *Field and Study* are my favorites. In the chapter "Phases of Animal Life" in *Field and Study*, which was published in 1919, Burroughs speaks with perceptive hopefulness, yet almost naively, about environmental balance: "The natural balance of life in any field cannot long be disturbed. Though Nature at times seems to permit excesses, yet she sooner or later corrects them and restores the balance. The life of the globe could never have attained its present development on any other plane. A certain peace and harmony have come out of the perpetual struggle and warfare of opposing tendencies and forces. When one force pulls down, another force builds up." While things now look more ominous for the global environment than they did in 1919, one would hope that Burroughs's observations and predictions might in the long run be correct—that nature can hold her own against the destructive forces of industrial expansion and human failing as they exist a century later.

Along with Burroughs were other prolific writers of his era who also made their mark on the twentieth century's collective consciousness. Emerson's essays "Self Reliance," "Nature," and "Prudence" were cornerstones upon which Thoreau, Muir, and later Leopold, Eiseley, and Carson built their word temples to Nature, and which such administrators as Theodore Roosevelt used as a bully pulpit to extol governmental programs to leave large tracts of American wilderness undeveloped and undisturbed for posterity. Emerson stands as a lighthouse on the rocky shores of the American psyche where environmental ethics are concerned. His writings are the launchpad for Thoreau's fireworks, which came soon after, as well as for the elevated message of Thomas Berry, who emerged at the forefront of the spiritual-environmental movement a century and a half later.

In 1841 in his essay "History," Emerson was already preparing us for the dilemma we find ourselves facing today regarding commerce and the environment.

> Broader and deeper we must write our annals, — from an ethical reformation, from an influx of the ever new, ever sanative conscience, — if we would trulier express our central and wide-related nature, instead of this old chronology of selfishness and pride to which we have too long lent our eyes. Already that day exists for us, shines in on us at unawares, but the path of science and of letters is not the way into nature. The idiot, the Indian, the child, and unschooled farmer's boy, stand nearer to the light by which nature is to be read, than the dissector or the antiquary.

Emerson's words speak today even more profoundly than they did during his own lifetime, as the world's and this country's population have far exceeded carrying capacity, and unchecked commerce has ravaged the land, air, and waters. Able to see for himself our current situation, Emerson would be appalled yet would have earned the right to say in response, "I told you so."

John Muir was a man who "walked the walk" as well as one who wrote about it, hiking and traveling thousands of miles across North America through uncharted wilderness. How many boots the man must have gone through! His "thousand-mile walk," trailblazing down the eastern United States (which brought him within a stone's throw of my place) when he was twenty-nine years old, is itself statement enough of his exuberance and dedication to the cause of the environment, to say nothing of what he went on to do for the remaining forty-six years of his life. "Such an ocean of wooded, waving, swelling mountain beauty and grandeur is not to be described," Muir would write—reminiscent of William Bartram before him—about his first impressions of the mountains of western North Carolina. "Countless forest-clad hills, side by side in rows and groups—all united by curves and slopes of inimitable softness and beauty. Oh, these forest gardens of our Father! What perfection, what divinity, in their architecture!"

Thoreau and Muir became the godfathers of the American environmental movement, spawned at the end of the nineteenth century by Muir's Sierra Club. In the early 1960s Rachel Carson's *Silent Spring* gave new vigor to the movement, which was joined by poet Robinson Jeffers and the whole bioregional movement on the West Coast—with poet-activist writers such as Gary Snyder, Peter Berg, and Lee Swenson leading the way. Snyder in particular, with his Zen approach to wilderness, has taken the torch of deep ecology and run with it through the 1960s—and a generation of protest marches and social actions—on into the present day. And in such seminal works as *The Real Work* (1980) he has handed the torch of sustainability to a whole new generation of activist nature writers.

"If you would learn the secrets of nature," Thoreau wrote, "you must practice more humanity than others." That credo more or less sums up the ethos of the "new naturalists," who are not only writing prose and poetry that evoke the spirit of the old naturalists and their tenets for a premeditated and sustainable future, but are also engaging in a kind of activism that is at once literary and biographical. They are, through their writing and their deeds, inspiring, organizing, and participating in nonviolent activities that provide alternatives to community apathy and destruction of natural habitat.

Many such voices from my generation have surfaced to speak out on behalf of the natural world. Rick Bass is a voice for stewardship in the plains region of Montana. Southeast of there is Wes Jackson, in Kansas, who writes about sustainable agriculture (*New Roots for Agriculture*, published by Friends of the Earth) and earth stewardship. In Kentucky, Wendell Berry (who is more of Snyder's generation) is writing about preservation of rural community and family farms. These are but some of the new naturalist voices that have emerged in recent years to stretch the paradigm of protection and proper proportion out into the twenty-first century.

Closer to my Green River home, addressing itself to the quality of life in the Southeast and following in the footsteps of adventure-naturalists William Bartram and Horace Kephart, a new generation of nature writers is distinguishing itself as new naturalists. Over in Swain County — in the environs of Bryson City — George Ellison has already established himself as part of this new breed of nature-activist writers with his poetry and prose, particularly his journalism. If anyone has embraced and embodied the writing of Thoreau and Kephart, it is George Ellison. As someone who has long lived without electricity and running water in a cabin approachable only by foot, Ellison has a nearly encyclopedic knowledge of nature lore and Native American history. Driving the bookmobile for the regional library system is his primary means of support, but his newspaper columns, frequent nature-walk workshops, and contributions to the living folklore of the region are invaluable in educating the public about its past as well as in celebrating the region's botanical present.

Over in Whittier off Camp Creek Road, John Lane, white-water enthusiast, wilderness and recreation writer, poet, and publisher of Holocene Press, has taken up residence in the midst of a former herb and native plant nursery that has run wild, and is engaged in water and land issues. His recent writing, destined for publication, is full of very human stories ("the new true Jack Tales," as I've referred to them) that take place in what he calls his "weed patch," as well as in the Nantahala Gorge, creating poetic petroglyphs on place-based awareness. His more activist and investigative prose is written on behalf of ecological issues here in the mountains with an awareness harkening back to his native turf on the other side of the Blue Wall in the South Carolina Piedmont of Spartanburg County. In both poems and prose pieces Lane writes in attack mode. While his journalistic work is brash, aggressive, and unmovable, his poetry written in and about these mountains is equally gentle, sensitive, fluid.

WAKING IN THE BLUE RIDGE

In the animal light of early morning
dreams persist but I am quickly
victim to the world's precision—

how oaks become one
in a web of blue above,
and the fox bursts
toward the nested quail,
or in tricks of color
copperheads coil
where they could not be.

All this in the hour
before breakfast, in the heaven
of unnoticed verdancy and light.

From a bit farther afield, in Virginia, Christopher Camuto's love of fly-fishing and the Great Smoky Mountains National Park has brought him down into western North Carolina. His writing on both these subjects is the stuff of supernovas. His rise to prominence as a southern Appalachian nature writer is becoming legendary. His whip-cracking intellect and inspired vocabulary have been a wake-up call for other writers and for readers of regional and natural history. His mix of autobiographical and scientific writing offers the next best thing to being there. The visual images he creates with language go beyond being merely photographic. They linger in the mind's eye for months and years.

Finally there is a core group of cultural and environmental activists here in the mountains working to create bioregional awareness and a sense of responsibility for our ecosystem. Their principal vehicle is to be a monthly newspaper-type publication espousing the values, ethics, and hands-on particulars of the bioregional and green movements. A sister organization to other bioregional groups across the country, the Katuah group has at its heart such writers as David Wheeler (a former resident of the Farm in Summertown, Tennessee), Marnie Muller (a student of Jean Houston and Thomas Berry), ecoscholar and teacher J. Linn Mackey, and Sam Gray, who writes convincingly on myth and metaphysics of place while heading up the Mountain Heritage Center over in Cullowhee.

Katuah's main emphasis is on teaching, and its main vehicle is the newspaper, which has an intelligent mixture of articles on plant lore, environmental issues, gardening and farming tips, regional geographic history, and Native American culture—focusing on life here in this southern Appalachian mountain watershed, which includes my own smaller ecosystem adjacent to the Blue Wall escarpment and straddling the Green River.

While the amount of work to be done in cleaning up our environment in the mountain and Piedmont regions of the Southeast might at times seem overwhelming, these new naturalists and others like them are more than equal to the task. This focused and dedicated "wild bunch" has taken on the heavy yoke of unchecked progress, growth, and development and, in exemplary bioregional fashion, with strong shoulders is pulling the ecology wagon in which everyone rides. "May it continue," as the old Apache ceremonial chant goes. This nature-activist tradition. This beautiful place. And these people who live here well.

Meanwhile I go on about my daily business, as we all must, taking care of the microcosmic world around me. Trying to live here with the other life-forms by which I am surrounded in conscious awareness, unswerving diligence, and grace.

PRAYER FOR THE EARTH

The earth is my body, and I
shall not want;
it beckons me to lie down in green pastures.
It shares with me its clean waters, and
it nurtures my soul.
It leads me along the paths of right-thinking
for its own sake.

Even though I walk through
valleys among shadows of darkness,
I fear no evil,
for the earth is with me;
its mountains and its seas,
they comfort me.

O, great Earth, you have set a banquet before me
on the table of this Garden,
have filled my mind with revelations,
and my wonder grows!
Surely the deer and the seasons shall
follow me
all the days of my life;
and I will live in the beauty of
this world
forever.
E-man'u. Amen.

ANIMAL STORIES

The animal creation . . . how wonderful is the mechanism of
these finely formed self-moving beings, how complicated
their system, yet what unerring uniformity prevails through
every tribe and particular species!

WILLIAM BARTRAM
Travels

The Boomer and the Blacksnake

I've been having a hard time sleeping lately. It's not because I'm not
tired after working all day, fixing a meal, setting a fire for the night,
and reading myself silly; it's the overhead drama being played out in
the ceiling at night. It begins as I turn down the wick of my kerosene
lamp after climbing into bed. The lowering of the light must be the
signal, as that is when the nuts begin to roll. Like a little bowling alley
in my attic. The only thing missing is the crashing of pins. The round
nuts roll, and something scurries to catch them. The game would
probably go on without interruption were I not to throw back the
covers, stand up on the bed, and pound on the ceiling. Then the game
playing stops, only to start up again just as I'm nodding off, and the
scene plays itself out once more. So it goes throughout the night.

I know who the player in this drama is, as I have seen him coming
and going during the daylight hours. The bowler is a reddish brown
squirrel, a "boomer," that appears on the roof and in the locust tree
over the south end of the cabin, chiding me — with a walnut in its
mouth — as if I were intruding on his space. He's been stashing walnuts in my attic for over a month and must have quite a hoard, judging
by the aftershocks of my pounding on the ceiling. Not able to find the
place where he's getting into the house, I'm left to suffer his midnight
antics.

Lately, however, another sound has come from the ceiling at night.
A soft sliding like something moving through snow. When this sound
occurs, I've noticed that my bowler does not work at stacking his wal-

nuts. At first I thought this new noise might be the boomer smoothing out his nest or maybe rolling around in his sleep. But then the other day, when walking down the pine-needle path to the backyard of the cabin, I glimpsed something moving around the underpinnings of the house. As I got closer I could see clearly a large blacksnake winding around a locust post and making its way up into the outside wall on the north side of the cabin. Worried that the blacksnake would get into the living area of the house, I stepped inside and went to the bedroom, waiting to see the old snake emerge. After a while what I heard instead was the same smooth sliding of a few nights before. The blacksnake had found a way into the cabin walls and up into the attic, where it has been hanging out ever since — coming outside during the day to hunt or to get quality time in the direct sun.

With this dynamic having gone on for some time, I went to bed a few nights later skeptical about getting any sleep. As usual, as soon as I blew out the lamp the bowling began. The nut-rolling had been going on a while when I finally heard the slow sliding of the blacksnake right above my head. As the nuts rumbled overhead on the far side of the room, the snake eased across the Sheetrock. Roll, roll . . . slide, slide . . . This surreal serenade went on for several minutes, concluding abruptly with flopping and thrashing followed by a choked squeal. The boomer's bray got louder and more frantic as the sliding and slapping continued. Then there was silence. And nothing moved overhead again for the rest of the night.

The next night and the night after that no noise came from my ceiling. No bowling. No slithering. Just an occasional breeze blowing through the screens in the windows on the west wall. A day or so later, coming down the path where I had first seen the blacksnake, I encountered it again. This time it was stretched out underneath the cabin and looked to be headed for the woods. There was a large bulge in the snake's midriff. Still digesting.

Happy for the quiet these nights since the brouhaha in my attic, I'm finding that I kind of miss the little boomer, though not his nightly games of boccie. The old blacksnake still hangs out up there, as the fall weather turns colder and he's found a warm place to lay out the winter — which is okay with me as long as he doesn't get greedy and decide he wants to trade up for my pillows and quilt.

Deer in the Orchard, Wild Turkey in the Field

My nights have been quiet since then, but meanwhile I have plenty of nonhuman neighbors to keep me company. Natural neighbors, you might say. My closer friends. My preferred company.

Only last week, as I peered out my cabin window on a dreary afternoon, a flock of wild turkeys stalked into the field from the pines. Cautious, yet seeming to know where they were going, and with a mission, they processed into the open in single file, led by a majestic old gobbler. As soon as they were all into the field, they spread out and began pecking around in the grass like domestic chickens looking for late lunch. It didn't take them long to make their way to the end of the field near the cabin. While I had seen this particular flock roosting in some tall oaks in the woods along the old dirt road that rides the ridgeline, I had never seen them over here. But they acted like they'd been here before — probably when I was off in the woods somewhere or working in the orchard or the grape arbors. Clearly the turkeys knew where I spread cracked corn at the edge of the field just below the woodshed. Within minutes the whole group was feasting on my maize.

Every day I spread cracked corn and sunflower seed on a bare spot of ground to attract the larger birds and give the smaller birds a better chance at the raised feeders closer to the house. This strategy has worked, with doves, crows, blue jays, towhees, thrashers, and thrushes all preferring to eat off the ground rather than up in the air. So word had gotten out in the bird community that ole T. Crowe had laid out a banquet in Zoro's field, and the turkeys were here in all their finery and, true to their nickname, were gobbling it up.

Little table talk went on during the meal, the hens cackling now and again, getting the tom's attention but not his response. I heard no gobbles and only a few faint clucks that for the women passed as gossip. Despite the discrepancy in size, the tom let the hens have first crack at the corn, moving around behind them eating what they missed. In this way the hens ate their fill first, and then the tom went in and cleaned their plates. All the while, the tom strutted around, his tail splayed, proud of the spread he had found to gorge his harem — and making certain the grazing girls didn't ignore him.

Now that ole tom and his hens have found this formidable feeding place, they will be back again, and often, especially since there aren't many open grassy areas on the ridgetop with such good food. Their usual meal of fall grapes and branch lettuce at this time of year will be supplemented with my cracked corn grown down in the drover's inn field. I'll see them roosting in the oaks early in the morning on my walks out the ridge road and in the evening when I come home from down on the river. And they will no doubt see me. I'm sure it won't be long before they know who I am and where I'm headed, hoping that my first business will be to throw corn into the dirt at the edge of the field.

As I watched the turkeys eat in my yard, I was reminded of Zoro's maxim about how staying in one place long enough allows you to see the whole spectrum of wildlife "march before you like a parade." I certainly have a front row seat for observing the wild turkey and everything else that comes into my field. When they were here, eating, they showed no fear or concern about who or what might lurk in the little cabin only a stone's throw from where they ate. Perhaps they sensed that I am not, for the most part, a hunter. Although they must have heard the shots I have fired from time to time at greedy squirrels and the odd rabbit, groundhog, or raccoon pillaging my garden, this didn't keep them from coming into the field and right up to the house for their helping of the "cracked delight."

After everyone had their fill and cleaned their plates, the flock left the field as it had entered—with ole tom leading the way across the plowed garden (which had long since been laid by) and up the far side of the field, disappearing into the pines. I enjoyed their company on that solitary afternoon, even in the absence of intercourse. And even though I stayed hidden in the cabin, I sensed that they knew I was here, and in that assumption I imagined we are neighbors and even a kind of kin. It promises to be a sociable, if formal, friendship I will have with these wild birds who came up the mountain to dine at my table and engage amongst themselves in mild conversation before returning home at a reasonable hour.

The turkeys knew where to come for their main course, and the deer know where to come when hankerin' for dessert. While they are scarce during the spring and summer months, in the early days of fall when the apples become ripe and begin to fall off the trees, the deer appear in the orchard. Usually I see them at the far end, which is just over a little rise where they are hidden from both the road and the surrounding woods to the north.

Along the unpaved ridge road, an orchard of ole-timey apple trees has been left to fend for itself for many years. Originally part of the Guice family orchard when Zoro was a boy and a young man, these trees are in various stages of ill health and disrepair. Despite the negligence, some of them still bear fruit. The deer appear like clockwork as the first ripe apples fall from the branches. Here amongst a few old limbertwigs, several wild crab apple (*Malus sylvestris*) and southern crab apple (*Malus angustifolia*) trees, and a lone Carolina cherry that stands in the dead center of what is left of the original orchard, the sweet-toothed deer bob for drops in the high grass and, like short-necked giraffe, reach up into the branches of the unpruned trees, drawing down the fruit.

Having come up from the woods and their perennial hiding places, the small tan-coated, white-tailed deer seem almost inebriated from the sugar-saturated apples when I appear in the orchard in late September. At first all I can see are their legs, looking like thin trunks to the apple trees behind which they are standing while they eat. Knowing which direction intruders might come from, they keep the trees between themselves and the road. When finally they sense that I am here, their ears perk up and they look in my direction. Normally, upon an unexpected encounter in the woods, we would stand there looking at one another like gunslingers waiting for the other to make the first move. But when the apples get ripe, the deer prefer satiation to self-protection, and so they almost ignore my presence. They are used to seeing me when they come here and must recognize my smell, knowing that I have come, too, for apples and not for venison.

While the deer graze cautiously, white tails wagging, I move about slowly and pick up drops from the tall grass. They are fine with my being there as long as I don't get too close. I know that if I do, or when they have had enough to eat, whichever comes first, one deer, followed by the whole herd, will bolt for the west wall of the woods. Meanwhile I use one hand to fill my flannel shirt with red and yellow apples and the other hand to eat a bittersweet limbertwig. We are all there in the orchard just chompin' on apples—I having become one of the deer, the deer having become my companions in this abandoned orchard. Since there are more than enough apples to go around, my ungulate neighbors suffer my presence and we will all get our fill of the fall fruit. I will go home with a shirtful of unsprayed organic apples that I will either make into rich brown applesauce or dry for winter eating.

Birds

Of all the animals in the woods, birds are the closest and most constant neighbors and companions. I wake up with their song and go to bed with their silence. They possess the woods around my cabin and are flitting ornaments adorning the trees throughout the day. A flash of color. An aria of sound. Ever and always there.

Over the years, by growing enough sunflowers and field corn down in the drovers' inn field, and by providing stations around the cabin for them to feed, I have been able to observe their behavior and their bacchanal close at hand. Particularly in the winter, when I am homebound and spending hours on end in my rocker or at my desk near the living-room window that looks out where I have mounted a shelf of rough-cut wood onto a maple sapling that grows up against the house, I can watch the coming and going, the play and perturbations of the birds. They don't seem to be bothered by my hairy visage staring at them through the panes as they eat their weight in seed each day. At such close quarters I can almost see the anger in their eyes, can see the strut of their carriage and the single feather out of place. It is an ornithologist's observatory.

I not only have noticed the general nature of the species, but have been able to single out patterns of behavior and even the specific behavior of certain individual birds. In fact, I have learned a lot about people as a result of observing birds. I have noticed, for instance, that birds, like humans, have frailties, failings, and personalities unique unto themselves. The dynamic of the bird community in and around Zoro's field is not unlike that of a human community, with all manner of interesting characters and personality types.

While every bird of a species may look, at a distance, exactly the same, upon inspection they are different in appearance. The length of each one's legs, the inexact replication of certain markings. Movement. Flexibility . . . Such variations become evident upon observation over time. But besides physical characteristics, behavior sets one bird apart from another. So much so in fact that I have taken not only to naming individual birds, but to renaming certain species in conjunction with their idiosyncrasies and actions. To the nuthatch, for instance, I have given the name "white-breasted quick-snatch," in reference to its physical appearance and its method of taking seeds from the feeder. Like a playful thief, it absconds with bounty quickly, flying to a nearby locust or walnut where it positions itself upside down and inserts the seed in a crack in the bark so it can peck the husk off the seed and gobble the meat down its white-feathered gullet. To the towhee I have given the name "brown-winged buckdancer," a direct take on the towhee's jiglike shuffle-dance as it forages the forest floor. And the chickadee I have renamed the "come-and-go bird," after its habit of coming to the feeder, snatching up a seed in its beak, and flying to a nearby tree to eat it before returning, never staying at the feeder to eat but always preferring "take out" to "dining in." The blue jays I have named the "blue-breasted bully," as they aggressively chase away smaller birds from the feeder when they get the notion to come and eat.

With a great variety and wealth of birds at the feeders now, it is increasingly interesting to watch the various feeding habits and personalities of individual birds. Their temperaments, much the same as their human counterparts, are each unique and quite telling. In his 1921 treatise "Psychological Types," Carl Jung created a general outline of human personality. Jung breaks human personality into two basic orientations: introverted and extroverted. And he identifies four so-called psychological functions: feeling and thinking, and sensing and intuiting. The two orientations and the four functions combine in individuals in different ways to produce eight psychological types: the introverted feeling and extroverted feeling types, the introverted thinking and extroverted thinking types, and so forth. Jung says all human personalities can be described with these general types. A similar outline can also be created, I am finding, for the bird personality.

I have noticed amongst the birds specific behavioral traits that help to delineate who they are. While I don't identify my birds here in Zoro's field as feeling, thinking, sensing, and intuiting, I do see certain behavioral traits that make each one unique, including what might be called introversion and extroversion tendencies. For example, the house wren is chatty and flighty, a kind of "party animal" that can be at times obnoxious—a trait that can easily be seen amongst humans, especially in large groups where one individual may stand out by virtue of the quality and carry of voice alone, as he or she flits about the room making small talk. Within the sparrow community I have seen that while certain sparrows are aggressive and even bullyish, others can be passive and easily chased from the feeders. Perhaps the most dramatic example of aggressiveness in the bird population is that of the hawk, as seen particularly in the relationship between the hawk and the dove. Many times I've been sitting by the window and from the corner of my eye seen a flash of dark color outside, sometimes accompanied by much winglike commotion and squawking. Often I look outside to see a red-tailed hawk or a Swainson's hawk standing in the field atop a stunned dove—the dove serving as easy prey for the faster hawk. When doves are congregated on the ground below my feeding station, they're easy pickings for hungry hawks. The picture in my mind of a hawk standing atop its prey perfectly symbolizes "hawkish" behavior: aggressive, warlike, preemptive. Similarly, when we refer to people or organizations as "doves," we think of naive passivity, peacefulness, nonviolence. Though the blue jay doesn't prey on its smaller feathered cousins as a source of food, I have noticed that within the jay family some are downright haughty, while others come off as narcissistic.

Moving at nature's pace, I have been able over time to identify individual birds by both their behavior and their markings. In some cases I have been watching individual birds for the whole time that I have been here, as they come and go, migrating north and south, returning seasonally and reliably each year. My "psychological types" list for birds includes polarities such as wise vs. social (exemplified by owls vs. finches, for instance), aggressive vs. nonaggressive (the blue jay vs. the mourning dove), high-strung vs. calm (nuthatch vs. oriole), chatty vs. pensive (crow vs. hawk), athletic vs. clumsy (barn swallow vs. grackle), neurotic vs. confident (turkey vs. falcon), elegant vs. ordinary (cedar waxwing vs. starling), and psychopathic vs. well-adjusted (typified by the differences between members of the hummingbird community). I have seen all these characteristics in any number of species as well as in individual birds within a single species.

The behavior of people and animals is much the same. This line of thinking brings to mind the animal tales of Native American peoples and the Uncle Remus tales that my mother read to me when I was a boy — stories written in an African American voice by Joel Chandler Harris, derived from tales he had heard from the Cherokee, Creek, and Catawba Indians here in the Southeast. In these narratives, animals are given human qualities and behavior, which makes them fascinating to readers like my mother and myself. But in the Harris stories the animals don't really take on human traits, as I thought when I was young. They behave as animals do naturally in the wild. Living amongst them wildly, I have come to see that it may be we humans who have learned to act like them.

Taking one step further the idea that humanity may be mimicking our animal neighbors, recently I realized where Beethoven found the first four notes of his famous Fifth Symphony. For a short time last year a family of thrushes made its home in a pile of brush about twenty yards from the cabin. During this time, and particularly in the afternoon when the sun was straight overhead, I would hear the song of at least one of the wood thrushes, its emphatic *ta-ta-ta-ta* echoing through the woods. Having heard this refrain repeated now many times, I am convinced that the composer heard the German cousin of the American wood thrush singing the same song and stole it for the beginning of his symphony. This kind of theft is fairly common in the realm of artists, as they appropriate from nature and from one another as a matter of course. Surely Shakespeare must have gotten material for his human characterizations in such plays as *A Midsummer Night's Dream* and *Much Ado about Nothing* from observation of wild and domestic animals. In the case of the "Beethoven bird," as I now call the wood thrush with its rusty brown back and spotted breast, I have been inspired to write a short poem for which I stole not only from the bird and from Beethoven, but from the words of Percy Shelley — carrying on the time-honored tradition of artistic thievery.

Here in Zoro's field, as well as in the woods and waters surrounding, I have identified many different birds. Such diversity! The abundance added to the various types presents a plethora of possibilities for the ardent bird-watcher. Better than any tale from a book or any story from the screen, the dramas of the bird world are played out daily like a soap opera staged by Pan. And we who watch them are not only the wiser for it, but are inexhaustibly entertained.

Close Encounter

On an unseasonably warm morning late in winter, I decide I will take time off from wood gathering and go for a walk in the woods. A spot about a mile and a half from my cabin is a favorite of mine for its magnificent view of the Green River Gorge and the mountains beyond. Since I haven't visited this place in some time and the sun is shining bright and the view will likely be good on such a day, I head out from the field and down the ridge road toward the bluff.

The rarely used ridge road ends about three quarters of a mile from my cabin, becoming a well-worn deer track and fisherman's trail running downhill into the woods. Once on the trail, I pass a spring branch that comes out of the ground under a lone boulder and then makes its way energetically down into a lovely bottom full of mature second-growth tulip poplars, where I often find ginseng in the fall. In March, however, there is no evidence of ginseng, as it has gone dormant for the winter. With no "sang" to dig or berries to pick, I make my way through the quiet poplar grove, still following the main trail as it makes its way further downhill, eventually ending at the river. A few hundred yards beyond the poplar grove, I take a smaller, less visible deer trail that peaks on a ridge parallel to the road ridge and extends closer to the Green River. The animal trail is rough hiking amidst thick undergrowth, and in several places it is easy to get sidetracked. But I've been here before and know how to make my way through the laurel and huckleberry until the trail starts descending through huge rocks, which necessitate careful negotiating if not rappelling. Having clambered over and around the "elephant rocks," as I have come to call them, it isn't long before I find myself standing on a granite bluff, my destination. From this spot I can see the Green River far below, winding its way like a mythical green snake in the direction of Tryon Mountain—which stands as a sentinel high in the distance, a beacon for the flatlands and the Piedmont, which lies beyond.

It doesn't take long to write about this hike, but it is, in real time, a long and rigorous one. Having stopped along the way to take notice of animal signs and to dig a few roots, I arrive at the overlook at midday. Tired and with the sun shining directly overhead, I find a comfortable spot on the moss-covered granite outcropping and sit down—admiring the view and the faint, meditative musical sound of the river as it rushes through the Narrows a couple thousand feet below. The moss is an inviting mattress, and the sunshine is a warm sedative, and soon I have fully reclined and am drifting into daydreams that become sleep.

By the time I awake, the sun has moved considerably to the west. Still stretched out on the rock and a little disoriented from my midday snooze, I find myself looking up into the branches of a shortleaf pine (southern yellow pine) that stands like a lone soldier at attention on the rock escarpment where I lie. As I am looking up into the pine . . . directly overhead on the lowest and longest branch of the tree sit two turkey vultures (*Cathartes aura*). As I emerge from sleep with the birds so close, the whole scene seems more like a dream than something that might occur in the light of full consciousness. The presence of the two birds is eerie as they sit there like specters looking down, their red heads and necks bent, while making a vulgar hissing as if gloating over a potential meal.

Through my altered state and from my supine position, the vultures look to be the size of pterodactyls. I am envisioning a worst-case scenario and becoming defensive, imagining that I am not only outmanned, but outsized in this potentially carnivorous encounter. Immediately my body becomes active and is producing adrenaline. Fright-and-flight or fright-and-fight reflexes well up in body and mind as if I were under attack. And in a sense I am, with two larger-than-life prehistoric-looking birds hovering over me licking their chops. At this point I am functioning 100 percent on animal instincts, million-year-old DNA memories kicking in, all sensory functions on red alert. In fact I can *feel* that the birds have come here to check me out. Having seen me from above while riding the thermals over the ridgetops and the gorge, they have come in for a closer carrion-inspecting look.

With adrenaline flowing and Poe's "quoth the raven, nevermore" running inanely through my mind, I jump to my feet, thinking this should startle the buzzards and drive them away. It does not. If anything my sudden actions aggravate their hissing and drooling, as now they are pissed. Their would-be meal has come back to life, and the vibes I'm getting from them indicate that they don't like it one bit. I'm still feeling like I'm out of my element with these big birds, deluded that I am outsized and outnumbered. And these guys aren't going away! In any other situation I wouldn't see turkey vultures as a menace. But out here, way off the beaten path and isolated in the woods miles from the nearest human, I feel vulnerable and more than a little frightened. This is their turf and it is past time for their lunch.

Since the buzzards aren't threatened by my aggressive gesticulations and loud cursing, I decide the better part of valor is in this case to retreat. Which I do. Quickly leaving the ledge, I make my way through the elephant rocks before finding the trail. Once back in the woods and away from the open, I'm thinking that I have put enough distance between myself and the birds to be out of danger. Not so. Looking back in the direction of the ledge, I see the birds have left the pine branch and are headed my way. This is not supposed to happen. Vultures are scavengers, living off carrion. With the two birds in hot pursuit, I break into a run up the ridge trail—heading for higher ground. As I get to where the trail begins to descend toward the grove of old-growth poplars, I stop to catch my breath. Having run maybe a quarter of a mile or so, I figure I should have left the vultures back near the bluff. Turning around and looking in the direction from which I have just come, what do I see but the buzzards on the wing and flying through the woods in my direction. I am being pursued!

The sound of wings coming through the trees seems thunderous, enhancing their size in my mind's eye, as they fly nearer, finally lighting in the branches of a buckeye tree not more than a hundred yards away. Not waiting around for any more casual conversation, I take off down the trail, headed for the poplars. From there I waste no time following the larger trail uphill alongside the spring branch, headed for the ridge road. Only when I reach it do I stop long enough to look back and take stock. My pursuers have followed me as far as the poplar grove, where they are sitting up in one of the biggest trees.

Back on the ridge road, I feel safer. At least I am out of the prehistoric woods and back on a path traveled more frequently by humans. I walk up the road that will take me back toward the cabin and sure safety. The turkey vultures don't venture up along the ridge. As I walk toward home I feel the imagined danger drop from my body and know that the birds are no longer in pursuit. Nevertheless, every once in a while I turn and look back. But I see no birds other than the conspicuous juncos flitting from branch to branch in the dogwoods and a pair of cardinals moving about in the old apple trees, feeding off the few prunelike apples still treebound in what was once the Guice family orchard.

By the time I reach home and the cabin, it is already approaching dusk, and despite my nap, I am worn out. I could easily go straight to bed but don't, as there are still chores to do and a rolling thunder in my belly that is calling for food. I, now the scavenger — of what I have stored in my root cellar — rather than the scavenged.

BEETHOVEN'S BIRD

The first thought.
The inner lake of open roses.
So-La-Ti-Do.
Or a symphony shaped and sculpted
from what we find like magic in the dirt.
Calling it ours.
Claiming copyright, like deeds
to an earth that no one owns.
Why, even on a good day
Beethoven must have stolen his song from birds!

SNOWED IN

In Lu Mountain's falling and scattering dark,
over night at East Forest: windblown snow.

PO CHÜ-I

The Selected Poems of Po-Chü-i, Tang Dynasty

*T*oday is the first day of spring, though you'd never guess it to look. What tricks nature plays on us and on our imagined schedules! On a day designated to celebrate the end of winter, when I might otherwise be out searching for the first blooming wildflowers or signs of early tree buds, Mother Nature gives us, instead, a winter wonderland: a blanket of new-fallen snow. In an hour's time the whole mountain world has been clothed in a saggy white suit. From my writing desk at the window, I watch the snow fall. Big leafy flakes settle on branches and ground, now more than an inch deep in white irony. How beautiful the pines and the laurels look half covered in this midday meringue!

Deciding to take advantage of this year's only substantial snowfall, I put down John Burroughs's *Indoor Studies,* fill the woodstove, throw on my greatcoat, gloves, and stocking cap, and walk out the door into a world of profound silence. How quiet the snowy world is! All I can hear are the flakes' gentle *ticks* as they hit the ground. Suddenly the silent spell is broken by the shriek of a cardinal calling for its mate—a solitary outburst cutting into the snow's whisper that is little more than the absence of sound. I can see the cardinal, his brilliant red feathers puffed against the cold, in a nearby holly tree: a gaudy cufflink in the sleeve of this first spring day.

The effect of the snow on the world is cleansing. It leaves your body and soul feeling spotless, without any sense of the usual bodily and spiritual grime. It has a purging effect on the inhibitions . . . and all I can think of is dancing! The crump of my boots in the soft snow seems resounding, and I think of the words of the great Russian dancer Vaslav Nijinsky: "I walked on the snow which crunched beneath my feet. I liked the snow and listened to its crunching. I loved listening to my footsteps; they were full of life."

Within a short time the snow is coming down dense as rain, so hard that I can't see to the far side of the garden field and the large pines and poplars beyond. At this rate there will be inches more by nightfall. With no weather reports to listen to or read, I depend on natural signs for prediction and surmise. I know that the birds anticipate a normal light snowfall by becoming unusually active, chowing down at my feeders and moving about energetically. But if the storm is to be substantial, their activity increases exponentially, and they become almost frantic, as if what few seeds they can find will have to last for days!

Having lived here three years, I can, with increasing accuracy, tell when a front is moving in and what the weather will do for a day or two to come. Right now the hyperactive snowbirds (juncos), the chatty chickadees, and the singing cardinals are forecasting more snow today and possibly overnight. For me this is not bad news. I relish the silence of the snowy woods and the robe that cloaks life here in Zoro's field. In snow I am secluded even further from the outside world. Monastic. Cloistered. The world forgetting, by the world forgot. With little or no movement along the dirt road that serves my neighbors half a mile away, life slows down to what it would have been a century ago—before cars. I look forward to a couple of days by my window in the rocker, reading, sipping lemon mint and springwater tea, watching the birds, studying their behavior and being entertained as much by their chatter as I am soothed by their songs.

As dusk creeps into the woods, displacing all that is white with a nocturnal gray, I chop wood for the stove and plan my evening meal. In addition to the usual winter staples of potatoes, canned green beans from the root cellar, and corn bread, I think tonight I will treat myself to a dessert of applesauce and sunflower seeds—à la mode with snow!

The next morning, just as my friends the juncos have predicted, I'm snowed in. Naturally imprisoned. Yet liberated in being so. I wake in brief panic to the crash of the mirror over the nightstand, blown down by a wind so strong it gusts through the gaps around my closed windows. The wind howled all night long and is still blowing hard enough to find a crack in the cabin and pluck the heavy mirror off its nail and onto the floor! Nature's bad-boy alarm clock . . .

When my feet first contact the hardwood floor, I know it is cold outside. The floor is like ice, and the shards of mirror glass scattered everywhere accentuate the effect. I look out the bedroom window at the thermometer: fifteen degrees! And with the windchill it's considerably colder than that. I tiptoe through the broken glass and into the living room.

Last night's fire is only embers in the little woodstove. I toss in a couple of small sticks from the indoors wood box, open the damper all the way, throw a flannel shirt over my shoulders, slip on my elk-skin boots, and hie me hence to the outhouse. I find that mice have been there during the night and had a ticker-tape party with the toilet paper I have been lazily leaving to one side of the large sitting surface instead of putting back on its twenty-penny nail, where it has never been bothered. Making my way back to the cabin, I notice that while the snow around the building has been blown into two-foot drifts, the trees are filled with singing snowbirds and the feeders are empty of seeds, suet, and leftovers from last night's corn bread. I will have to fill the feeders twice today. By the time I get back to the cabin my breath has frozen and encased my mustache Christo-like in ice.

Almost a foot of snow fell during the night. After stoking the fire and getting some heat in the house, I crack the north and west windows so I can hear, in stereo, the sounds of the birds feeding in the snow—an excited chorus of chirps, trills, and squawks. A symphony, in fact, as I watch their anxious state, resembling more a contest than a casual buffet. When the mountain world is covered in snow and ice, the birds still must eat each day their body weight in food; and with their normal food sources buried and gone, feeding takes on a more serious tenor. Their squabbling will go on as long as there is seed and as long as there is snow on the ground.

After a quick breakfast of last night's corn bread and the remains of a jar of peaches from last year's bumper crop, and after putting a quick coat of mink oil on my high-top cold-weather boots, I decide to walk down the hill to the spring to check my water supply and bring up two jugs of cold water for cooking and washing, and also to see who in the neighborhood has been up and around. Once outside I brush the snow from the birdfeeders and replenish the seed and suet, and no sooner do I disappear around the corner of the building than I hear the feeders coming to life with the sound of snowbirds.

As I lean down over the spring to take a drink and to fill my water jugs, a pileated woodpecker, like the gatekeeper of the spring, swoops into a nearby oak and lets out a raucous shriek, as if castigating me for not getting permission to drink. Startled, a flurry of cardinals and juncos retreats in haste. The ground around the spring after a fresh snow is a catalog of wildlife. In warmer seasons the mud here works the same way — revealing the comings and goings of animals who leave their scat as well as perfect imprints of their paws. Today the neighborhood around the spring is working hard to weather the storm, and visitors leave their calling cards in the form of urine trails and foot shadows in the snow. Throughout the surrounding laurel, which includes some mature poplars and oaks, are traces of rabbit, fox, and raccoon — all of whom have made trips to the spring to drink — as well as bird tracks leading away from the spring.

Under a large overhanging rock just up from the spring, signs indicate that a creature about the size of a bobcat spent the night here. I know this from matted mud and blurry paw prints under the rock. I have seen this kind of housekeeping by bobcats before, but I can't be sure who made this den, as it may have been occupied prior to last night's snow, and no prints come or go from the lair.

I walk out of the woods into my garden field, which is like an uncaged aviary. Dozens, maybe hundreds, of birds. Impatient small airplanes trying to land all at one time on the deck of a dry-docked aircraft carrier. Everywhere! Birds wrangle for position around the large feeder I have set up there and peck through the crust of snow to find food on the ground. Brawling and cussing, they crowd around the feeder, establishing their avian hierarchy. They are almost all juncos, with the exception of a female blue jay, who has learned the tactic of flying to the feeder, snatching a pumpkin seed, and then flying back to the nearby sourwood to eat in peace and privacy. When she tries to eat at the feeder, she is evicted by a gang of tackling snowbirds, enacting a strength-in-numbers drama, protecting what they claim as their turf.

Walking to the middle of the field, I get a gallery view of the surrounding woods. Heavy with snow, the branches of the evergreens bow deeply, the low branches touching the ground. The hemlocks especially look like they are bent in prayer. I proceed to the northern edge of the field, set down my water jugs, and walk into the grape arbors, enjoying the sound of my feet in the encrusted snow. *Boompfh . . . boompfh . . . boompfh . . .* The percussive rhythm of my boots compacting the snow serves suddenly as a springboard, and I spontaneously leap from one foot to the other. The rhythm escalates faster and faster, higher and higher. Soon I'm flapping my arms up and down, until the whole forward movement is a lumbering kind of earthborne flight. Down each terrace in a leap I go, arms stretched out like thin denim-covered wings—landing on one foot and then the other down the terraces, never breaking stride. I am high in the air and land in a run as I reach the bottom row of last year's as yet unpruned vines. This little burst of exhilaration has brought more joy than it has freezing sweat to my brow and beard.

With this unrehearsed display of reinhabitory theatrics, I feel more wild, more part of the animal world than of my two-legged kin's world. In fact, day by day over the passing seasons and years, the wilderness has invaded me. The mayhem and antics of the birds tell me much about myself as an animal. Who's to say that from watching the birds at my feeders over the course of days and years I may not one day leave the ground and fly—where my heart already soars!

Retrieving my water jugs at the edge of Zoro's field, where rhubarb and asparagus will rise up in a few weeks after a long sleep, I head back to the cabin. I have been gone a couple of hours and am hungry from the hard walking down and up the steep incline to the spring, not to mention the cold air, the brimming jugs, and the acrobatics in the arbor.

In the cabin I sit in the rocker with a bowl of applesauce and the last of the corn bread and add the birds and other animals I saw or saw evidence of this morning. The list I have been keeping since I took up housekeeping here runs into the dozens and includes a distinguished company.

BIRDS: blue jay, cardinal, snowbird (dark-eyed junco), black-capped chickadee, Carolina chickadee, white-eyed vireo, common crow, sparrow (house, chipping, song, white-throated), pileated woodpecker, red-headed woodpecker, downy woodpecker, purple finch, house finch, American goldfinch, grosbeak (evening black-headed and rose-breasted), northern oriole, wood thrush, hermit thrush, ovenbird, redwing blackbird, white-breasted nuthatch, indigo bunting, scarlet tanager, Carolina wren, house wren, tufted titmouse, cerulean warbler, yellow-throated warbler, common grackle, brown-headed cowbird, starling, belted kingfisher, cedar waxwing, yellow-shafted flicker, American robin, eastern bluebird, brown thrasher, barn owl, great horned owl, screech owl, hawk owl, mourning dove, mockingbird, eastern kingbird, barn swallow, purple martin, eastern phoebe, rufous-sided towhee, whip-poor-will, vermillion flycatcher, red-tailed hawk, Swainson's hawk, Cooper's hawk, chicken hawk, goshawk, sparrow hawk, peregrine falcon, turkey vulture, ruffed grouse, great blue heron, hummingbird (ruby-throated and rufous), bobwhite, mallard, black duck, Canada goose, wild turkey.

OTHER ANIMALS: gray squirrel, red squirrel, flying squirrel, red fox, silver fox (and hybrids of red and silver foxes), rabbit, opossum, raccoon, chipmunk, wildcat, bobcat, cougar (panther?), field mouse, jumping mouse, field rat, box turtle, snapping turtle, woodchuck, blacksnake, king snake, garter snake, ring-necked snake, water snakes, copperhead, rattlesnake, deer, skunk, mole, bat, trout (rainbow, speckled, and brown), bass, bream, catfish, tree frog, bull frog, beaver, and bear.

I finish off the day with chores—chopping wood, refilling the bird feeder out in the field, cleaning up the broken mirror. And as this memorable day of being snowed in comes to a close, I bring some apple cider up from the root cellar to quench my thirst and give relief to my aching snow-blind eyes and my chilled fingers and toes. This is the last of the cider that I put away last fall. By now it's truly fired up from almost six months of fermentation and aging in clay jugs in the constant fifty-five degrees of the root cellar. With the first swig, I know that this batch of cider has both the right amount of sugar and the kick! And it's not long before I'm relaxed and content. Ah . . . the miracles of putrefaction and decay! What wonders a little CO_2 and sugar can do for my ongoing struggle with solitude, the intercourse with my ego, and the courting of my soul!

With the combination of a hot woodstove and the intoxicating cider, I'm forced to go to the doorway for fresh air. From the vantage of my stoop, the stars are ablaze tonight—so clear is the sky from the cleansing of the snowfall. I imagine that the stars tonight are more distinct and more shimmering than they may have ever been since my arrival in this mountain lair. But it's probably just the cider. The snow and the snuggle of quiet isolation that it has brought to these woods turns me inward. Standing in the doorway of this little cabin and looking out and up into an equinox sky, I feel present. Truly here. And there is nowhere I'd rather be.

.

SNOW ON THE FIRST DAY OF SPRING

Spring will be a little late
this year.
Strings stretched across the bridge
of a rested body still wanting to sing.
Glass hugging the wood
in windows that reflect the snow.

The warmth from the stove
fuels a dream of yellow flowers
that disappear into the red grass—
Flowers burning, like desire,
too hot to touch and too young to pick.

With dawn,
I wake to the sound of
small fists knocking at my bedroom panes.
Looking out: the forest.
Covered in white.

A WALK IN THE WOODS

If ever a man minds his own business
it is when he is alone in the woods.

HORACE KEPHART

While any time of year is a good time to walk in the woods, winter is probably the best. "When the snakes ain't a-crawlin'," as Zoro would say. This time of year, with copperheads and rattlesnakes deep in their dens, one doesn't walk defensively or reach into blind crevasses with fear. With the leaves off the trees, the line of sight expands and vistas open up in the forest giving a better view of the lay of the land and of whatever is moving about. Rock outcroppings make themselves known, faint pathways expose themselves, and old home sites and log cabin ruins appear like rabbits out of a hat in places one has walked many times, unaware of the history hiding among bushes and trees in full foliage. Spring branches and small streams run high and noisy since the trees are dormant and not drinking from the soil. Walking is a soft pleasure with the forest floor thickly layered in damp decaying leaves.

I took many walks through the woods and over mountains this winter, discovering hidden treasures that only the spare season shares, but the equinox with its day and night of equal length has passed and we're already into spring. Still there's the possibility of dogwood winter, when the temperature drops below freezing after the dogwoods start to bloom. This morning I got up with the sun, the west wind blowing chill. Although it was cold enough that I burned a fire in the woodstove last night, with the sun shining it is warm enough to spend an enjoyable day in the woods. Yet cool enough not to encounter snakes. I have decided to hike to Camp Creek, to the falls, and then on down to the Narrows in Rocky Mountain Cove, passing a glen where wildflowers often bloom early—a circular route that will begin by roadway and end coming home through the back woods.

I have packed a light lunch of corn bread, walnuts, and dried apples for the hike and set out down the hill on the dirt road that joins Old

Howard Gap Road. I walk for a little more than a mile until I reach Camp Creek Road, where I turn left and proceed uphill for a quarter mile before arriving at Camp Creek and leaving the road on a scant path that goes into the woods and runs parallel to the creek. I make my way slowly downhill through laurel and stands of hemlock and holly. Unlike some places I visited this winter, the forest here echoes with early morning birdsong. I can make out the sounds of nuthatches, snowbirds, and chickadees, and see movement in the trees in every direction. Even at this early hour, the sun has climbed over the ridgetops to the east and is warming the woods.

After a twenty-minute downhill saunter, I come to the top of the Camp Creek falls. Here the water pools and then slides over a fifteen-yard stretch of smooth, moss-covered granite before disappearing among poplar and locust trunks below. As I make my way out onto a rock beside the stream and nearer to the falls, I can see the creek rushing off downhill on its way to join the Green River. But unlike the anxious water, I am content to take my time and stand at the edge of the falls looking down some fifteen feet into a pool that acts as a sound chamber. Here, as everywhere in nature, there is perfect pitch. A low G pervades the woods around the waterfall, drowning out the Ds and Cs of the winter birds still flitting through the trees upstream.

Having enjoyed the meditative roar of the cascade for a while, I climb down the steep bank, slipping and sliding in the dew-covered leaves, until I find a dry flat stone a few yards from where the pristine pool receives water from above. I have been here before and know that a narrow path passes tunnel-like behind the falls. Loving the feeling of being wrapped in water but not drenched, I ease back behind the white wall of water and stand breathing the mist as I revel in the intensity of the sound and energy. Being locked onto this ledge behind rushing water is one of those moments one finds, often unexpectedly, in nature, giving you a sense of your mortality and your kinship with the natural world. With the roaring silver sheet inches from my face, my senses are all engaged, a feeling I imagine surfers must experience beneath the curl of a giant wave. My pulmonary and nervous systems are running on all cylinders. Synapses firing like it's dusk on the Fourth of July. This moment, this place, is a complete work of art, what Richard Wagner called *Gesamtkunstwerk*. But this proscenium is grander than any man-made stage.

Though exhilarated, at the same time I am overwhelmed and take myself out from under the falls to regain my equilibrium and catch my breath. Heart rate back to normal in a couple of minutes, I set out down the fisherman's trail, descending deeper into the woods. Gray squirrels dart back and forth across the path ahead of me as blue jays cry mockingly overhead. Before long I come to one of my favorite spots in all the woods up and down the Green River Gorge: a place where the creek falls beautifully into a deep, quiet granite-lined pool before disappearing downhill steeply toward the river. The pool is defined by smooth, dark granite walls on three sides. The fourth side looks out into the tops of trees further down the slope. I've been to this place, snakes and all, during the hottest months of summer, using it as a natural bath — so perfectly are the walls formed with the quiet water reflecting the tall tulip trees that surround. I have luxuriated in the cool creek water in July and August, feeling like Pan or some kind of pagan prince lounging in his exotic bathhouse. In this font I have felt my troubles being washed away, as well as the sweat from the long trek to get here.

While I have previously seen several water snakes in and around this rectangular pool, today I encounter only a small frog, who, as I approach, falls almost awkwardly off his rock perch into the water and swims off, disappearing into the dark black depths. Scouting around the west end of the pool, I find that beavers have felled a birch in a failed attempt to dam up the lower end, but the pool is naturally dammed and there is little room to build a house. Besides the beavers' fruitless work, I notice signs of other animals. A decaying crow feather amidst the leaves. A jawbone and one orbital from a skull, vertebrae, and a couple of tibiae from what looks to be either a possum or a raccoon skeleton. Whichever critter it is, it had its last drink and found its end at the foot of this natural bath.

Since I'm not going to bathe here today, I walk back to where the fishing trail forks and joins an old logging road. Here the switchbacks begin winding down toward the river. I haven't gone far when I spot a large groundhog running along the upper bank of the logging road.

Having seen me, he's moving fast and quickly disappears into a hole under the lip of the high bank.

Traveling steeply downhill now, it isn't long before I come to a shelf in the woods where a stand of poplars presides. The tall, branchless trunks provide for an open floor with no appreciable undergrowth. The river roaring in my ears, I approach this fertile bottom all eyes. I am looking for early signs of spring wildflowers. In the rich damp soil of this area where the noonday sun sneaks through branches bearing new buds, wildflowers often get a much earlier start than up on the ridgetops or near my cabin. This glen somehow mimics the properties of a thermal belt, one of which modifies weather a few miles from here at a lower altitude. When I enter the dell, I notice a rise in temperature, a good five to ten degrees warmer than in other parts of the woods. There is no simple explanation for this phenomenon that I know of, so I simply enjoy the warmth and know I am in a special place.

Today I am in luck, as I see with a quick glance that much is going on under the dogwoods that have made a life for themselves in the shadows of the poplars. Walking into the glen, I immediately come across a large bed of newly sprouted trillium that spreads out of sight. Looking more closely at the expansive bed, I am amazed to find not just a single species of trillium, but three varieties. Scouting the area, I also find signs and evidence of dwarf crested iris, Canadian violet, purple mountain violet, silver bell, wild azalea, wood vetch, squaw root (red trillium), mountain Andromeda, sweetshrub, robin's plantain, and dog violet.

This treasure-trove of mountain wildflowers is a perfect place to recline, idle, and practice what Zoro calls "being in place" — which I do after finishing my paperwork, sitting down in the damp, soft leaves against a large tulip tree to eat my corn bread and dried fruit. But since it is already past midday by the time I've eaten and lounged a bit, I get up from my elfin seat, find the fishing path, and keep going toward the Narrows, which roars in the near distance.

Camp Creek empties into the Green River right above the Narrows. This time of year, the river is swollen by the runoff from the early spring rains, and the Narrows is a force majeure. With the human body being a natural converter of hydroelectricity, the energy here is palpable. I plan to get close to the most intense part of the sluice — something I've never dared to do (on account of snakes and compromised visibility) on other trips, which have been mostly in late spring or summer, fishing with Horace Pace. Today, the rocks to the sides of the river are relatively dry and the visibility good. In a few weeks leafy green shoots on the saplings and deciduous bushes will all but block visibility and easy approach to this perilous section of the river. I don't have any business doing this now, since I am alone and without aid should something go awry, but I've made up my mind and am already crawling through the dense mountain laurel and rhododendron to a rock outcropping that borders the most dramatic part of the Narrows.

Worming through a laurel thicket, I get out onto the rocks and crawl on all fours toward the edge, the river roaring only feet below. At this spot, there is a slightly elevated and smooth area of rock on both sides of the river, which is no more than ten feet across. This spot is the notorious nexus of the many stories I have heard about foolhardy youth trying to jump the river. Storied for would-be feats of derring-do to impress girlfriends and drunken chums, this piece of river has claimed several lives and has the reputation in these parts for being a "dead man's sluice." Stories I have heard rush through my head as I lie belly down at the precipice. Far from attempting to jump the river, I don't even stand up and risk the possibility of slipping. Instead I simply admire with awe the power of nature and sit as witness to this fabled spot, with the wet river-generated gale blowing into my face and hair, and the sound of the water's downhill rush through wild rock overwhelming my ears.

Having gotten enough of the wild part of wilderness for one day, and seeing that thunderheads are moving across the sky, I back off the rock and through the laurel and onto loamy land, get my bearings, and head upriver along the fisherman's path. This path parallels the river for a half mile or so, then turns uphill, following a spring branch until it passes the roofless ruin of a log cabin said to have been home to a bootlegger and his still, now half hidden in a stand of ivy. The well-worn path continues, meeting an old logging road that comes out eventually at Johnson's Pond. About halfway up the road I am already breaking a sweat and getting short of breath. Being much less active during the winter has taken its toll and is now showing up in my stamina on this walk. But I forge ahead.

Suddenly thunder crashes and the sky opens up, dumping a torrent of rain mixed with small hail. I am at a ford in the little overflow creek on my left—a ford that becomes an almost invisible animal trail leading to Zackey Dorton's cave. With the rain coming down in sheets and thunder and lightning going wild, I hurry up the trail and through the laurel hell to the rock overhang that was the hiding place for the local man turned draft resister during the Civil War. After scrambling and slipping for about three hundred yards, I'm at the cave. Soaking wet but not cold. I sit down in the dirt and enjoy the theatrics and energy of the storm, in awe and some fear at the lightshow, watching the water and hail play off the rock and rhododendron, reveling in the zestful ambiance of being wet. History haunts, in a friendly way, this cave, as the black smoke residue from open fires can still be seen on the ceiling stone. The ethers of human passage linger. The offspring of animals—bobcat, possum, busy birds—still scurry about, as evidenced by their footprints in the cave's dirt floor.

When the rainstorm finally stops, I leave the cave and make my way back through the rhododendron, eventually emerging from the canopy of the woods at the edge of Johnson's Pond into an opening of blue sky amidst late afternoon sun shining and wind sighing through the white pines and spruce. In a sunny area at the edge of the pond, I spot some Indian strawberries, the little yellow flowers with their faux berries nestled in a mix of grass clumps and sticks. Seeing this spring plant reminds me of its edible cousin the Virginia Strawberry (*Fragaria virginiana*) and an area over on the dam that usually yields an early crop of berries, owing to the moisture and direct sunlight. Wandering in that direction, I immediately see the delicate white flowers erupting from hairy stalks and points of deep red peeking through the leaflets. While the full crop of berries has not come in, a handful or two are ready to pick, and I quickly consume them. Nothing is so sweet and satisfying as a ripe wild strawberry! The ruby of the naturalist's edible gem collection. I will come back to this spot in a few weeks and gather enough wild berries to make jam—which will cover my corn bread for a couple of months thereafter.

Tongue and lips no doubt dyed red by the berries and my stomach definitely in motion, I begin to think about supper. With that thought driving me, I head across the dirt dam to the path that goes uphill to the gravel road and winds around a hill and up a ridgeline to where I will walk off into the woods and beyond, through dogwoods blooming, to Zoro's field and home.

THE ETHER OR

some kind of rock
are the sheets between which I lie.
And after sleep
or before time is
where I rest my head.

Knock three times on Nature's door.
Or twice on the sky.
You will find wild rivers flowing
way over their banks.
Mica in mountain streams.
Seas of ice.
And snow.

How can science eat
these trees?
These villages of wattle and clay
going in and out of sight.
That come to life and
the naked eye
only when we stop
and are at rest.
More birds flying in branches
than we'll ever see.

They are here. Everywhere.
All around.
Like the absence of time. Or
a man
who walks wildly through familiar woods.
At home.

EARTHQUAKE

What we add to Nature is easily peeled off,
but what Nature adds to herself sticks.

JOHN BURROUGHS
Field and Study

*S*urprise is part of the story of life in the woods. This and the constant reminder that at any moment we can become subject, even victim, to Nature's overriding eccentricities and whims. This was never more evident than in May of 1981, when Nature let loose with one of its more memorable paroxysms.

It was a sunny late spring day with the temperature in the low seventies. A little warm for early May but otherwise normal for that time of year. I was outdoors doing some exterior decorating in the woods around the cabin—cutting the vines and underbrush, thinning out the saplings, pruning dead limbs—to make way for a path that would lead from the cabin, over the hill, through the grape arbors and bean terraces, to the mailbox. Unnecessary work maybe, but I had been thinking of this project for some time, and today was the day I had chosen to get it done. By the middle of the afternoon I had accumulated enough branches and small trees to make three substantial piles close together near the edge of the woods on the cabin side of the field. A bevy of sparrows and a few titmice had already discovered the piles and were scouting it out as a possible nesting place—singing as they flew in and out of the mound of sticks. Up on the crest of the hill a pileated woodpecker burst out in its eerie laugh. In the pines on the other side of the field, a lone crow answered with a raucous caw. The ambiance of the day was palpable. Nature at its lackadaisical best.

Just as I was becoming accustomed to how gentle and relaxing the day and the work of woods-cleaning were, I noticed the sparrows in the brush pile jumping and flitting nervously and chirping madly, the air getting denser, the light dimming, as a yawning roar came from the ground. The world around Zoro's field shook with a sudden spasm. The woods heaved with an outburst of emotion as the ground beneath my feet rose and shook. With the trees swaying, the ground rocking and rolling, the birds frantic, and the air loudly yawning, the three brush piles, all clearly within my view, leapt into the air about a foot, levitating there for what seemed like a captured moment before hitting the ground again. Thrown almost off balance by the movement underfoot, I reached for a sourwood sapling a couple of feet from where I was trying to get my footing. But even the sourwood was unstable.

EARTHQUAKE! startlingly filled the blank page of my mind as I clung to the sourwood tree. Simultaneously came the thought: earthquakes aren't supposed to occur in the mountains of western North Carolina! Maybe this is the end of the world. I looked up to see whether falling trees or broken branches were headed my way. I'd experienced tremors during my years in San Francisco, when the pavement would roll and the streetlights flicker or the beer would slosh out of my glass—reminders of the devastating earthquake that practically leveled the city in 1906. But my experiences with earthquakes were on the extreme West Coast and in cities and towns. All of my mental associations with earthquakes were urban, which is part of why it seemed so strange to be standing in the woods with this shaking going on! What was happening around me was, if nothing else, surreal. And what a ride it was, as time and everything I'd previously considered real and stable went into a moving state of otherworldliness.

I was in uncharted territory, and my experience and frames of reference weren't working. I was on the deck of a ship at sea, rolling with an early summer squall—holding on to the mast for dear life, waiting for the next wave to wash over the bow and come aboard. In those long moments, the metaphors racing up from my feet to my head came, too, in waves, like the movement of the dirt and leaves underfoot, my sense of equilibrium gone overboard with everything else in my psyche that wasn't nailed down. I was able to verbalize these metaphors only later that evening, on paper and upon reflection, as while the earth was moving, every system in my body was working overtime: a tap-dancing cabin; the temblor like a train thundering through; brush piles high-jumping; wind rattling its bones . . .

Later after the train had passed, including a couple of aftershocks, I found that the quake had been substantial enough to do damage in the cabin. My new bedroom mirror had come off its hook and was lying cracked atop the washbasin on the nightstand. Ceramic cups had fallen from their shelf and lay in pieces on the hinged table where I ate my meals. Long, substantial cracks had rent the Sheetrock in the bedroom walls and ceiling—cracks that would serve as reminders of this day and what kind of havoc, without warning, Nature can wreak.

I would learn that the quake occurred within minutes of the death of the hunger-striking IRA leader Bobby Sands in Ireland—as if the two exclamatory events had some arcane, yet organic connection, and Bobby Sands's passing was electric enough to cause the Earth to moan. To grieve. Maybe even to show anger. A sonorous outcry for the dead soldier and son. Synchronicity, Jung would call it, suggesting that there might have been a parcel of predetermination, destiny or karma, if not an act of will somehow involved in the whole thing.

In the past, indigenous peoples on this continent and others embraced such numinous notions and incorporated them into their belief systems and behavior. And after my experience in early May "when the Mother moved," I better understand the animistic aspects of their mythologies and rituals. "Strong medicine," an aboriginal elder might say, referring to the awe with which such events are perceived by a pagan people. And it was strong medicine. Strong in the sense that it made an indelible impression on my psyche and body, and medicine in the sense that by going through the experience I have less fear of the world in general and more respect for the natural world in particular.

While scientifically we know what causes the earth to move so violently, an aspect of unknowability and mystery still surrounds such events as earthquakes. The force is so great, the scale so *über*-human, that the mind takes it to the level of myth instantly, in order to put it into some coping kind of perspective. Thus the shifting of tectonic plates becomes a supernatural event. We stand in awe. Feuds are forgiven. Prayers offered up.

In the world of nature many things occur for which no logical explanations are known. Walt, in all his canny queerness, was also a dowser. Although this seemed an unlikely side of his personality, he was able to find underground water with a stick, a divining rod. On more than one occasion over the years, he would veer off the trail during one of our walks in the woods and would snap off a forked branch from a young sumac. After announcing his intentions, he would take his pocketknife and whittle down the bark on all three ends of the stick to the moist, green, pithy heartwood. Taking the two closer ends of the tri-forked stick in a kind of backward grip, he would stretch his arms out in front of him and begin walking, the strange "rod" looking as if it was leading him, even pulling him along. "I'm divining for water," he would say. "This ole stick will show me where to look." He prefaced this pronouncement with, "You ain't going to believe this, but you'll learn something today," as if he'd never shown me this trick before.

"Now, follow close beside me and just watch this here rod," he'd say as he left the path and took out into the woods. After walking a short distance, he would suddenly stop and stand there completely stationary with arms outstretched and with the sumac rod bending down as if a heavy weight was hanging from its end and shaking while it pointed to a precise spot on the ground.

"You see that!" he would exclaim. "There it is! Water is right there. Right where the shoemake stick's a-pointin'. Ye see?" And I did. The dowsing stick clinched tightly in his fists pointed like a bird dog to a spot in the loamy soil and leaves. "Put a stob in the ground right there," he would direct me. "And then go to the house and bring back that mattock and shovel, and I'll show ye what we'll find." And I would dutifully go back to the woodshed, fetch the tools, and return to the spot where he and his faithful hound were waiting—Walt with a hand-rolled cigarette half smoked.

In the spot that I had earlier marked with the stake, I wouldn't have to dig too deep before the ground would become moist and then would bubble up with a small flow of water coming from deeper underground. "Ye see!" Walt would say, with a satisfied grin on his face. "Hit don't never fail. The water in this shoemake attracts the water in the ground and points it out. I never failed in findin' at least a tad of water with this here rod." And Walt was right. In my experience he'd always led himself, me, and the dog to some kind of water flow every time he'd used the dowsing stick, even if it was just dowsing the obvious—like a tiny spring branch flowing above ground. Whenever he would pass over such a flow of water, his rod would bend downward in his hands as if wanting to take a drink.

Walt was even good at finding old still sites, where whiskey had been made at one time and where barrel rings or other materials from the still were often buried under years of leaves and loam. On one of my trips off the beaten path with Walt and his shoemake stick, he was able to dowse out a crawdad that had made a home for itself under a large rock where a bit of water stood. I never failed to be impressed with Walt's dowsing abilities, which also never transferred over to me, as my attempts at dowsing resulted only in fruitless hours of walking in circles in the woods, never feeling a tug, the forked stick never moving an inch. Even though I don't know how Walt could find water, old still sites, and other things with a forked stick, I saw him do it again and again.

Another thing almost as mysterious as his knack for finding water in the ground was Walt's ability to predict the weather. While not as numinous (in the sense that most of his weather predicting acumen came from years of observation), nevertheless it was always impressive when Walt would look into the sky or over on the hill on the other side of the lake and say something like: "Hit's fixing to rain. Look yonder at them maples on the mountain. Pert nigh all the leaves are silver-lookin'. By mornin' we'll get a right smart of rain." And sure enough, the next morning I'd wake to the sound of rain on the roof of the old mountain house. He could also predict snow and the accumulation of snow by similar means—by the sudden appearance of a cool evening breeze, a certain formation of clouds, a shift in wind, by barometric sensation or the behavior of forest animals. Although he often sensationalized his predictions, Walt was rarely wrong.

The realm of the numinous in nature also includes lightning. On this topic the old-timers have a hefty share of stories, some being more theatrical or believable than others. While most stories concern the depredations of storm-generated lightning—the jagged thunderbolts of Zeus—I have also heard fascinating tales of ball lightning: a kind of inland Saint Elmo's fire. No matter what the story or who the source, these tales are some of the best one is likely to hear in the mountains. The unpredictable, uncanny, and surreal behavior of lightning after it reaches the ground often leaves one confounded. Walt told the story of a lightning bolt that hit the chimney of his old home-place down on the lake and raced through the electrical lines in the house before exiting by the back door, going down the steps, and leaving a burned track across the yard for about a hundred yards to the lake, where it killed a mallard sitting on its nest, fried the eggs, and then proceeded into the water, killing several fish (bass, catfish, bream). The dead fish floated to the surface, and Walt picked them out by hand and took them to the springhouse to clean for supper that night.

A few months ago I heard a story from a linesman who was working a half-mile or so up Macedonia Road on electric lines that had been taken down by an ice storm. As I stood at the bottom of the pole talking to the linesman overhead in his climbing shoes and safety belt, he proceeded to tell me of a time several years before, when he was working at the top of a power pole and a summer storm came up over the mountain out of nowhere. He didn't even have time to get down from the pole before a large ball of light came out from the looming cloud and hit the electric line on top of the hill not more than a quarter of a mile away. "I saw that ball lightning come out of the sky and hit a pole way up yonder on the hill. Then it commenced to travel right down the wires — a big red and blue ball of light — toward where I was stuck up on that pole. Strapped in like this, I didn't have time to unhook and climb down. So I was sittin' there watching it when that ball of lightning got to me. Blew me clean off that pole with a loud clap. Burst the big ole belt that had me tied to the pole right in two. I went flying off that pole and hit the ground about twenty feet out. I was lucky though and missed that thorny Japanese rose that grows all over the place and hit soft ground. I was unconscious for a pretty fair while. But the good thing was my partner was down the road with the truck. He heard the lightning and came to see if I was all right. He found me lying beside of the Japanese rose unconscious with my britches and shoes all burned. I was awake by the time they got me to the hospital but was in pretty sorry shape. Took me a few weeks to get my bearings and to get back on my feet. When I did, I was only able to limp around. I walk all right now but the limp is still with me. Probably always will be. But I guess I'm lucky to have got off with only a bum leg. The doctors at the hospital said it was a miracle I was alive at all. I took off work for a couple months. During that time I found out strange things had happened to me. I could read people's minds. You know, tell what they were fixin' to say and stuff such as that. I also found out I had developed a talent for dowsing. Never had tried that sort of thing before and wasn't interested. But for some reason I started thinking about it while I was settin' around the house there all those weeks. So I tried it out. Used an old plumb bob I had in my carpenter's box. Right away I could find water and tell just how many gallons per minute the flow was and how deep down you'd have to dig. All that. Pretty soon I had well-drilling companies calling me, wantin' me to dowse for them. And they paid me right smart amount of money for it. Still do. Now I can dowse for almost anything. The sheriff's department had me out the other side of town last month or so lookin' for a young woman where there was suspicion of wrongdoin'. I didn't find anything in the woods or along the ravine over there, but they had me out there dowsin', hoping I would find something."

Only two of the many lightning tales I've heard since I came to the woods, these typify the curious and extreme nature of the beast. Neither the linesman nor Walt could account for why the lightning did what it did. Nor can any experts. The stories stand on their own as witnesses to what in Nature is mysterious and cannot be explained.

TREMORS

for Bobby Sands

Just when everything seems at peace
and my body and my life are at rest,
the Earth moves!
My little home tap-dancing on the dry May soil.
Brush piles high-jumping the wind.
The wind rattling its bones
as the tremor moves over the land
like a train.
Its whistle roaring
like a fed lion who is ready for sleep.

going to die," he confided one day, "as Bessie will be here alone when I'm gone, and she'll need a clean place to sleep. It won't be fittin' for her to have to sleep in the same bed where someone has died." He seemed to like me there, as he knew I wasn't much of a talker. He liked the fact that I respected his desire not to be bothered with end-less, painful questions but was there as a supporting presence, neither making small talk nor expressing sentimental grief. Sometimes after we'd been sitting together in silence in the little room, he would turn his head to the right and his eyes would twinkle and he'd say some-thing like: "You still here?" or "What you think about a man in such a mess?" But as his days neared their end Zoro had less and less to say, and the pain from the cancer — which even the painkillers he was taking couldn't finally override — made it increasingly difficult for him to do anything, including talk. When he did want to communicate something, he would do it through his eyes or with a slight smile, or with only a word or two. "Dang," he'd say, as I watched a wave of pain roll over his outstretched body. "Sheeeitt," he muttered once or twice when he heard someone who had come to pay their respects saying something about him or his situation that he didn't particularly like. "Not true," I heard him say once to something that a local preacher uttered in the next room.

During those last days, something happened between Zoro and me that hadn't before. We bonded. Instead of being teacher and pupil, or old man and young man, we became simply friends. Age and experi-ence melted away into the necessities of silence and quiet companion-ship. Maybe he saw a little of himself in me, sitting there in my cov-eralls with my long beard, that reminded him of his youth. Or maybe it was just that he knew that I knew he didn't want to talk and didn't want people making a fuss, and that I honored that wish, giving him time and space to confront death on his own terms and with dignity. Whatever the case, the communication between us was profound, and I felt privileged to be in his presence and to be with him at the end. My experience watching Zoro die alleviated any fears I had regarding death. Dying as he did, with such relative grace (even though he was in great pain), was maybe the greatest teaching, the greatest gift that Zoro gave me over the short years that we spent time together. Along with the practical things I learned from him, he also taught me, by allowing me to watch him work through his death, a great spiritual lesson.

Zoro wasn't much of a churchgoer in his later years. He'd come to a place regarding his religious beliefs and convictions that was, like his lifestyle, self-sufficient. He didn't have any use for the social and economic structures inherent in present-day religions, nor in preachers who were paid or kept by their congregations. Not unlike the distinctions between church and state set down in the Constitution, Zoro's spiritual politics embodied a separation of church and economy. After many years of being a respected member of the Baptist church on Macedonia Road where his family had gone to services, attended homecomings, and buried their kin, he left the flock when the church began paying their preacher a salary. Zoro believed that spirituality didn't have a price and that a man who was called to preach or spread the word of God should do it purely and without pay. So when the Macedonia Baptist Church began paying their preacher, Zoro walked away and never returned.

Even after such a theatrical and controversial exodus, Zoro was buried at the old church on Macedonia Road alongside his kinfolk, although with no grave marker—which was one of his last requests. The little church was overflowing on the day they held the burial service. On an unseasonably warm sunny day, as if it had been ordered by the Divine especially for the occasion, I watched and listened to the service from the front steps. Somehow this seemed appropriate to me—to be outside, where Zoro had spent the majority of his life. A man of the fields and the woods, Zoro seemed almost out of his element within the walls of any building, even his own home. Wild, yet beautifully refined in that wildness, he belonged to the out-of-doors and was a prince there. For me he carried a saintly shroud to his grave. He was my inspiration and my role model. For three and a half years he had taught me how to live.

I have taken the long walk up Macedonia Road more than once these last several months to visit Zoro's grave. To get his quiet counseling and friendship through graveside osmosis. To keep our correspondence alive. Sometimes when the breeze blows over the roof of the church and through the gravestones I can feel his presence. And as I sit in the churchyard where he is buried, thinking lofty thoughts or wondering about people and what they do and say, I can hear a windy voice saying, "Not true."

It seemed like no sooner had Zoro died than Mac followed him abroad, to the other side. With both my woodsman-mentor and my Emerson now gone, the social structure of my world in the woods was being undone by time and entropy. For years I'd watched the way things had returned, full circle, back to the world of composted soil, and had studied it and accepted it as the inevitable way of all flesh. But I found it different when my own kind, my friends, began their fall. To watch a bird decay, reposing alone in a leafy sepulcher, or an old jack pine rot as it lay in state somewhere in the woods, is somehow different than seeing a member of one's family or community die. And now I had lost in quick succession two of the foundation posts holding up my life in the woods.

Unlike Zoro's slow descent into silence and the churchyard, Mac died suddenly and in an odd way, perhaps willfully. I had been over at his place tightening up the wires on the bean trellises for his half-runners while he was finishing with his spring planting of corn on one of the upper terraces of the garden. I had finished tightening the wires and was sitting on the bank by the cornfield having a drink of water that I'd gotten from the well and blowing the soft white seeds off a dandelion while watching Mac drop kernels of Silver Queen seed corn into the furrowed rows. As I watched him stooping there over the plowed earth, something he had said months before popped into my mind: "I want to die in my garden. But I don't want to go until I've planted the last seed of the last crop in the spring." At the time, I took what he was saying to be the kind of philosophical platitude he was fond of uttering as part of normal conversation. As I watched Mac working the next to last row of the upper terrace, the last terrace to be planted, I noticed a grimace come over his face, and suddenly his hands and forearms jerked and pink inoculated seed corn went flying in every direction. Shaken from my spring reverie, I jumped to my feet and ran to where Mac stood clutching his body as if checking to see if it was still there. When I asked if he was okay, all he said was, "It's just this damn angina again. Promise me you won't tell anyone." I assured him I wouldn't, but the grimace and the clutching became more pronounced, and he dropped to his knees uncharacteristically as if in prayer. "I did it. I got in all the corn," was all he said, kneeling there in the dirt.

After a couple minutes, in obvious pain Mac forced himself to his feet with my assistance and said again, "I'm okay . . . I got the corn planted," and ambled out of the cornfield, disappearing onto the back porch where he loved to sit each day at dusk, smoking his pipe and sipping a large yellow tumbler of scotch and water while contemplating his garden and planning his work for the next day. This was the last time I saw Mac. It wasn't more than fifteen or twenty minutes until a red and white ambulance drove up the drive to the McHugh house, as I was covering over the corn rows to bury the remaining unplanted seed. The ambulance took him to the Hendersonville hospital, where he died from heart failure and a stroke. His last words to me seemed like a verification of prophecy from some ancient text. In looking back over these past weeks since his death, it seems to me he chose to die when he did, that after planting the last row of corn (which in actuality he came just shy of doing, being short of his goal by a row and a half) he put an exclamation point at the end of the long, unpunctuated sentence that was his life. And closed the book.

While letters were sent out announcing Mac's death, and his memorial service drew a crowd of a couple hundred, only a small gathering of family and friends assembled several days later to scatter his ashes over the orchard as he had wished. Mac was not fond of organized religion or its dogma, so this pagan ritual seemed realistic, seemed right. It was a bright but blustery day, with the wind whipping through the orchard and bending the pine trees at the edge of the woods. The ashes, as we scattered them beneath the drip lines of apple, plum, cherry, and apricot trees, blew back on us—got in our hair and on our clothes, as if a part of Mac wanted to remain here disembodied in the Polk County mountains, living vicariously through us. I was okay with the idea that, as I inhaled his ashes into my lungs and had the white dust of his bones commingle with the follicles of my hair, maybe some of this wise and traveled man became a part of me. What ashes didn't come to rest around the fruit trees or on us blew up into the air and off into the woods, everywhere. Even in death Mac was cutting a wide swath. Leaving his mark and part of himself scattered through memory and the old mountaintop farm that he so loved.

With Zoro and Mac gone, things around here are not the same. I feel like an orphan, a babe in the woods, without the two wise old men around. It's an eerie feeling. Almost ominous. Maybe I'm being melodramatic or overly sensitive, but it feels like something, some kind of energy or aura, has disappeared from these woods. Like a protective scrim has been lifted—letting in all manner of goblins from the world outside. With old Walt Johnson also gone from these hills, a whole patriarchal cultural tradition has disappeared. All of the viable role models of this way of life have left the rest of us at the top of the Green River Gorge to our own devices and vulnerable to the modern world.

> Who will separate, now
> the wheat from the chaff?
> These men whose sweat
> watered grain.
> These women
> whose milk was the strength in human bone.

I recently wrote these lines as part of an elegy for a generation and a tradition gone. No longer will we see oxen and mules pulling plows across slopes and along bottomlands here in these hills. No longer will families earn their living by what they make, build, and grow. I have witnessed and been part of a watershed moment here on the upper end of Old Howard Gap Road. A transition. With one kind of life being traded out for another, for better or worse.

With these three old mountain men gone, things will irreversibly change. Important skills will vanish. Time-honored mores will melt into a greater monocultural ethic. Long observed customs will cease. And a way of speaking will become lost in the undertow of a rising tide of a common English speech. The rich and marvelous human diversity I have known and witnessed here will be irreparably diminished. This will all happen quickly, as "the seeds saved / from great grandparents to be given / to children not yet born / are eaten by the fiery incinerators of banks." This, I fear, is the destiny of this community and this landscape. All is change, and all things must pass. Sage wisdom for time immemorial.

As my life has been altered with recent events and I am left with some of the music gone from the symphony of these highland fields, I plant my seeds this year in Zoro's field. My dreams and body are full of foreboding as my memories of these halcyon years push away my fears.

LEARNING TO DIE

To be prepared for dying,
and yet live! the wise ones will say.
And so I go on.
Too busy to stop and cry, or
sometimes to even rest.
Ice ages come and go between each breath
as I hoe the corn rows.
Mountains
rise up and then melt again into sand
in the time it takes to drink
one drink from the pure stream
that runs nearby.

How can my friends find time
to dream of being rich?
To bad-mouth the moon.
Or chase women around all day —
I tell them that good sex is
having only a small house to sweep.
And a bowl of hot soup at the end of the day.

They think I am foolish
living alone out here in the dark and
wolf-ridden woods.
And they go on with their dying.
More lonely than any moonlit night.

Here in my forest home,
I sit by the fire and listen to the rain
falling from the maples onto the roof.
I am learning to die from the simple things
that keep me each night from sleep.
In each shadow that dances through the woods.
Preparing for the day when darkness
makes of me: a feast.
Knowing this I am already loam.
A spade in an endless soil.
Digging destiny from the speed of light.

AFTERWORD

When a naturalist is thoroughly comfortable
and settled, it is time to uproot him.

DONALD CULROSS PEATTIE
"A Transplanting," *Flowering Earth*

*N*ot long after Mac died, the veil of protection lifted, confirming my premonitions and exposing the pristine world where I was living to the gremlins of postindustrial and monocultural America. Various family members appeared from across the country, and soon there was talk of clear-cutting the 250-acre mountain farm as well as cutting down the old orchard in order to graze some Scottish breed of long-haired cattle. And sure enough, it wasn't long before the sounds of chainsaws and timber trucks could be heard from holler and ridgetop all across the land. While this was going on, I raised another garden and tried to carry on as usual. But as the song says: the thrill was gone. With the changed consciousness of a younger generation and the loss of my mentors, the woods around me had taken on a different personality. Even though in many respects things remained little changed, the subtle and not so subtle differences were enough to put me on edge. The comfort zone of wildness that I had felt for four years was gone. Instead of living in nature, I felt like I was simply living in the country — with an increasing amount of machine noise, development, and unenlightened vibes. While it was true that I had been spoiled during the almost four years I had lived next to Zoro's field, and was living, some would say, on borrowed time, I found it difficult to sit still and watch what had taken generations to build and to protect falling away around me.

I was generously given the opportunity to stay and live on in the cabin that I had helped Walt Johnson build, but in my mind I had already left and so respectfully declined the offers to remain and work the old mountain farm essentially as a hired hand. With my mind made up I faced the problem of where to go and what to do. Luckily, or unluckily as the case may be, I knew a fellow on the other side of

Saluda who worked as a carpenter for a small construction business, and it wasn't long before I was riding to work every morning (while still living in the cabin) all the way to Black Mountain, where his boss was building a house and where I was now working as part of the construction crew. Just going back to work for someone else on a regular basis was a huge adjustment, not to mention I was spending the better part of my days out in a world alien to my energies and more primitive values. While the people I worked with were good-hearted enough, the pace and quality of life they led and that surrounded me each day was a true shock to my system.

I felt a little like Dersu Uzala in the 1970s film of the same name about a Siberian woodsman who is brought into a Russian city for the first time to live in the apartment of a military surveyor who befriends him. All Dersu does is sit on the living-room floor and stare into the window of the woodstove, watching the fire—the fire being the only thing in city life to which he can relate as a reminder of his former life. The kind of shock I was experiencing was much like the kind of culture shock I had experienced when reentering the United States after living abroad following my graduation from college and before I set out for California. Then, as now, I felt a stranger in a strange land.

I have been back in what most people consider the real world for more than twenty years. The real world of the twenty-first century is very different from the world and the "real work" I did and experienced in the cabin next to Zoro's field, and in some ways I'm still getting used to it—if one ever really can get used to such a world, with its mindlessness, its madness and machines. Twenty years ago, when I finally said my good-byes to my bee-loud glade, my Walden Pond, I took my culture shock and moved across town into the attic of an old two-story farmhouse owned by a couple who had come there from Indiana to get away from the rat race and start a family and a health-conscious bakery. Living with the Thomases, I became an extended family member and, in essence, became Thomas Thomas. I liked my attic room and the time I lived with the Thomases and their young family, and it served as a soft transition between the world I had come from and the world into which I was headed. And while the Thomases were gentle and of the earth, I had a hard time acclimating and adjusting to modern life. Still with my long hair and a very long beard, I scared people on the streets of Hendersonville and Black Mountain where I worked. And their reactions to my appearance scared me.

But it was mostly the noise and the pace of life that was so disturbing during those first weeks and months away from the woods. And I'm not sure twenty years later that I'm any more comfortable with it. The difference may be that now I can tune it out, or at least pretend to. Then, I hadn't developed the coping skills and so was thrown into the world of commerce and crass materialism like a baby tossed into deep water to learn how to swim. I was newborn in this modern world and was being bombarded with all manner of sensations and sensibilities that I had not confronted for years. Imagine taking a monk who had lived most of his life in a secluded monastery in the mountains of Tibet to a Nine Inch Nails concert as his introduction to contemporary society. In a sense this is what my reentry into twentieth-century America in 1982 was like. And I was for a long time depressed.

My body was as depressed as my mind during that transition time, as I had to struggle to distance myself from my former life in order to stay sane. Just as separation in a love relationship causes emotional suffering, so I suffered from the loss of my relationship with the woods. Every day I wanted to go back, even knowing that it wouldn't be the same as during the idyllic years. So attuned and accustomed had my mind and body become to the quiet, the calm, the slow natural pace of things, that it was going to take a rewiring of some sort, a makeover, in order for me to fit into the workaday world.

In time I began my makeover by cutting my hair short and shaving off my beard—an act born of necessity in order to find a job. While solving one problem this act of desperation created another: an identity crisis caused from seeing myself essentially hairless for the first time in many years. By this time, I had made my way to Jackson County after having lived in Black Mountain and then in the hills around Marshall and Mars Hill, where I was the victim of a major car accident—yet another shock to my system. While recovering from the accident, I threw in for a time with a renegade band of Sufis helping to stage large healing conferences that brought spiritual and medical teachers from all over the world and from many religious backgrounds. This connection too, I think, helped me in some ways to adjust or, if nothing else, to heal, as I participated in spiritual practices designed to help sensitive people become balanced in a brash world.

Little by little, day by day, year by year, I've made my way back into the "real" world. But as much as I have found a way to function here, I still think of the natural world that I knew beside Zoro's field as the one that is real. This modern world seems little more than a dream by comparison. An illusion. Now even though I am living in a remote farming community in the back country of Jackson County, I still have to get in my old pickup truck and drive many miles to shop or to send packages for my publishing business—in short, to do everything that needs to be done to stay functional. My days are spent in front of a computer or on the phone or in recording studios. My spare time is spent working outdoors with a chainsaw to cut my firewood and with a noisy gas-powered tiller to plow my garden. The cars on Highway 281—which used to be a gravel road that runs in front of my 130-year-old farmhouse—go back and forth all day, leaving only short periods between cars when I can hear unadulterated natural sounds such as the birds singing in the trees or at the feeders. In short, I have become a citizen of the industrial world.

Yes, a part of me longs for my wild life in the woods, but now at age fifty-five I can't go back. Even if given the perfect opportunity, I couldn't sustain myself in the way I did when I was living beside and growing my food in Zoro's field. My body won't do all I ask of it anymore. Just growing a small garden gets more difficult each year. A day behind the tiller leaves me exhausted for twenty-four hours, if not longer. A few hours hefting a chainsaw sees me the next day in the office of the chiropractor. Hoeing a row of corn, I have to stop and rest before I can go on to the next row. So, to think about living a self-sufficient life at this age would be pure fantasy.

For years after I left the woods, I dreamed of the cabin and hollers and hills near the Green River. Only many years later did I go back—to revisit the place as I began writing this book from diaries and notebooks I had filled. A friend advised me not to go. "You'll only be disappointed," he said. I wish now that I had listened to him and had kept my impressions of the place in my mind's eye. What I encountered on that return visit was a cabin that was a disintegrating shell. Roof collapsed from a tree that had fallen on it and entered the bedroom. Door akimbo and off its hinges. Inside ravaged by animals, wind, and weather. An outhouse that lay on its side, more useful to a snake. And Zoro's field grown up in heavy grass and locust saplings, as if it had never been tilled. Like Zoro, Mac, and Walt, the old place had succumbed to the inevitable entropy that plays the card that inevitably trumps all others.

I have been back only one other time since that initial return, and what I saw on the last trip was a horror almost beyond reckoning, yet at the same time so indicative of the nature of the beast we call "progress." Not only has the cabin been razed, but Zoro's field has been replaced with a gravel lot and a large metal building that is used to store earthmoving equipment—bulldozers, backhoes, dump trucks, and cherry pickers. So much out of place is this building, painted a gaudy orange, and so out of context with everything around it, that it is not only surreal, it is the stuff of nightmares. "They paved paradise / and put up a parking lot," words in a song from 1970, came to mind as I stood dumbstruck by this monstrosity where broccoli and Brussels sprouts, cauliflower and corn had once grown. As I brushed aside the tears that were rolling down my cheeks, I was wishing I had not come back a second time. This image would remain with me, salt in the wound.

Although the air quality here in the mountains has gotten worse and the housing developments more invasive, my life these days in Tuckaseegee is a good one. This place too has its own natural beauty, even with the constant traffic that rushes by the house at sixty miles an hour, and the house-shaking sound of Black Hawk helicopters using the river basin as practice for their inane games. While I live very much in the technological present, I've brought a few things with me from my life in Polk County, and they have continued to be part of my day-to-day life for the past twenty-five years. I have continued to use a woodstove and to heat with wood. I have fed the birds through all seasons with a series of bird feeders and a variety of seeds. I continue to work with the Cherokee over on the reservation in various ways regarding a variety of cultural issues. I have cultivated a garden every year, growing enough food to supplement diet and income. And I still don't wear a watch.

The biggest difference from my days living alone in the wild is that now I live with a woman I love and with whom I share many passions and interests, and who also loves nature and the wild world. On this little farm, I live in the world of the here and now, which, while it may sound oh so Zen, is really the only one there is. I learned this from Zoro and from living next to Zoro's field. There is no future and there is no past. There is only the moment we consciously live in—which is a part of the singularity of all other moments. I live in this moment, extended, here along the Tuckaseegee River in the Little Canada watershed, trying as best I can to be steward of my behavior, this place, and the conservation values I hold dear. Over the years, I have become involved in activist cultural and environmental organizations, and I speak out by writing letters or editorials to regional newspapers and by writing articles for magazines—taking what I learned from my years in Zoro's field and applying those lessons to the present in the larger world of western North Carolina and beyond.

Looking back now, I'm thinking that Thomas Wolfe may have been right after all, and you can't go home again. In some ways Zoro's field will always be home to me. Those years, the most informative and profound of my life. But I can't go back to Zoro's field. This farm in Tuckaseegee is my home. Instead of pining away for my halcyon years in Polk County, I write about them, hoping they will entertain or nurture others who have been less fortunate than I in experiencing such a life. Every day I pray for a conversion experience deep in the psychic structure of the human population that will be a catalyst for the healing of the natural world. Anything short of this won't get the environmental conservation job done. May these words, along with those of my naturalist writer friends, be a start toward the restoration of beauty as an innately embraced value. And in turn may the rivers flow and the flowers bloom. And may it continue . . .

MAY IT CONTINUE

May the brown earth and the green leaves
thrive in color and in grace.
May it continue.

May the clear air and the cumulocirrus clouds
be there in the sky and in each breath, always.
May it continue.

May the water made of sweet minerals and salt
in small streams and large rivers
flow forever and forever flow to the seas.
May it continue.

May the sun shine warm and bright
and the moon give light at night — *shining from shook foil.*
May it continue.

May the beautiful birds of Hawaii and
the luminous parrots of Peru fly far and fast
and may their number grow.
May it continue.

May the deer and the elk, the antelope and the ibis
move and migrate, leap and lope across plain
and wooded plateau.
May it continue.

May the whale and the dolphin and the manatee
swim deep in dark oceans and lagoons   and sing.
May it continue.

May the elephants forever in families roam,
trunk to tail, trumpeting bliss.
May it continue.

May waves of warm frost linger in bush and blaze
that puts fire in the peat of loam.
And let lick cry from ripe vine.
May it continue.

May the rose climb through
the cold murmur of morning dirt.
May dark mulch coax tendrils from sleep.
May it continue.

May wild words come flying on green coils and
may juice in rock rustle with blue moss
in the sound of song.
May it continue.

Thomas Rain Crowe
Tuckaseegee, North Carolina
February 2004

CREDITS

Some chapters and poems in this book have previously appeared in the following publications: *Smoky Mountain News, Nantahala Review, The Elemental South* (University of Georgia Press), *Virginia Library, Voices of the Mountains* (*Asheville Citizen-Times*), *Salamander, Katuah Journal, Southern ARC, Eco-Logic, Lights in the Mountains, The Blue Ridge Parkway: Agent of Transition* (Appalachian Consortium Press), *New Native* (New Native Press), *Heartstone, Rivendell,* and *Poems for Che Guevara's Dream* (Holocene Press).

ABOUT THE AUTHOR

Thomas Rain Crowe, one of the Baby Beats of the 1970s San Francisco Renaissance and the editor of *Beatitude* magazine, was born in 1949 and is a poet, translator, editor, publisher, and recording artist. His twelve books of original and translated works include *The Laugharne Poems* (which was written at the Dylan Thomas boathouse in Laugharne, Wales, and published in Wales by Gwasg Carreg Gwalch), *Writing the Wind: A Celtic Resurgence* (The New Celtic Poetry), and *Drunk on the Wine of the Beloved: 100 Poems of Hafiz* (Shambhala). He is a former editor-at-large for the *Asheville Poetry Review* as well as a regular feature writer for the *Smoky Mountain News* and a book and music reviewer for several publications including *Jazz News* and the *Bloomsbury Review*. His work appeared in an anthology of nature writing, *The Elemental South*, published in 2004 by the University of Georgia Press. His literary archives have been purchased by and are collected at the Duke University Special Collections Library in Durham, North Carolina. He lives in the Tuckasegee community of Jackson County, North Carolina.